THE WILD HORSE
OF THE WEST

The Wild Horse of the West

WALKER D. WYMAN

Illustrated by

HAROLD E. BRYANT

UNIVERSITY OF NEBRASKA PRESS • Lincoln

First Bison Book printing: February 1963

Most recent printing shown by first digit below:

6   7   8   9   10

Bison Book edition reprinted by arrangement with Caxton Printers, Ltd.

To

HELEN BRYANT WYMAN

A genuine product of the West, who, like the wise old ones of the wild "bunches," guards well our herd.

Preface

For the past few years the press has been carrying stories from the mountain and desert country telling of the removal of thousands of wild horses. From the public domain and Indian reservations came the cry which e c h o e d throughout the West: the wild horse must go! Stockmen's associations and various governmental agencies have been active in the final phase of the destruction of the horse herds that frequent the mesas and breaks of the Rocky Mountain empire. In this recent period two scholars have published material on the introduction of the horse into America, and have reopened the question of the distribution of that animal by Indian tribes. But what happened to that pony since the Indian came into possession of it, what happened to it when the cattleman spread across the plains and valleys of the mountain country, what has happened to the Spanish horse as its blood was chilled by ranch stock, this has not been told. Even the story of the removal of thousands of starved, often degenerate horses, has not appeared in sober print. The purpose of this study is to set forth the main outline of the history of the wild horse of the West in the period between 1600 and the present. This is not a record of the mustang alone. It is a partial record of the feral, or wild horse, whether it be of Spanish or American ancestry. What has happened to that horse since 1890 is the chief contribution of this study.

To the staffs of the following institutions the writer wishes to express his appreciation: River Falls State Teachers' College Library; St. Paul Public Library; James J. Hill Reference Library of St. Paul; Library of the College of Agriculture, University of Minnesota; the state historical societies of Minnesota, Kansas, and Colorado. To Lois M. Fawcett, Head of the Reference Department of the Minnesota Historical Society; Lyle H. Miller, Research Director of the Kansas State Historical Society; and William R. Hogan, of the University Libraries of the State University of Louisiana, is given an especial word of appreciation for information which they sent to the writer. To the fifty-five Grazing Service officials, professors of history and animal husbandry, Indian agents, officers of stockmen's associations, and others who were so considerate in answering questions by mail, recognition is gladly given in the footnotes and bibliography. The researches of J. Frank Dobie, Robert M. Denhardt, and Francis Haines have contributed much to this study. The artist's map reproduced on the end leaves showing the northward spread of horses among the Indian tribes is based on one by Haines that appeared in his monumental work in the *American Anthropologist.*

Lastly, a word of appreciation is due the artist, Harold Bryant, native Coloradan, whose paintings show a love for horseflesh not possessed by many people. Out of the goodness of his heart and the love of the mustang he turned aside from a busy life to produce these illustrations.

To that little horse, dean of the mammals, which has had such great influence throughout history, especially in the range country of the West, the writer bows with a respect bordering on veneration.

WALKER D. WYMAN

River Falls, Wisconsin
February 3, 1945

Table of Contents

List of Illustrations

In the first place, reflect on the circumstance that the horse has been a resident of the planet for approximately forty million years longer than man. Remember also that the horse reached his physical prime some twenty million years before man learned to stand on his feet. Finally, bear in mind that, of all the mammals still inhabiting this globe, the horse is dean in point of residence. There is no existing mammal older than the horse. There is none younger than man. On this purely temporal basis alone, the horse is entitled to a respect bordering on veneration.

Arthur Vernon, *The History and Romance of the Horse* (Boston, 1939), p. 8.

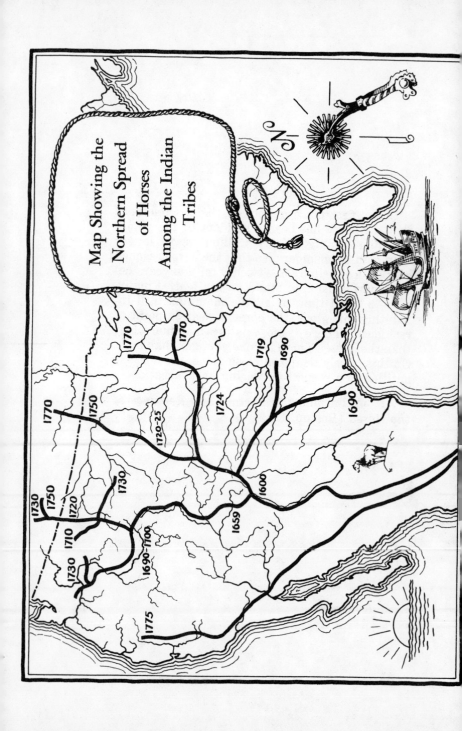

Map Showing the
Northern Spread
of Horses
Among the Indian
Tribes

CHAPTER ONE

Wild Horse: Old Model

Millions of years before man came on to the scene the history of the horse began, a history that has been written largely by those scholars who work with fossils and rock strata, trying to piece together the evolution of animal life. The modern horse found in America was introduced by way of Europe, not only by the Spanish but also by those nationalities that settled the Atlantic seaboard. Among the first animals brought by these peoples was the horse. From the Spanish settlements the horse that escaped or was stolen by the Indians became the wild mustang that was so numerous on the Western plains. In a real sense it was not a wild but a feral horse, a horse that formerly had been domesticated, or its descendant. It may have developed some markings and senses that characterized its ancestors living in the wild, but it was still the modern *equus*.

That the horse of today was introduced from

Europe is not disputed at this time, but in the eighteen-thirties it was. At that time an army officer stationed at Fort Gibson on the Arkansas River, spoke of the "true American horse, equal to Arabia's best and fleetest sons . . . ." found on the plains.[1] Another argued that these horses could not have developed from the "escapes" from the Spanish, but were "indigenous to these fertile plains even as was the buffalo. The peculiarly favorable conditions in the Southwest for horse culture lead to the conclusion that these horses were not of the same stock as the Arabs brought over by the Spaniards."[2]

The true wild horse, the remote ancestor of the domesticated and feral horse of our era, was indigenous to the American continent. In those remote years, when semitropical woodlands and lush vegetation provided a hospitable environment, and after the herbivorous dinosaurs weighing several tons had gone, the first horse was about the size of a fox. The forefoot had four toes and the back foot had three. Thousands of crushed skulls and skeleton fragments of this tiny animal, called *Eohippus*, have been found in the rock formation of the West. Another distinct type of the early horse is the three-toed creature, the size of a prairie wolf or a sheep, and well adapted for speed. The tenth and last stage in the development of the horse appears in the Pleistocene Age. The skeletons found show it to range in size from the small-

They roamed the primordial forests

est Shetland pony to a large draft horse. One mounted in Yale Museum is fifteen hands high "having somewhat the proportions of a western broncho, but with a very large head and with teeth greater than a modern dray horse....."[3] This one-toed animal roamed not only the North and South American continents but also Europe and Asia. Clark Wissler, famed anthropologist and specialist in Indian life, believes the Indian migrating from Asia to North America "spread through lands overrun by wild horses..... Whether these early hunters," he continues, "who ate wild horses, reached Cape Horn five or ten thousand years ago we leave to those speculatively inclined; we do know that they reached the southern tip of the New World before the wild horse and the sloth were extinct. At least it was so long ago that the historic Indians had never heard of it."[4]

The evolutionary data show a gradual change in the bones, teeth, and skeleton of the horse, as well as the development of special parts of the body affecting his ability to run and to eat—for the preservation of his life by escape, fighting, and grazing. Why the horse disappeared in both North and South America and not in Asia is not known. Theories have been advanced that they were destroyed by glaciers, but this does not explain their extinction in southernmost parts of the Western Hemisphere. "That no permanent change of environment occurred to render the earth unsuitable to these creatures," according to Richard Swann Lull, "is evident from the amazing way in which the few imported horses [of the Spanish] .... multiplied and spread..... We look naturally therefore for some other cause of the extinction and the one of all theories that seems most plausible is the bringing in by migrating animals of insect-transmitted disease, such as the sleeping sickness of Africa or the Surra disease which attacks domestic horses in India..... "[5] We might now be in a horseless age had not there been a migration of the prehistoric horse to Asia and Africa, where the line of development continued, producing not only the modern *equus* but also the zebra and the ass. One writer concludes:

It is inferred that the Old World horses came from America, because of their appearance in England, Northern Italy and Northern India in the same geological period in which they were found so abundantly in America, and also from the fact that a distinct connecting link between this horse and his three-toed ancestors has been found only in America..... At the end of the Tertiary Age [or period] .... there was a land connection between North America and Asia, and it is then that our American wild horses are supposed to have started on their journey to the Old World.[6]

There is no unanimity of opinion among anthropologists relative to the ancestral home of the horse. Some have concluded that the Tarpan or the Equus Przhevalski,[7] found on the Gobi Desert in recent years, is the true progenitor of the modern horse.[8] This animal was found by the Russian army officer, Przhevalski, and brought to England and the United States for study. It was dun-colored with spinal stripe, twelve hands high, and had a roached mane, large head with chin whiskers, convex profile, short neck and back, and strong legs. These horses may still be found in considerable numbers in the steppe country of Asia. They can

be captured but no evidence exists to show that they can be domesticated.

Presumably modern horses have their origin in several wild species rather than in the Tarpan alone. Scholars point out the existence of the steppe (or Tarpan), desert, forest, and possibly one other type of horse from which have sprung modern horses.[9] Regardless of the particular line of descent, the horse spread to Europe from Asia. It is known to have come into Mesopotamia from

Persia about 2500 B. C., to Egypt from there in about 1700 B. C., and thence it spread over North Africa.[10] The history of the European horse from this date is that of the incorporation of it into civilization. In the times of Herodotus wild horses were said to exist.[11] During the Middle Ages, St. Boniface was rebuked by Pope Gregory III for permitting his German converts to eat the flesh of wild horses. Various writers have pointed out the existence of wild horses throughout most of Europe as late as the sixteenth century.[12] Teutonic knights hunted them for their skins, while the Duke of Albert in 1543 "sent an order to the commander at Lyck bidding him to take measures for the preservation of wild horses, whilst far into the 17th century the horse was hunted in Poland and Lithuania."[13]

It is probable that these horses were *feral* horses, so called because they are either escaped domestic horses or the offspring of them. Feral horses have existed all over the world since the domestication of the horse. In Australia, soon after the occupation by the English, many of the horses introduced by them were wild. Known as "brumbies" they have been numerous ever since.[14] When Philip of Spain, attempting to invade England, rounded the Scottish coast, one ship was wrecked off the peninsula of Galloway. The ponies swam ashore and gave rise to the famous breed, the Galloway horse. Called the "Forester," they existed in a half-wild state.[15] The "Russar," Sweden's wild horse, is still found on the island of Gothland. Protected by law, they multiply. When the increase is great enough to warrant it, a rodeo is held and the supernumeraries are disposed of.[16] Feral horses may still be found in considerable numbers in parts of North and South America. But the true wild horse exists in only one place, Mongolia. There is found in large numbers a pale brown horse of small size with slender legs, a large and ugly head, and a roached mane.[17] He stands as the only representative of *equus* which has resisted the mighty forces of civilization. The story of the wild horse in America then becomes that of the feral horse. Introduced by the Spanish, the horse was taken by them to the northern frontier, whence he escaped or was stolen by the Indians and distributed by them throughout most of the trans-Mississippi West. In large herds these feral horses roamed the plains threatening to compete with the buffalo, but the American ranchers came on the scene to dispute their control over the grass. Into these Spanish "escapes" there filtered the "escapes" of the emigrants, miners, ranchers, and travelers, leavening the mass beyond description. It is this wild horse that has so excited the lovers of Western romance. However, it is not so exciting to look at this horse as just another "plug," or perhaps thoroughbred, that left his home range.

FOOTNOTES—CHAPTER I

1. E. B. Nowland in a letter to the *American Turf Register and Sporting Magazine*, VII (1835-36), 60-62.

2. *Ibid.*, VI (1834-35), 118-24.

3. Richard Swann Lull, *Organic Evolution* (New York, 1932), p. 600. Quoted by permission of Macmillan Company. For the evolution of the horse *see also* W. D. Matthew and S. H. Chubb, *Evolution of the Horse*, issued by the American Museum of Natural History, and Arthur Vernon, *The History and Romance of the Horse* (Boston, 1939).

4. Clark Wissler, *Indians of the United States* (New York, 1940), pp. 8-9. Quoted by permission of Doubleday, Doran and Company, Inc.

5. Lull, *op. cit.*, p. 602. Quoted by permission of Macmillan Company.

6. B. M. Underhill, "The Evolution of the Horse," *Scientific American*, LXIV (1907), 413.

7. This name is spelled several different ways.

8. J. C. Ewart, "The Possible Ancestors of the Horse Living Under Domestication," *Science*, XXX (1909), 219-23; *Independent*, LXXVI (1913), 171; *Scientific American Supplement*, LXXI (1911), 18; W. H. Carter, "Story of the Horse," *National Geographic Magazine*, XLIV (1923), 462.

9. E. N. Wentworth, "The Horse—From Then to Now," *The Producer*, December, 1933.

10. A. L. Kroeber, *Anthropology* (New York, 1923), p. 473.

11. E. L. Trouessart, "Wild Horses," *Popular Science Monthly*, XXXVI (1890), 629.

12. *Ibid.*, also William Ridgeway, *The Origin and Influence of the Thoroughbred Horse* (Cambridge, 1905), p. 16.

13. Ridgeway, *op. cit.*, pp. 16-17.

14. National Live Stock Association, *Prose and Poetry of the Live Stock Industry* (Denver and Kansas City, 1905), Vol. I, p. 138. The chapter, "Domestic and Wild Horses," is a good survey.

15. E. T. Sheaf, "The Ponies of the New Forest," *Outing*, XLI (1903), 415-18.

16. Holgar Lundbergh, "Last of Sweden's Wild Horses," *Nature Magazine*, April, 1934.

17. Ernest Schwartz, "The Story of the Horse," *Nature Magazine*, March, 1938.

One thing is certain; of all the monuments which the Spaniard has left to glorify his reign in America there will be none more worthy than his horse . . . . the Spaniard's horses may be found to-day [1888] in countless thousands, from the city of the Montezumas to the regions of perpetual snow; they are grafted into our equine wealth and make an important impression on the horse of the country.

He graces the Western landscape, not because he reminds us of the equine ideal, but because he comes of the soil, and has borne the heat and burden and the vicissitudes of all that pall of romance which will cling about the Western frontier. As we see him hitched to the plow or the wagon he seems a living protest against utilitarianism: but unlike his red master, he will not go. He has borne the Moor, the Spanish conqueror, the red Indian, the mountain-man, and the vaquero through all the glories of their careers; but will soon be gone, with all their heritage of gallant deeds. The pony must meekly enter the new regime. He must wear the collar of the new civilization and earn his oats by the sweat of his flank. There are no more worlds for him to conquer; now he must till the ground.

Frederic Remington, "Horses of the Plains," *Century Magazine*, XXXVII (1888-89), 338 and 343.

CHAPTER TWO

Introduction of the Horse into America

The area which was to become the United States was in 1600 lacking the animals that have made such great contributions to its conquest. The original horses apparently had long since disappeared. Excluding the fur-bearing animals that drew trappers to new frontiers, the buffalo was the only animal present that was to have considerable influence in the conquest.

On the Atlantic seaboard there is no record to show that the original settlers in Jamestown brought any horses or cattle. In 1609, however, a letter from Virginia to England shows that the first horses had been introduced there: "Arrived Plymouth 20th day. We took the 'Blessing,' being the ship wherein I went 6 mares and two horses."[1] The Dutch brought cattle to New Amsterdam in 1625. Four years later twenty-five mares and stallions were introduced into Massachusetts Bay Colony. On July 1, 1630, John Winthrop noted in

his journal: "The 'Mayflower' and the 'Whale' arrived in Charlestown harbor. Their passengers
were all in good health, but most of their cattle were
dead; whereof a mare and a horse of mine. Some
stone horses [stallions] came over in good plight."[2]
Importation of horses by the French had preceded
that of the English, Dutch, and Swedes, for in 1604
horses had been taken to Nova Scotia, and in 1608
to Canada.[3]

It was not from this stock, however, that any
considerable feral horse herds were to be established, nor is it from this stock that the Indians
of America were to be given herds of horses. That
development was to come from the Spanish horses
introduced from Spain or the West Indies.

Columbus deserves the credit for introducing
the horse to the Western world. On his first trip
he was instructed to take 6 mares, 4 jackasses, 2
she-asses, 4 bull calves, 2 heifers, 100 sheep and
goats, 80 boars, and 20 sows.[4]

On his second trip to the Indies he brought a few
horses along to establish ranches in Santo Domingo. His request that they be given free transportation to the New World, which was honored in
1504, shows his firm belief in ranching and his
disbelief in basing the colonial economic life on
gold alone.[5] Since every ship carried horses to the
New World, it is probable that by 1500 a fair beginning had been made in ranching. The threat-

ened depletion of the horse population in Spain caused the king some alarm by 1505, for in that year he forbade shipment of horses to the colonies and decreed anew the old Spanish law that all gentlemen should ride horses instead of mules. The cavalry had been reduced to less than one half that of former years.[6] This decree seems not to have been enforced for several years, for, whereas horses and other livestock had come on nearly every ship for the first quarter century or more, only occasionally after the expedition of Hernando Cortez were horses exported, excepting stallions for breeding or horses for a wealthy nobleman.[7] The demands made by the expeditions outfitting in the West Indies apparently depleted the limited supply of island horses.

Local stockmen found a ready market for both dried beef and horses. After 1510 prices began to increase. A horse that could have been purchased for four or five pesos in that year sold for 200 in 1530 and for 500 in 1538.[8] Bernal Diaz complained years later that in 1523 there were "no horses to be got . . . . except at great price, and that was why we embarked no more horses for there were hardly any to be had."[9] Fernando De Soto imported 100 out of his 115 from Spain for his expedition in 1538. To overcome this shortage, no doubt, Don Alonzo Luis de Lugo and perhaps others contracted with Charles V to bring along with 1500 men, 200 horses as well as mares for breeding purposes. It does seem reasonable to conclude that horses were being shipped to the New World during most of the first fifty or seventy-five years. This probably is no indication of the failure of the local supply to multiply but rather indicates the heavy demands upon the stock.

A few writers of the modern period who have seen or have heard about American wild horse herds have assumed that the Spanish stock was purebred Arabian. John Warrington, writing in the *American Weekly*, speaks of the gorgeous spectacle a herd of the 1940 horses provides, for in "the veins of many wild horses that still roam the plains and mountains flows some of the splendid blood of the Barb-Arab horse....."[10] An English writer says that without doubt "most of the horses of the first Conquistadores came from the plains of Cordoba, then as now the great horse-breeding part of the peninsula. Cordoba is but a short way from Cadiz, Seville and San Lucar, the chief ports of embarkation for the Indies....." The horse of the Americas was uniform in type. "Thus, a horse from the plains of Venezuela or Northern Mexico, placed in an Argentine corral, would hardly be distinguishable....."[11]

Another student, who no doubt had looked at the paintings of Velasquez, says the Spanish horses were of the "great Andalusian breed, round-chested, paced to the *paso castellano*, 'which is something

more than a walk, and less than a trot, and is truly
sedate and sedan-chair like, and suits a grave Don,
who is given, like a Turk, to tobacco and contempla-
tion.' "[12]

It is a general opinion that these horses were not
"plugs." The high prices—as much as two to four
hundred dollars—is not proof of that point, however. It would seem that "no sane don would have
preferred a coarse-jointed great Flemish weight-
carrier for use on the hot sands of Mexico to a light
and supple Barb..... "[13] The dangers and expense
of importation, the calms or "horse latitudes"
which often necessitated throwing the horses over-
board, the bad effect upon a horse of being carried
in swings on such a long journey—these may have
discouraged the introduction of the blooded stock.
Since the Spaniards had long used for war the
descendants of the Moorish horse it is probable that
the quality brought to America was high despite
the danger and expense.[14] Denhardt describes
them as having short backs, "without much day-
light showing beneath their bellies, and admirably
suited for the hard work of a campaign. Their
lengthy posterns made them comfortable to ride,
and their legs not too long, and firmly jointed,
showing that they were sure on their feet..... "[15]
Since these horses carried not only the men but
weapons, cloaks, Moorish saddle, and armor, no
weaklings could have endured the rigors of a con-

tinental campaign, existing as they did largely on the country.

When possible, the conquerors took to the mainland the horses that had been acclimated or raised in the Indies. Most of the explorers were themselves stockmen and had an appreciation of the type of horse necessary for the campaign. Santo Domingo became the point of embarkation and the horse capital of the New World until superseded by Mexico.

Hernando Cortez is credited with landing the first horses on the North American mainland. Near Vera Cruz, Mexico, March 13, 1519, he took from his ship the famous sixteen horses. Here he was joined by Alvarado with twenty horses and 150 men. The diary of the expedition reveals a love for horses, for the description of each horse given was, in the words of Prescott, "minute enough for the pages of a sporting calendar." Gray, brown or chestnut, sorrel, roan, overo (denoting more than one color), dappled, white, and black were represented among the eleven stallions and five mares, two of which were jennet bred.[16] Two of these were killed in the first battle. What happened to the rest is not clear, but in 1524, Cortez sent a message to Charles V, his emperor, saying that he was dispatching a ship to Cuba "for supplies, especially horses."[17]

Sailing under Pánphilo de Narvaez, the expedition led by Cabeza de Vaca, starting in Florida in 1527, introduced horses to the present United

With the Conquistadores the horse returned to the New World

States. These steeds were killed for food and their skins were used for water containers when the expedition embarked in boats to explore the coastline.[18]

The legends concerning the beginnings of wild horse herds stem not from De Vaca or Cortez but from De Soto and Francisco Vasquez de Coronado. This viewpoint is shared by most writers on the subject. Arthur Vernon in his *History and Romance of the Horse* states that the horses escaped from De Soto's band in 1543 while on the Mississippi, immigrated south, and mated with the horses of Cortez. Theodore A. Dodge holds that "De Soto's horses abandoned on the Mississippi, bred on the plains and were lost to civilization."[19] John Warrington, writing in *Travel*, points out that two of the six horses liberated from De Soto's band were stallions. He says:

[There is] every reason to believe that these six gallant mounts retained the freedom they had so gloriously earned. Moving westward from the woody, swampy region surrounding the Mississippi, it is altogether probable they wintered in warmth and plenty somewhere on the eastern plains of Texas. And here when spring again returned to cover the earth with a mantle of greenness and loveliness, four little fuzzy colts, mostly legs, romped with their elders in the wide rolling plains. These four colts became the first Western horses.[20]

Mark Van Doren has put this legend to poetry in his "The Distant Runners."

Ferdinand De Soto lies
Soft again in river mud.
Birds again, as on the day
Of his descending, rise and go
Straightly West, and do not know
Of feet beneath the fainting thud.

If I were there in other time,
Between the proper sky and stream;
If I were there and saw the six
Abandoned manes, and ran along,
I could sing the fetlong song
That now is chilled within a dream.

Ferdinand De Soto, sleeping
In the river, never heard
Four-and-twenty Spanish hooves
Fling off their iron and cut the green,
Leaving circles new and clean
While overhead the wing-tips whirred.

Neither I nor any walker
By the Mississippi now
Can see the dozen nostrils open
Half in pain for the death of men—
But half in gladness, neighing then
As loud as loping would allow.

On they rippled, tail and back,
A prairie dog, and swallows knew
A dark, uneven current there.
But not a sound came up the wind,
And toward the night their shadow thinned
Before the black that flooded through.

If I were there to bend and look,
The sky would know them as they sped
And turn to see. But I am here,
And they are far, and time is old.
Within my dream the grass is cold;
The legs are locked; the sky is dead.[21]

These accounts treat rather lightly the presence of Indians and the natural enemies of the horse. Harcilasco, the Spanish historian, says in regard to De Soto's horses that the "Indians pulled off their halters and saddles, set them running through a field, and hunted them down with arrows until they had slain them all. Thus perished the last of the three hundred horses which had entered Flori-

da."[22] Had these horses escaped and attempted to join the horses running loose in Mexico at that time, as Vernon states, one would of necessity accredit them with stronger instincts of survival than horses are known to possess. The distance from the Mississippi to the plains of Mexico is no short one and a fairly well-baked desert lies between the two. And natural enemies of the horse frequented much of the area. The call of the wild is not sufficiently strong to permit the conclusion that either the horses of De Soto started the herds of America or that there was a union of the Mexican and Mississippi "escapes."

Not quite so improbable is the conclusion reached by others that the estrays and abandoned horses of Coronado provided native horse stock. Starting in 1540 this adventurer with 250 or more horsemen and perhaps 1,000 extra horses and pack mules trekked through the valleys of north Mexico, across the desert, across the Rio Grande, and up to Cibola, to the Pueblo Indian tribes of Arizona.[23] A small part of the expedition made the remainder of the trek into Kansas and back. It was the main body that had most of the difficulties with the horses. In western Mexico a hailstorm caused nearly all of them to break away. A number died from exhaustion and lack of food. Others strayed at night and were lost.

Will C. Barnes, a well-known authority on the Western horse, believes that these estrays produced the wild horse herds that were to become so plentiful in the eighteenth and nineteenth centuries. The Spanish never practiced gelding, as is done today, so it would be possible to start herds if it could be proved that these "escapes" in the grazing country of Arizona were not so few and far between but that instinct could unite them. If they had wandered loose individually, it is likely that the wolves would have destroyed them or driven them back to the main herd. If these horses survived, why did not Juan de Oñate when he was establishing his Northern empire above the Rio Grande sixty years later see some of the horses or hear about them? That must be explained before Coronado's horses can be accredited with being the progenitors of the wild herds. Professor Arthur S. Aiton throws some light on the subject when he states that the muster roll of the Coronado expedition shows that of 558 horses taken, only two were mares.[24] If this may be accepted as true, the possibility of horse herds originating from the estrays is reduced to a point further than it has ever been before.

The Spanish expeditions to South America, as in Central and North America, were equipped with horses. The legend persisted for some time that the original horse there had not disappeared but was to be found in Brazil. When John Cabot visited the La Plata in 1530 he reported seeing horses.[25] Since no future navigators reported seeing native horses, and since the Indian obviously had not known the horse before the Spanish introduced it, it seems clear that Cabot, in the words of E. L. Trouessart, "is a liar."[26] This adventurer wanted to impress the king of Spain and later the king of England so he reported both mines and horses which did not exist.

Horses became plentiful in Chile, Peru, Honduras, Brazil, Argentina, Venezuela, and elsewhere in South America. Nicaragua became a horse-breeding area of note. In the valleys and plains of

Mexico was established a great ranching industry that was to extend north of the Rio Grande. Robert Tomson, an English trader, wrote in 1555 that in New Spain there was "a marvelous increase of cattell which daily do increase and they are of greater growth than ours. . . . . They have many horses, mares and mules which the Spaniards brought thither. . . . . "[27]

The governor of Nueva Viscaya, appointed in 1562, is given credit for the rapid spread of livestock in Durango, Sinaloa, and parts of Chihuahua and Sonora, the provinces bordering the Rio Grande,[28] while Oñate in 1600 was the pioneer of the ranching interests in New Mexico.

The Jesuits led the way in the colonization of California, being followed by settlers. Stock ranches were established in lower California in 1696, and in the next century fifteen missions existed there as evidence of Spanish expansion. In 1769 missionaries began the settlement of Upper California. All these missions had livestock and "their flocks and herds first were increased in size until their numbers were numbered by thousands. . . . . "[29]

It is probable that the wild horse herds emerged from the ranches or mission ranches of the Spanish in the Americas, not from some tired horses of the conquistadores. In the southwestern part of the United States where there are natural enemies, a lack of rainfall, and limited grazing, the stock arose that was to give Western America its horse. It was here, as well as on the grass-covered pampas and the plains of Venezuela, that the horse herds were to become nearly as numerous as was the native buffalo of North America.

FOOTNOTES—CHAPTER TWO

1. Quoted by W. C. Barnes, *The Story of the Range* (Washington, D. C., 1913), p. 4.

2. Quoted by Joseph A. Bursey, "Horses of the Southwest," *New Mexico Magazine,* September, 1933, p. 12.

3. *Loc cit.*

4. Robert M. Denhardt, "The Southwestern Cow-Horse," *The Cattleman,* December, 1938.

5. Robert M. Denhardt, "Spanish Horses and the New World," *The Historian,* Winter, 1938, p. 9.

6. *Ibid.,* pp. 7-8.

7. R. B. Cunninghame Graham, *The Horses of the Conquest* (London, 1930), pp. 110-11. Early expeditions had been bound by agreement to bring stallions and mares.

8. Denhardt, "Spanish Horses and the New World," *The Historian*, Winter, 1938, pp. 14-20.

9. Quoted by Cunninghame Graham, *op. cit.*, p. 52.

10. "Still Time to Save America's Wild Horses," *American Weekly*, issue of January 14, 1940.

11. Cunninghame Graham, *op. cit.*, p. 131.

12. Morris Bishop, *The Odyssey of Cabeza de Vaca* (New York, 1933), p. 31, quoting Ford, *Spaniards and Their Country*. Quoted by permission of D. Appleton-Century Company.

13. Frederic Remington, "Horses of the Plains," *Century Magazine*, XXXVII (1888-89), 333.

14. This viewpoint is held by Denhardt and Cunninghame Graham, careful students of the Spanish horse.

15. Denhardt in *The Historian*, Winter, 1938.

16. W. H. Carter, "The Story of the Horse," *National Geographic Magazine*, XLIV (1923), 551-52; and Denhardt, "The Truth about Cortés's Horses," *Hispanic American Review*, XVII (1937), 525-32.

17. Will C. Barnes, "The Passing of the Wild Horses," *American Forests and Forest Life*, XXX (1924), 624.

18. Morris Bishop, *op. cit.*, p. 51.

19. "The Horse in America," *North American Review*, CLV (1892), 668.

20. "Wild Horses of the Old Frontier," *Travel*, November, 1939.

21. Given in Louis Untermeyer, ed., *Modern American Poetry* (New York, 1930), pp. 690-91. Quoted by permission of A. and C. Boni, Inc., publishers of the volume in which it originally appeared.

22. Quoted from *Historia de Florida* by Bishop, *op. cit.*, p. 31, footnote 4.

23. This account is told by Petro de Casteñeda, historian of the expedition, in G. P. Winship's "The Coronado Expedition, 1540-1542," *Fourteenth Annual Report of the Bureau of Ethnology*, Part I (Washington, D. C., 1896).

24. Taken from Francis Haines, "The Northward Spread of Horses Among the Plains Indians," *American Anthropologist*, XL (1938), 249, footnote 2.

25. R. C. Auld, "As to the 'Extinction of the American Horse,'" *Science*, XX (1892), 135, quoting Flower's manual *The Horse*.

26. "The Fiction of the American Horse and the Truth on this Disputed Point," *Science*, XX (1892), 188.

27. Quoted by Joseph A. Bursey, "Horses in the Southwest," *New Mexico Magazine*, September, 1933, p. 12.

28. Denhardt, "The Southwestern Cow-Horse," *The Cattleman*, January, 1939.

29. National Live Stock Association, *Prose and Poetry of the Live Stock Industry* (Denver and Kansas City, 1905), chapter on the "Introduction of Live Stock into the Domain of the United States."

Try to think of the west absolutely without horses . . . . the west of song and story and familiar fact, the west of the buffalo, the antelope, the grizzly bear and the Plains Indian. But throughout the length and breadth of it there is not so much as one horse, and the Plains Indians . . . . move slowly, ploddingly, on foot.

Then drop the curtain.

A miracle has happened. The plains are alive with droves of wild horses, in places almost rivaling the buffalo in numbers. . . . . The Indian nations of the plains, who just now were earthbound footmen, are nations of mounted warriors, perhaps the finest cavalry in the world.

H. R. Sass, "Hoofs on the Prairie," *Country Gentleman*, July, 1936, p. 5. Quoted by permission of the *Country Gentleman*.

CHAPTER THREE

The Indian Gets the Horse

There is a legend that near Oaxaca, Mexico, an Indian scout stood on a hill to report on the advancing Spanish. What he saw as the cavalcade passed was one of the most extraordinary sights his eyes had ever beheld— he had seen the horse. According to the legend he went inside the near-by cave and there on the wall in white pigment he drew this new monster that was to revolutionize his life in the new world.[1] If the Indians of the Americas had ever seen a horse before the Spanish came, they had long since forgotten even the legends connected with it.

When Pánphilo de Narvaez was given the task in 1511 of pacifying the Indians of Cuba he had need of nothing except his mare. Because of the treatment of the Indian women by the Spanish several thousand warriors made an attack at night. Narvaez mounted his mare, clad only in a shirt, and with bells in his hand, rode among them. The braves fled in great confusion.[2]

When Hernando Cortez invaded Mexico, the Indians killed one of his horses, which they cut to pieces and exhibited in the villages. This showed them the horse was mortal. If this fact had been generally known at this time the conquest of America might well have taken a different course. The Indians played safe on this occasion, however, and gave the horseshoes to their idol.[3]

Later, when Cortez came to the island of Petén to subjugate the Indians, a horse which was disabled was left behind. The missionaries had brought Christianity at the same time, so the Indians associated horses with the deity. They garlanded the horse with flowers and fed him poultry, only to see him die within a short time. One hundred years later the Spanish returned to this island, there to find the Indians worshipping in their temple an image of the horse as the god of thunder and lightning.[4]

At one time when Cortez was in a precarious position in respect to the Indians, he had a stallion brought rather close to the place of the powwow where a mare was tied. The mare was then removed. The stallion, scenting the mare, began to neigh, prance, and paw the ground. The Indians, not understanding this strange behavior of the horse, were terrified. Cortez rose to the occasion, commanded his men to take the horse away, then told the natives that the horse had been instructed not to harm them since their mission was for peace.[5]

When Chief Isquin of a tribe of Yucatan Indians saw the horse for the first time, he "almost ran mad with joy and with astonishment. Especially the jumps and bounds made by the animals moved him to admiration, and going down on all fours he skipped about and neighed. When tired of the manifestation of his joy and astonishment, he asked the Spanish name of the mysterious animals. When he heard it was Caballo, he forthwith renounced his name, and from that day . . . . to his dying day was called Don Petro Caballito."[6]

Fernando De Soto gave a Florida chief an experience new in his life when he put him on a horse and took him for a ride. The chief was so long-legged that his feet touched the ground. The historian of the expedition recorded that the chief could not have been pleased "because the Indians looked upon these animals as if they had been lions or tigers, and feared them mightily."[7]

Consternation seized the natives when they saw one of Francisco Pizarro's cavaliers fall from his horse. They were not prepared for the division of what they had considered one and the same thing, a man on horseback.[8]

The Pueblo tribes of Arizona were so impressed at the sight of the horses of Francisco Vasquez de Coronado that they smeared their bodies with sweat, taken from these wonderful animals, perhaps for the purpose of thereby gaining some of the magic of the white man's horse.[9] The historian of the expedition admitted that horses were "the most necessary things in new countries, and they frighten the enemy most."[10]

That the horse was the most important factor in the conquest of the Americas is obvious. The contemporary records show that the cavaliers believed that next to God the horse was most responsible for their victories. The tribes held the horses in such terror that a cavalry charge could route an Indian army—until they learned the horses were mortal. There is one incident which shows that two or three loose horses, galloping close to a village, dispersed the whole settlement. Cortez regarded the loss of one horse equal to that of twenty men.[11] When in the siege of Mexico a riderless mare of Cortez' ran toward the enemy and was struck by arrows before she returned, he wrote: "Although we feel her death deeply, for the horses and the mares are our salvation, our grief was less because she did not die in the hands of the enemy, as we feared would be the case."[12]

In life and literature the horse had meant much to the Spaniard. For over one thousand years the Spanish gentleman had traveled on horseback. Even beggars called their superiors *caballero*, a gentleman on horseback. There is a story about a Spanish governor of an American province who

fell when walking, only to exclaim, *"Caramba! eso
es camina sobre terra*—This is what comes of
walking on the ground."[13] It is not strange that
after the Spaniards established their ranches in
the new world they prohibited the Indian from
riding horses. Ironical it is, though, that while the
conquest of the Americas was made possible
through the use of the horse, it was the horse, when
it became the possession of the Indian by theft,
through estrays, or from wild herds, that prevented the conquest of many of the Indians north of the
first Spanish frontier in the present United States.
Not only did the Spanish empire stop here, but it
found difficulty in protecting settlements from the
horse Indians. The savages not only held the Great
Plains until the Texas Rangers or the United
States Army came on the scene, but they made life
and property unsafe on a frontier from Canada to
the country below the Rio Grande.

Just when the Indian overcame his fear of the
horse is not clear. This probably occurred when
each tribe learned that an arrow could kill either
a man or a horse or both. The Spanish ruse perhaps worked but a short time after the first contact with a tribe was made. After the missions and
ranches were established the Indian herdsmen soon
learned to use horses and gradually the tribes to
the north came into possession of them. From these
sources it would seem the Indian secured his horse,

The Indian looked upon the horse for the first time

not from wild herds composed of estrays from Coronado or De Soto.

There were wild horses on the plains of Mexico in the early seventeenth century, long before they were present in southwestern United States.[14] Soon after the establishment of the livestock industry in the northern Mexican provinces in 1562 the natives were stealing great numbers for their own use. On one foray alone they succeeded in getting 250 horses.[15] It is not probable that the American Indians received any of their stock from this source because of the lack of communication with these tribes, nor is it probable that any of the estrays wandered across the arid lands which separate the American Southwest from the Mexican plateau. When Coronado came across the plains in 1540 he found the tribes traveling "like Arabs, with their tents and troops of dogs loaded with poles and having a Moorish pack saddle with girths. When the loads get disarranged, the dogs howl, calling some one to fix them right. . . . . "[16] Juan de Onate, who was the next Spaniard to lead an expedition into this part of the world and who founded Santa Fe as a great trading center, found no traces of horse culture. It is possible that there could have been isolated bands of horses that had survived from the Coronado expedition, but it is not probable.[17]

The period from 1680 to 1750 saw the conquest of the horse by the Indians. By the time of the

Pueblo Revolt in 1680, the Pueblos and Apaches had acquired some horses; how long before is uncertain. It is not probable that these horses were coming from the missions since there were none in Texas prior to 1690, or in California before 1769, while those in New Mexico established after 1598 had few if any horses. The conclusion seems to be

warranted that the natives were getting horses by theft or from estrays during the latter part of the seventeenth century, not from missions but from the settlements and ranches of New Mexico and perhaps from the southern provinces of Coahuila, Sonora, and others.[18]

Regardless of just how the first horses came into the possession of the plains tribes, it seems evident that they did not come from wild-horse herds. Most of the tribes had horses before the feral herds had spread over the western plains. The Apaches were the first to get horses. In 1659 the Navajo Apache made raids on ranches in the Santa Fe area, and these became a common practice.[19] The Pueblo Revolt of 1680 may have accentuated this trend, for the horses could be traded to the adjoining tribes who were either without horses or had an insufficient number. Because of the close relations between these Indians and the Texas tribes it is probable that the horses were distributed there first in greater numbers. When the Mendoza-Lopez expedition moved northwest across Texas from the Rio Grande in 1683, horses became more plentiful as they progressed, there having been none on the Rio Grande. Henri de Tonty found a few horses among the Red River Indians in 1690. "It would seem, then, that by 1690 all the Plains tribes of Texas had horses, but that the animals were quite scarce to the south and east, indicating that they had but recently reached those areas."[20]

The Comanches probably were the horse brokers of the plains. By 1850 they "were boasting in all seriousness that the horse was created by the Good Spirit for the particular benefit of the Comanche, and that the Comanche had introduced it to the whites."[21] Their herds always had a good sprinkling of Spanish brands among them, indicating that their legend was groundless. The Poncas have a legend that the horse came to them from the Comanches. When Claude Charles Du Tisne visited them in 1719, he found that the 400 warriors had

300 highly-prized horses.[22] With them he traded goods for two horses and a mule bearing a Spanish brand.[23] According to the Ponca legend they saw the horse for the first time when they sighted a band of Comanches. "The Comanche charged, wielding their stone battleaxes. The breasts and sides of their 'kawas,' as the Poncas called the strange-maned animals, were protected with over-lapping plates of rawhide to ward off the Ponca's arrows; but the latter, though they were much afraid, fought desperately and at last, when neither side could win, the battle ceased. Peace talks were held, a truce was arranged, the Ponca bartered some of their bows, which were very fine, for horses and persuaded the Comanche to teach them how to ride. Then they made war on the Comanche again and drove them from the region....."[24] The Kiowa Indians, who probably got their first horses by 1748 from the Crows when they lived in the north mountain country, were thus rebuked by a Comanche chief in 1868 for stealing horses: "When we first knew you, you had nothing but dogs and sleds. Now you have plenty of horses, and where did you get them if they were not stolen from Mexico?"[25]

The Pawnees, whose range adjoined the Comanches and who therefore were able to steal more easily from that tribe, became the distributors to the Osages to the east and the Dakotas to the north. That this was the horse frontier is indicated not only by the fact that the Pawnees prized their horses so highly, but also by the report of a traveler years later who said that at that time the poorest families had two or three horses, many braves and chiefs had eight to twelve, and one chief had thirty, some being wild, some Spanish, and three of American origin.[26] Etienne Vanyard Bourgmont, who made a trip up the Missouri and across the plains in 1724, could get only seven horses from the western Kansas Indians. This indicates that here was the upper limit of the horse country.[27]

The northward movement of horses (shown on map on cover leaves) seemed to have been along two routes, one paralleling the eastern slope of the Rockies, the other to the west of the Continental Divide.[28] The Snake or Shoshoni Indians apparently were the brokers through whom the Saskatchewan and most of the tribes north of the Platte River and of the Pacific Northwest directly or indirectly gained horses.[29] The Blackfeet of Montana have a tradition that their horses came from the Snake and the Flathead Indians. The Crow, Teton, Arapaho, Kiowa, Pawnee, and Nez Perce got them from the Shoshoni. When the Blackfeet were first contacted in 1754 they had many horses.[30] As early as 1742, Pierre Le Vérendrye's sons on a trip west from the Mandans in the Dakota country saw horses most of the way to the Rockies.[31] By 1776, Assiniboins to the east of the Blackfeet had herds or horses "in number" feeding on the plains.[32]

These were probably stolen from or gained through trading with the Indians to the west.

When Jonathan Carver approached the Minnesota country from the east in his 1766-68 expedition he found no horses among the Eastern Sioux bands. However, he was informed that the "Indians that inhabit still farther to the westward, a country which extends to the South Sea, use in fight a warlike instrument that is very uncommon. Having great plenty of horses, they always attack their enemies on horseback. . . . ."[33]

That the tribes in the north Rocky Mountain area had horses before most of the upper plains tribes seems certain. The Coeur d'Alenes, living between the Spokane tribes on the west, the Nez Perces and Palouse to the south, and the Pend d'Oreilles to the east, had horses by 1760. The first horses came from the Kalispel, according to the following legend:

The first horse came to the Coeur d'Alene country at a place about 3½ miles northwest of De Smet. A large number of people were gathered there, digging camas. They saw a man approaching on horseback, and became greatly excited. The rider was a Kalispel Indian, who remained several days with the Coeur d'Alene. The people examined the horse closely, and wondered at the strange animal. As the horse was gentle, many people tried to ride him; but when he trotted, they fell off. . . . .[34]

The legend goes on to explain that no Coeur d'Alene ever went east to the plains until the tribe had horses. At the time when they did make the first trip they found the Shoshoni and Flathead had many horses. The Blackfeet and some other Eastern tribes often sold horses to the plains tribes but they did not procure any from them.

A recent student of the distribution of horses by the Indian tribes, Francis Haines, believes the Shoshoni had horses by 1700, which was about the time the horse reached the Oklahoma-Arkansas border and twenty years before it reached the Kansas-Missouri frontier. Thus he concluded that the traffic in horses which supplied the Indians of the northern Rocky Mountain and plains area occurred west of the Continental Divide.

This evidence does not explain how those among the Indians east of the Mississippi acquired their horses. As has been stated before, horses were introduced into the seaboard colonies soon after the first settlements were made, near the time Oñate was establishing the first permanent settlement there.[35] The wild horses allegedly found by the pioneers of South Carolina probably were "escapes" from Virginia or were from the wild herds ranging the hinterland.[36] In 1829, on the island chain lining the seaboard from Delaware to Georgia, many wild horses known as beach ponies were common.[37]

Among the Northern Indians there seems to have been no evidence of early horse culture. Colonel John Johnston is quoted as saying that the Wyandotts of the Ohio country did not have horses before

1775, but acquired them at that date from the troops, at Braddock's defeat.[38] The Kansas, Osages, and others, according to an Osage chief, had to eat horses on their way home from that campaign.[39]

Yet it appears that at the same time, and much earlier, horses were in general use among the tribes below the Ohio River. James Adair, a trader among these Southern Indians for forty years, tells in his book published in 1775 of the superb horsemanship of the Choctaws, which would indicate that the horse had long been among them.[40] In 1774, one traveler who bought a beautiful horse from the Chickasaws, said they "are very careful of preserving a fine breed of Spanish horses they have long preserved, unmixed with any others."[41] William Bartram, a famous early American botanist, saw in 1773, "the most beautiful and sprightly species of that noble creature perhaps anywhere to be seen, ... a small breed, and as delicately formed as the American roe buck."[42]

Since the horse was the most numerous in the South, was Spanish in appearance, and wore the Spanish type of saddle, the ultimate source probably was the Spanish settlements west of the Mississippi or the West Indies. It is known that in this spread of the horse the "French were a negligible factor because they settled at the mouth of the Mississippi after the horse had reached the Missouri. Even the English settlements in Virginia scarcely reached a point where they could supply horses to the Indians of the East before horses are reported in the West....."[43] The Mississippi River, while not prohibiting horse stealing or trading, did discourage such intercourse. Evidence cannot disprove that these horses were not introduced and propagated from those escaped when De Soto lost fifty horses in the Chickasaw attack in 1537, but the probability is that the De Soto horses were destroyed by the puma and wolf and natives in the thick cover of the region. Professors Bolton and Marshall say that the trade in "Pawnee and Spanish horses extended to the English seaboard colonies, Governor Patrick Henry being among the purchasers of thoroughbred Spanish stock....."[44] Z. M. Pike, who went into North Mexico on his expedition of 1807, spoke of the abundance of wild horses there which supplied the savages of Texas and the Spaniards in other provinces, and which were "also sent into the United States, notwithstanding the trade in contraband."[45] In 1789, the well-known Daniel Boone was reported "at Monongahela with a drove of 'lose horses' for sale," the source of such animals being unknown.[46] It is doubtful, however, if the traffic between the Spanish-Indian frontiers and that of the seaboard ever was of much significance.

Thus it would seem that the horse, while introduced by the Conquistadores, was established in the Southwest by Oñate and his followers in the first years of the seventeenth century, and by the English and French on the Atlantic at approximately the same time. The lack of intercourse, the nature of the country, and the lack of prestige of the horseman served to prevent the Northeastern tribes from acquiring them until after the Revolutionary War. Spreading upward from the New Mexican ranches and trading centers, the horse was distributed by the tribes until it reached the northernmost plains tribes by approximately the time the Northeastern Indians had horses. Horse culture spread like a fan from the Rockies to the eastern Gulf area. From these herds as much as from the Spanish horses grew the feral herds that have been such a lodestone to American romantic interests.

FOOTNOTES—CHAPTER THREE

1. Given by J. Frank Dobie, "The Spanish Cow Pony," *Saturday Evening Post*, November 24, 1934.

2. This incident is given by Morris Bishop in his *The Odyssey of Cabeza De Vaca* (New York, 1933), pp. 17-18.

3. R. B. Cunninghame Graham, *The Horses of the Conquest* (London, 1930), p. 60.

4. M. Oldfield Howey, *The Horse in Magic and Myth* (London, 1923), pp. 193-94; also given by Hartley B. Alexander, "The Horse in American Indian Culture," in the volume *So Live the Works of Man* (Albuquerque, 1939), edited by D. D. Brand and Fred Harvey.

5. Robert M. Denhardt, "Equine Strategy of Cortés," *Hispanic American Review*, XVIII (1938), 551, quoting Bernal Diaz de Castillo.

6. Taken from Villagutierre, the Spanish historian, by Cunninghame Graham, *op. cit.*, pp. 35-36.

7. Quoted by Cunninghame Graham, *op. cit.*, p. 75.

8. Basil Tozier, *The Horse in History* (London, 1908), p. 171.

9. Hartley B. Alexander, *op. cit.*, p. 67.

10. Quoted by G. P. Winship, "The Coronado Expedition, 1540-1542," *Fourteenth Annual Report of the Bureau of Ethnology*, Part I (Washington, D. C., 1896), p. 546.

11. Cunninghame Graham, *op. cit.*, pp. 23-24.

12. Quoted by Denhardt, *op. cit.*, p. 552. Permission to quote given by Duke University Press.

13. "The Inheritance of the Centaur," *Atlantic Monthly*, LXXII (1893), 576. No author given.

14. W. D. Matthew, in a letter, "The Horse and the Llama," *Outlook*, CXXIII, (1919), 318-19.

15. Denhardt, *op. cit.*, p. 39.

16. Winship, *op. cit.*, p. 527.

17. This viewpoint is held by four scholars, Wissler, Denhardt, Haines, and Alexander.

18. This opinion is given by Professor Lansing Bloom, University of New Mexico, in a letter, May 22, 1940.

19. Francis Haines, "The Northward Spread of Horses Among the Plains Tribes," *American Anthropologist*, XL (1938), 431.

20. *Ibid.*, 432.

21. E. Douglas Branch, *The Hunting of the Buffalo* (New York, 1929), p. 24. Quoted by permission of D. Appleton-Century Company.

22. James R. Mead, "The Pawnees as I Knew Them," *Transactions of the Kansas State Historical Society* (Topeka, 1910), X, 107, footnote.

23. Anna Lewis, "Du Tisne's Expedition into Oklahoma, 1719," *Chronicles of Oklahoma* (Oklahoma City, 1925), III, 318-22.

24. H. R. Sass, "Hoofs on the Prairie," *Country Gentleman*, July, 1936, p. 6. This and subsequent quotations from the *Country Gentleman* are used with the permission of the publisher.

25. James Mooney, "Calendar History of the Kiowa Indians," *Seventeenth Annual Report of the Bureau of Ethnology* (Washington, D. C., 1898), pp. 160-61.

26. C. A. Murray, *Travels in North America During the Years* 1834, 1835, & 1836 (London, 1841), II, 353.

27. Mead, *op. cit.*, footnote.

28. Haines, *op. cit.*, pp. 435-36.

29. Clark Wissler, "The Influence of the Horse in the Development of Plains Culture," *American Anthropologist*, XVI (1914), 24. Spanish brands were found on the horses of the Saskatchewan in 1784. *Ibid.*, p. 21.

30. Haines, *op. cit.*, p. 433.

31. L. J. Burpee, ed., *Journals and Letters of Pierre Gaultier de Varennes de La Vérendrye and His Sons....* (Toronto, 1927), p. 420.

32. Alexander Henry, *Travels and Adventures in Canada and the Indian Territories between the Years* 1760 and 1776 (New York, 1809), p. 295.

33. Jonathan Carver, *Travels Through the Interior Parts of North America in the Years* 1766, 1767, and 1768 (London, 1781), p. 294.

34. James A. Teit, "The Salishan Tribes of the Western Plains," *Forty-fifth Annual Report of the Bureau of American Ethnology* (Washington, D. C., 1930), p. 109.

35. Will C. Barnes, "The Passing of the Wild Horse," *American Forests and Forest Life*, November, 1924, p. 645; Wissler, *Man and Culture* (New York, 1923), p. 115.

36. Sass, *op. cit.*, p. 68.

37. "Natural History," *American Turf Register and Sporting Magazine*, I (1929), 20.

38. Ray Merwin, "The Wyandott Indians," *Transactions of the Kansas State Historical Society* (Topeka, 1906), IX, 79, footnote 2.

39. George P. Morehouse, "History of the Kansa or Kaw Indians," *ibid.* (Topeka, 1908), X, 330-31.

40. James Adair, *The History of the American Indians* (London, 1775), p. 426.

41. Quoted by Sass, *op. cit.*, p. 69.

42. *Loc. cit.*

43. Wissler, "The Influence of the Horse in the Development of Plains Culture," *American Anthropologist*, XVI (1914), 8.

44. H. E. Bolton and T. M. Marshall, *The Colonization of North America*, 1492-1783 (New York, 1927), p. 400. Quoted by permission of Macmillan Company.

45. Z. M. Pike, *An Account of Expeditions....* (Philadelphia, 1910), Appendix to Part III, p. 29.

46. John Bakeless, *Daniel Boone* (New York, 1939), p. 333.

The horse has come. Almost overnight, it seems, he has captured the west; and by his coming the west has been awakened, transformed.

It was one of the most dramatic and one of the most momentous transformations that ever took place in any land under the sun. The bare facts of the coming of the horse and the transformation thus wrought constitute the greatest animal epic ever enacted in the world.

H. R. Sass, "Hoofs on the Prairie," *Country Gentleman*, July, 1936, p. 5. Quoted by permission of the *Country Gentleman*.

CHAPTER FOUR

Indians on Horseback

Anthropologists call the period between 1600 and 1880 that of Indian horse culture. In these years the Indian not only acquired the horse but made it a part of his everyday life. In this period he prevented further encroachments of the Spanish upon the Southwestern frontier, and for a number of years kept the Texas Rangers and a fair segment of the United States Army busy. The horse changed the whole life of the aborigine. It was as important to him as the coming of steam was to the white man. The consequence was "a general upward swing of the culture, which put it, as regards outward appearances, on a par with the cultures of other areas that in purely aboriginal times had outranked the Plains. . . . . "[1]

The plains Indians, before the advent of the Spanish horse, were nomadic and warlike, not agricultural, except in a limited way. With the acquisition of the horse, these traits were intensified greatly; they became "outwanderers, raiders, and splendid thieves. . . . . "[2]

The horsemanship of these Indians is a trait most often commented upon by contemporary observers. While most of the tribes became adept at this art, sufficiently so to be called the greatest cavalry in the world, it was the Comanches that elicited the most praise. Captain R. B. Marcy on his Red River trip in 1849 spoke of them in what seems to be admiring terms:

It is when mounted that the Comanche exhibits himself to the best advantage: here he is at home, and his skill in various manoeuvres which he makes available in battle—such as throwing himself entirely upon one side of the horse, and discharging his arrows with great rapidity towards the opposite side from beneath the animal's neck while he is at full speed—is truly astonishing. Many of the women are equally as expert, as equestrians, with the men. They ride upon the same saddles and in the same manner, with a leg upon each side of the horse. . . . . Every warrior has his war-like horse, which is the fleetest that can be obtained, and he prizes him more highly than anything else in his possession, and it is seldom that he can be induced to part with him at any price. He never mounts him except when going into battle, the buffalo chase, or upon state occasions. On his return he is met at the door of his lodge by one of his wives, who takes his horse and attends to its wants with the utmost care. . . . . I once made an effort to purchase a favorite horse from a chief of one of the bands of the Southern Comanche (Se-na-co), and offered him a large price, but he could not be persuaded to part with him. He said the animal was one of the fleetest in their possession, and if he were to sell him, it would prove a calamity to his whole band, as it often required all the speed of this animal to insure success in the buffalo chase; that his loss would be felt by all his people, and he would be regarded as very foolish; moreover, he said, (patting his favorite on the neck), "I love him very much."[3]

The Sioux were considered by General George Crook as being the best natural cavalry the world had even seen, and in their games they were likewise the superior of other Indian tribes. But the Comanches surpassed them and all others in riding and racing. George Catlin, traveling among them a few years before Marcy, spoke glowingly of their ability to throw themselves from an upright position to the side of their horses, from there throwing spears or shooting arrows. This practice of taking all their exercise on a horse caused them to look as awkward on the ground as a monkey.[4]

Washington Irving was most impressed by the Crows who approached his camp for the purpose of showing their skill on horseback, "careening at full speed on their half-savage steeds, and dashing among rocks and crags, and up and down the most rugged and dangerous places with perfect ease and unconcern."[5]

Even the Choctaws, east of the Mississippi, as observed by James Adair, boasted of "the swiftness of their horses, and their skill in riding and guiding them, much better with a rope than with a bridle....." These Indians, however, mounted their horses from the "off side, claiming it was the more natural than mounting from the left side."[6]

Horse racing was a sport much practiced by

the Indians of the plains. It assumed a position in their life that athletics do in the collegiate world. More than one contemporary observer was thrilled or horrified at this sport. Catlin, when among the Mandans of the Dakota country, was pleasantly shocked at this "sin that is so familiar in the Christian world of sporting with the limbs and the lives of these noble animals. *Horse-racing here* .... is one of the most exciting amusements, and one of the most extravagant modes of gambling." He stated that he had just been a spectator and had been "not a little amused and pleased with the thrilling effect which these exciting seenes have produced amongst so wild and picturesque a group."[7] When once a miserable appearing wild pony of a Comanche chief defeated a thoroughbred ridden by an army officer, it is "small wonder," says R. M. Denhardt, "that among the Indians the horse was worshipped *and his name* became synonymous with God."[8]

The immediate effect upon the Indians of the acquisition of a few Spanish horses by trade or theft was to discourage what little agricultural work they did, and cause them to rely upon the buffalo more than ever before. When they used the dog to drag tepee poles and pack burdens, their migration had been limited to the season. With the horse they roamed for miles, encroached upon others' hunting grounds, went to war, and otherwise became marauders of the plains. While agriculture was never completely abandoned, the ease with which the whole camp could be moved by using the pony as a pack horse or a travois discouraged it.[9] It may have given an impetus to agriculture in the case of those Indians who clung to settled life, preferring to trade their surpluses for the jerked meat of the hunting tribes. This new food supply was withal a new standard of wealth and well-being, all of which came to be measured by the number of ponies possessed. Ponies became to the Indian what the automobile was to become to this civilization. With them he bought his wives and paid his debts. "It was the greatest ambition of an Indian to be the owner of a band of horses; his chances of success were nil without them; his wealth and social position was determined by the number he possessed. . . . . ."[10] A chief showed his position in part by having more horses than anybody else.

Hunting the buffalo became a picturesque practice. For this type of hunting each brave had as "top horse" one which in many instances had been trained as a cow pony by some rancher. At the sight of a herd the rider would advise the horse to run well, to have no fear, to try to keep from being gored.[11] As the two lines of hunters rode in, one on each side, the horse took his rider along one buffalo until it was killed, then on to another, all the while leaving his master's hands free to throw the lance, stretch the bow, or reload the rifle. He also learned equestrian tricks that amazed white observers. Writing in 1829, Don Alphonso said that often the arrows passed through the buffalo and fell to the ground. "When this occurs, the assailant stoops, lifts his arrow as he passes onward at half speed, and preserves it ever after as evidence of divine favor....."[12]

Down in New Orleans, about 1840, a budding poet tried to describe an Indian buffalo hunt. The poem rambles and speaks in the language of another day, but it does give a romantic touch to this sporting business of making a living:

> Silence, beneath the noon-day moon, is keeping
>   Watch o'er the untrod prairies of the West,
> Where myriads of Buffalo are sleeping,
>   Or grazing on earth's green and flowery breast;
> And their low bellowing doth the stillness break,
>   As Zephyr moves the lake.
>
> A thousand hunters, on their fire-eyed steeds,
>   With barbed arrows and with bended bow,
> Shrieking as each new victim falls and bleeds,
>   Are dealing death among the buffalo!
> See the wild herds, swift crossing as they fly,
>   The verge of land and sky.
>
> See the Comanches, with a fiend-like ease,
>   Flying on half-wild steeds across the plain;
> Their long dark scalp locks streaming to the breeze,
>   Red as the sun-beam with vermillion stain;
> Now distant far, then instant flashing nigher,
>   Like mounted flames of fire!
>
> And see the phrenzied buffalo at bay,
>   After his savage hunter madly rushing;

Vainly he fights or seeks to 'scape away,
  With the red stream from his wide nostrils gushing!
He pauses, staggers, pants and glares around,
  Then headlong seeks the ground!

Around them see the red Comanches crowd,
  To the huge victims' horns their wild steeds tied;
With flashing knives and yell of triumph loud,
  Tearing the warm skin from his reeking side.
See the red devils, with the brute's own hoof,
  Knocking his rump ribs off![13]

Buffalo hunting may or may not have been that exciting, but it was more sport for the Indian than the old method of stalking the game, driving them into an enclosure, starting a prairie fire, or stampeding them over a cliff. Now, if the herd left the region, the tribe went too, following the meat supply wherever necessary. While the Indian did not give up the jerked meat for fresh meat, the horses came close to bringing the advantages of refrigeration to the plains. The prestige of the medicine man declined, his machinations no longer being necessary in order to fill the larder.[14] Camps could now be large and the men, with more leisure on their hands than ever before, could loaf, gamble, or engage in war against, or steal horses from, both whites and neighboring tribes.[15] Washington Irving believed that the red men, "continually on horseback scouring the Plains, gaining their food by hardy exercise, and subsisting chiefly on flesh, are generally tall, sinewy, meagre, but well-formed, and of bold and fierce deportment...."

while the fish-eating Indians of the Columbia River, "lounging about the river banks, or squatting and curved up in their canoes, are generally low in stature, ill-shaped, with crooked legs, thick ankles, and broad flat feet. They are inferior, also in muscular power and activity, and in *game* qualities and appearance, to their hard-riding brethren of the prairies."[16]

It was this leisure time, the rise of the pony as the measure of wealth, and the infringement upon one another's buffalo range that was a cause of intertribal war. From this time on there was little peace among many of the tribes of Indians. Horse stealing became a part of the mores of most tribes, and provided an outlet for the energy stored up in leisure time. One old chief told Captain Marcy that his four sons were a comfort to him because they could steal more horses than any other members of the tribe.[17] A contemporary spoke of this trait as follows:

An Indian, if well mounted, feels an aristocratic pride, which has its parallel no where but in the bosom of a ragged Circassian prince. . . . . A band of braves may go out on foot, but they are rarely observed to return pedestrians. Give an Indian a halter, or a thong, and the precepts and practice of the sages of his tribe teach him how to procure a horse. . . . . The virtues that Lycurgus taught are prized and refined upon by the braves and warriors; for they are not only thieves, but they glory in the character. There is this in their favor: they do the thing on a large scale, making it a business of their lives, and they rarely serve as foot-pads.[18]

The horse changed the whole life of the Indian

The Blackstone of the Indians, or perhaps their own Hebraic law, held that if thirty horses were stolen by the neighbors, the tribe thus affected might steal thirty from the first herd they saw.[19] Irving noted that the Arikara Indians traded horses to the whites for ten dollars worth of guns, tomahawks, and powder, but replenished the supply by raiding the Sioux.[20] Picture writing of the Indians give accounts of Oglalas stealing seventy horses from the Crows in 1822-23, and the Utes stealing all of the Brûlés' horses in 1874-75.[21]

It has been said that the Indians of South America were "probably the greatest horse thieves that ever lived, and those of Central America can easily be favorably compared with our own Sioux ....,"[22] but it is doubtful if any surpassed the tribes of the plains. Their herds were probably the greatest. The Comanche, Assiniboin, Sioux, Arikara, and Shoshoni Indians were most notorious among the thieving tribes.

The methods used perhaps varied, but usually a group of braves, who had been specially anointed by the medicine man, moved across the prairie to the enemy Indian camp where the choice horses were tied. They would look over the herds grazing in the open country. Then two or three men wrapped in buffalo robes would go into the camp after dark, and work at cutting loose the horses until they got as many as they wanted, or until a dog barked or a sentry saw them. Mounted, the thieves would drive the loose horses ahead of them in the darkness and start for new frontiers. Dogs barked, Indians yelled, lodges were overturned. If everything went well, confusion and the absence of riding horses kept the enemy in camp a sufficient length of time for the raiders to escape.

An old Assiniboin told in 1935 of a horse-raiding expedition in which he participated in 1869 when he was eighteen years of age. He said a medicine man told of dreaming of a successful expedition against the Piegans. A warrior, by coincidence, had a similar dream. Accordingly, an expedition was organized, a powwow was held, and the band started off walking. That night the sound of wolves and the neigh of a horse encouraged them. They knew they would be successful. But dampening of spirits came in the morning when the leader reported a dream in which the Piegans followed and killed one of them. Some of them decided not to go any farther, and left the band. The raid, because of these manifestations of an unfriendly spirit, was unsuccessful.[23]

It is not to be inferred that the Indians stole only from other tribes. It would seem that in stealing horses as well as other booty, the rules of the game set no restrictions on the source of supply. Texas colonists had to guard their horses carefully. Traders sent their horses several miles away under guard when the tribes came to the post to buy goods. The incessant raids upon the Spanish settlements by the Apaches caused the authorities to offer a bounty for scalps. In a treaty with the United States in 1804, the Black Hawks and Sauks agreed not only to cede the lands in Wisconsin but to return all stolen horses.[24] Various other treaties made had the provision that horse stealing was to cease.

The horse affected the war practice of the tribes, making them a dangerous cavalry. The presence of the horse in large numbers was in itself assuring. In 1837, when the Comanches came to Ft. Gibson and saw a white settlement for the first time, the small number of whites and the few hundreds of horses as compared to their thousands, failed to impress them. The government made plans to take some of them to Washington, as it did so many others in subsequent years, to see if the power of the white man as evidenced there would not impress them.[25]

The well-trained buffalo horse was an excellent fighting horse. He was fast and could be controlled by a movement of the knee, leaving the rider free to use both hands. With one leg supporting him as he lay on the side of the horse, the hunter could hang there nearly completely obscured from his enemy, and shoot beneath the neck of the horse as he circled the beleaguered troops, overland freighters, or emigrant train. If the ammunition of the enemy became spent the circle closed, the death blow being given in a final rush. There they had only to fear the bayonet of the trooper. If the enemy were mounted and attempted to outrun the attackers, so much the better, since the buffalo horse could usually outrun the grain-fed horse. The warriors could even bring away their dead and injured without stopping, by reaching down, picking them up by one hand, and dragging them to safety.[26]

It has been held that in the history of Indian warfare the six-shooter in the hands of the army was the symbol of the conquest of the plains Indians as long as the tribes possessed only arrows and lances.[27] But they soon acquired guns which they used against white men and other tribes, and also for hunting. They preferred short ones, some of them even cutting off the gun barrels with files, thereby making it easier to load a muzzle-loader while riding.[28] Much better suited for horseback use was the breech-loading rifle which the Indians had when the army met them for the death blow. The six-shooter, first used by the Texas Rangers, did not become standard equipment until after the Mexican War. While it must be admitted that the revolver had considerable effect upon the Indian cavalry, it was not the factor that explains the ultimate triumph of the white man. Superiority of white troops, well-mounted, and the destruction of the buffalo herd explain the Indians' fate. The buffalo rifle stands as a better symbol than the six-gun.

The Indians of South America seem to have had a closer affinity to the horse than did their North American relative. They ate horse, drank melted horse fat, shampooed their hair in horse blood, used twisted horsehair for rope, and made their beds, saddles, shoes, and clothing from the hide.[29] Few of the plains tribes ate horse meat. The Sioux followed this practice, according to Wissler. In 1878,

when the buffalo were scarce, the Kiowas ate their ponies during the summer. Indians on the Pine Ridge and Rosebud reservations stated that they first ate horse meat in the winter of 1928-29. Charles Yellow Boy, telling of this, said that when the Pine Ridge Indians ate 2,000 horses, their faces became black, and that he ate so much that in his sleep he could "hear the horse heh-heh-heh-heh."[30]

For their clothing, tepees, and the like they used the buffalo. The horse occupied a different position. From the first they regarded it with wonder, calling it elk-dog (since they had used the dog prior to the coming of the horse), the divine dog, or "Shoon-ka wah-kon," the wonderful dog. The Dakota bands had horse songs and they even prayed to horses.[31] The Arikaras believed that the souls of horses would arise in judgment against cruel riders.[32] The burial rites of a number of tribes indicate well the position of the horse. The warrior's horse would be buried with him so that he could ride to the happy hunting grounds. Manes and tails were cut off as testimony of grief.[33] Longfellow in his "Burial of Minnisink" tells of this practice.

But in spite of these sentiments the Indian was not a kind master. In the winter months, when the plains were covered with snow, the horse was provided with no fodder, and was forced to find food by pawing away the snow. A pictograph of the Dakota Indians' history shows horses starving when the snow was so deep they could not get grass.[34] There were some exceptions. The Assiniboines did put their horses in wooded river bottoms for protection in the winter, while the Comanches and Kiowas, and perhaps others, established winter quarters on the Red River where the horses could live on the grass and the bark of the cottonwoods which were so plentiful there. The Mandans took their favorite horses inside a compartment in their winter huts in the evenings and fed them maize. In the daytime the herd was driven to the prairie.[35]

Decoration of the horse was practiced by some tribes. The Coeur d'Alene Indians put on tassels of dyed horsehair and tail feathers of hawks and eagles. War bonnets and paint adorned some. Manes and tails were clipped. Some Indians even put perfume on their favorite mounts. Spotted Wolf, a Cheyenne, had his son get some blue clay from the hill, then painted a kingfisher on the withers and back quarters of his war horse, and tied a scalp to the lower jaw. All of this presumably was to prevent the horse from becoming winded.[36]

The horse of the Indian came from Spanish range herds. Stolen and passed from tribe to tribe, horses with Spanish brands were to be found all over the plains. This preference for trained horses may have been stimulated by the natural indolence of the Indian or by his inability to train a horse. In the testimony on this point there seems to be only one voice against that of E. B. Nowland, an officer at Ft. Gibson in 1835, who maintained the true "wild herds were highly prized by the Indians, and when taken, it is rarely they will part with them."[37] However, a major in the army contended at about the same time that the tribes southwest of Ft. Gibson valued most the horses stolen from the whites "whilst those they have caught wild, they will sell for a blanket and a half a plug of tobacco."[38]

The sources of horses, however, were not limited to the Spanish ranches. "It is significant to note that where wild horses were abundant, the Indians were mounted. The explanation seems to be that when the horses could live in a wild state, the Indian could possess them. He could not store food for them or stable them. . . . . He considered the animal capable of rustling for himself. In the northern latitudes the long winters presented something of a problem. The buffalo and the wild horse survived by drifting here and there where dry grass was to be found, but the domesticated horse was restricted in his movements by tying and herding. . . . . "[39]

While the first horses came from the Spanish, many of the Indians, except among the Southern tribes, built their herds from wild stock. Catlin, speaking of the Mandans, said that scarcely "a man in these regions is to be found, who is not the owner of one or more of these [wild] horses; and in many instances of eight, ten, or even twenty. . . . . " Near the Mandans were "invariably wild horses, which are in great numbers on the prairies. . . . . "[40] C. A. Murray observed that among the Pawnees in 1840 even the poorest families had two or three horses, and one chief had thirty, some being wild, some Spanish, and three American.[41] Irving spoke of the great number of horses grazing around the village of the Arikaras, each chief and warrior owning a "great number."[42] Even the Cayuse

Indians, on the banks of the Columbia, traded salmon for horses, one being thought poor who had but fifteen or twenty. "One fat, hearty fellow," said one observer, "owns something over two thousand; all wild except so many as he needs for use or sale."[43] Among the Flathead and Nez Perce Indians even children over three were reported to have horses. One chief among the Piegans owned so many he could not keep track of them, while the Sioux had so many that forty were traded for a medicine pipe, "and a warrior in love might send twenty fine ones over to her tepee."[44] In the winter campaign of 1868-69, General Custer surprised a band, captured 800 ponies, and destroyed all of them excepting enough for the women captives to ride.[45] An early observer noted that the Comanches had 3,000 in one valley, most of them being of poor quality.[46]

Catching the mustang became sport. There is no evidence that the tribes ever went to war over grazing grounds for horse herds, for apparently only intermittent warfare resulted from stealing. They seemed to have preferred the grey and the pinto because these colors blended into the background and took paint better.[47] There were apparently two methods of catching wild horses: the relay and "ground circle" hunt. In the case of the relay when a group of riders sighted a herd, individual riders would scatter over the range, and pursue until their horses were winded. Then the next rider would take a turn for a while. When the wild herd was nearing exhaustion, the rider would take a short cut, throw the loop of his rope over the horse and try to hold him. A Pawnee, who once had succeeded in roping a mustang, had the sad experience of having the captured horse become so frightened upon the approach of the other riders that he jerked his captor's horse down, and in the melee, the Pawnee hero was killed.[48] The lasso was used not only by those Indians close to the Spanish from whom it came, but also by the Northern Indians. In the pictograph records of the Dakota Indians they used the lasso, and after 1812 it became the "conventional sign for wild horses."[49] The Mandans, according to Catlin, could throw a rope well while running at full speed.[50] It is not certain whether the Indians snubbed the rope to the saddle, but it would seem that tying it was necessary in order to hold the horse.

The Osages used a modified form of this method. Each rider was supplied with a noose at the end of a pole. According to one writer, "they take their stations on every side of the wild horses, and commence running them, until they overtake and noose some among them. Of course, in this chase the good horses invariably escape, while the mean ones are taken. . . . "[51]

Down in the Panhandle country, James Pike, scout and ranger, participated with the Anadarko Indians in a "grand circle" hunt which he believed the only one which ever resulted in much success.[52]

The wild herds from which the Indian replenished his *remuda* were to increase until the days of the cattleman; then the unceasing war against them was to begin. But in that period the Indian had his day. His culture was based upon the horse. This animal affected his food supply, his relations with both friend and foe, his nobility, his religion, perhaps his stature, and even the size of his dwelling. The dog continued to be present in every camp —but the horse was the evidence of "having arrived." From a skulking Indian stalking game a few miles from camp he became a warrior proud who caused the military forces of America to consider him for what he was—a worthy adversary.

FOOTNOTES—CHAPTER FOUR

1. A. L. Kroeber, *Anthropology* (New York, 1923), p. 387. Quoted by permission of Harcourt Brace and Company.

2. Walter Prescott Webb, *The Great Plains* (New York, 1931), p. 61.

3. Grant Foreman, ed., *Adventure on Red River, Report on the Exploration of the Headwaters of the Red River by Captain Randolph B. Marcy and Captain G. B. McClellan* (Norman, 1937), pp. 156-58. Quoted by permission of University of Oklahoma Press.

4. George Catlin, *North American Indians* .... (Edinburgh, 1926), I, 495-97.

5. Washington Irving, *Astoria. Bonneville. The Complete Works of Washington Irving* (New York, n.d.), p. 186.

6. James Adair, *The History of the American Indians* (London, 1775), p. 426.

7. Catlin, *op. cit.*, p. 161. This quotation and the following one from Catlin are used by permission of John Grant Booksellers, Ltd., Edinburgh, Scotland.

8. Robert M. Denhardt, "The Southwestern Cow-Horse," *The Cattleman*, February, 1939. Quoted by permission of *The Cattleman*.

9. From the chapter "The Horse in American Indian Culture," written by Hartley B. Alexander, given in Donald D. Brand and Fred Harvey, *So Live the Works of Man* (Albuquerque, 1939).

10. James R. Mead, "The Pawnees as I Knew Them," *Transactions of the Kansas State Historical Society* (Topeka, 1910), X, 108.

11. E. Douglas Branch, *The Hunting of the Buffalo* (New York, 1929), p. 43.

12. "Horsemanship of the North American Indians," *American Turf Register and Sporting Magazine*, I (1829), 73.

13. New Orleans *Picayune*, quoted in *American Turf Register and Sporting Magazine*, XI (1840), 648-49.

14. Branch, *op. cit.*, p. 41.

15. *See* both Alexander, *op. cit.*, and Clark Wissler, *Indians of the United States* (New York, 1940), p. 262.

16. Irving, *op. cit.*, p. 69.

17. Told by Webb, *op. cit.*, p. 66.

18. Don Alphonso, "Horsemanship of the North American Indians," *American Turf Register and Sporting Magazine*, I (1829), 73-74.

19. C. A. Murray, *Travels in North America During the Years 1834, 1835, & 1836* (London, 1841), I, 302.

20. Irving, *op. cit.*, p. 155.

21. Garrick Mallery, "Picture-Writing of the American Indians," *Tenth Annual Report of the Bureau of Ethnology* (Washington, D. C., 1893), p. 658.

22. Robert M. Denhardt, "Spanish Horses and the New World," *The Historian*, Winter, 1938, p. 12, based on Roy Nash, *Conquest of Brazil* (New York, 1926).

23. David Rodnick, "An Assiniboin Horse-Raiding Expedition," *American Anthropologist*, XLI (1939), 611-16.

24. Mrs. Ida M. Ferris, "The Sauks and Foxes in Franklin and Osage Counties, Kansas," *Transactions of the Kansas State Historical Society* (Topeka, 1910), XI, 354.

25. Grant Foreman, *Pioneer Days in the Early Southwest* (Cleveland, 1926), pp. 232-33.

26. Wissler, *Indians of the United States* (New York, 1940), p. 262.

27. Discussed by Webb, *op. cit.*, pp. 167-79.

28. Wissler, *op. cit.*, pp. 262-63.

29. Denhardt, *op. cit.*, p. 12.

30. U. S. Congress, House Committee on Indian Affairs, *Indians of the States.* Hearings before the Committee on Indian Affairs, I, 2804, 2913. House of Representatives, 66th Congress, 1st Session.

31. J. Owen Dorsey, "A Study of Siouan Cults," *Eleventh Annual Report of the Bureau of Ethnology* (Washington, D. C., 1894), pp. 433 and 479.

32. Chas. Smith, *Horses* (Edinburgh, 1841), p. 181.

33. M. Oldfield Harvey, *The Horse in Magic and Myth* (London, 1923), pp. 201-2.

34. Mallery, *op. cit.*, p. 656.

35. *See* Alexander Henry, *Travels and Adventures in Canada and the Indian Territories Between the Years 1760 and 1776* (New York, 1809), Part I, p. 295; Grant Foreman, ed., *op. cit.*, p. 142; and Reuben G. Thwaites, ed., *Travels in the Interior of North America by Maxmillian, Prince of Wied*, from the series *Early Western Travels* (Cleveland, 1904-7), Vol XXII, Part 2, p. 272.

36. For these practices, *see* G. B. Grinnell, *The Fighting Cheyennes* (New York, 1915), pp. 324-25, and James Teit, "The Salishan Tribes of the Western Plateaus," *Forty-fifth Annual Report of the Bureau of American Ethnology* (Washington, D. C., 1930), pp. 110-45.

37. E. B. Nowland, an officer at Ft. Gibson, in a letter to the *American Turf Register and Sporting Magazine*, VII (1835-36), 62.

38. Major R. B. Mason, letter in *ibid.*, VI (1834-35), p. 166.

39. Wissler, *op. cit.*, p. 264. Quoted by permission of Doubleday, Doran and Company.

40. Catlin, *op. cit.*, pp. 160-61.

41. Murray, *op. cit.*, II, 353.

42. Irving, *op. cit.*, pp. 151 and 155.

43. T. P. Farnham, *Travels in the Great Western Prairies, the Anahuac and Rocky Mountains, and in the Oregon Territory* (New York, 1843), p. 82.

44. H. R. Sass, "Hoofs on the Prairie," *Country Gentleman*, July, 1936, p. 68.

45. Robert M. Wright, "Reminiscences of Dodge," *Transactions of the Kansas State Historical Society* (Topeka, 1906), IX, 71.

46. "Santa Fe Trail Traveler," letter from Little Rock, Arkansas Territory, dated November 5, 1835, appearing in the *American Turf Register and Sporting Magazine*, VII, 204-5.

47. This view is given by Denhardt in *The Cattleman*, February, 1939, p. 45.

48. Told by J. C. Henderson, "Reminiscences of a Range Rider," *Chronicles of Oklahoma* (Oklahoma City, 1925), III, 284.

49. Mallery, *op. cit.*, pp. 656-57.

50. Catlin, *op. cit.*, p. 160

51. "Santa Fe Trail Traveler," *loc. cit.*

52. Carl L. Canon, ed., *Scout and Ranger, Being the Personal Adventures of James Pike* (Princeton, 1932), pp. 96-97.

This was the pony that followed millions of longhorns northward from Texas and, as the buffaloes were killed and the Indians hemmed up, made the lands stretching from the Missouri River to the Pacific Ocean a cattle empire. This was the pony that brought the pony express into legend and song and made it a flaming part of the great American tradition. This, too, was the pony ridden by the Texas rangers, sheriffs of every Western state, and usually by the cavalry when they were effective against savages.

J. F. Dobie, "The Spanish Cow Pony," *Saturday Evening Post*, November 24, 1934. Quoted by permission of the author.

CHAPTER FIVE

The Rancher and the Mustang

The number of wild horses that grazed on the plains and in the valleys between the Missouri and the Pacific will never be known. Never so great as the buffalo except on certain ranges, they probably numbered in the millions. Apparently they were constantly increasing. When the cattleman came into the range country he found an abundant supply of native grasses on the desert and plains, which would indicate that the wild horses might ultimately have multiplied so much that they would have struggled with the buffalo for existence. At least it is known that natural enemies or lack of forage had done nothing to decimate the herds.

These horses ranged in immense herds in the Southwest. One old-time cattleman spoke of the scene during the rise of ranching in Texas when great herds "of wild ponies, some duns, some blacks and grullas, but mainly bays with dark manes and tails, swept over the trail to the north. Wherever they passed, with long manes tossing and tails streaming almost to the ground, they stirred the imagination of men as surely as their hoofs stirred the dust of the trail."[1] They were never so numerous in the North, but they were still plentiful. As late as the 1880's Theodore Roosevelt spoke of them in the Dakota Bad Lands. "In a great many —indeed, in most—localities there are wild horses to be found," he wrote, although most of them were "escapes" or the descendants of such estrays.[2] Bancroft speaks of the numerous semi-wild herds in California about 1890.[3]

When Pike led his expedition to Mexico in 1806 he found the wild horses so numerous that it was necessary to keep an advance guard of horsemen in order to frighten them away, for "should they be suffered to come near your horses and mules which you drive with you, by their snorting, neighing, etc., they would alarm them, and frequently the domestic animals would join them and go off, not withstanding all the exertions of the dragoons to prevent them. A gentleman told me he saw 700 beasts carried off at one time, none of which was ever recovered. They also in the night frequently carry off the droves of travellers' horses in the vicinity."[4]

An English traveler had a unique experience with a wild-horse stampede. After having tied his horses for the night as he stayed in an Indian camp, he heard a sound similar to distant thunder. To quote him:

As it approached it became mixed with the howling of all the dogs in the encampment, and with the shouts and yells of the Indians; in coming nearer, it rose high above all these accompaniments, and resembled the lashing of a heavy surf upon a beach; on and on it rolled toward us, and partly from my own hearing, partly from the hurried words and actions of the tenants of our lodge, I gathered it must be the fierce and uncontrollable gallop of thousands of panic-stricken horses: as this living torrent drew nigh, I sprang to the front of the tent, seized my favorite riding-mare, and in addition to the hobbles which confined her, twisted the long *lariett* round her forelegs, then led her immediately in front of the fire, hoping that the excited and maddened flood of horses would divide and pass on each side of it. As the galloping mass drew nigh, our horses began to snort, prick up their ears, then to tremble; and when it burst upon us, they became completely ungovernable from terror; all broke loose and joined their affrighted companions, except my mare, which struggled with the fury of a wild beast, and I only retained her by using all my strength, and at last throwing her on her side. On went the maddened troop, trampling, in their headlong speed, over skins, dried meat, etc., and throwing down some of the smaller tents. They were soon lost in the darkness of the night, and in the wilds of the prairie, and nothing more was heard of them, save the distant yelping of the curs, who continued in ineffectual pursuit.....[5]

It has been held by some of our popular writers that these wild herds served as a great reservoir from which the American cattleman took the necessary cow ponies for his own use. One even goes so far as to say that the "mustang was highly prized, particularly as a saddle pony."[6] That might have

This was the pony that followed millions of longhorns northward

been true in regard to the best representatives of the herds but to most cattlemen a wild horse was something to shoot, not to capture, while to the cowboy and settler he was a source of income and fun.

Wild horses were caught by the early settlers in Texas for both sport and profit. When "broke" to ride (they killed one out of every three in so doing) a wild horse was worth $10 to $12, a "Mexican" horse raised from wild stallions brought $10 to $30, while an "American" horse sold for $150 to $300.[7] An old cowman, Charles Goodnight, tells of a wild colt caught by his brother in 1828. "After feeding it with milk by hand to keep it from starving," it was broken to ride. Before he mastered it, the horse had thrown him over a hundred times.[8]

Cowpunchers chased horses for both fun and money. If they could thereby acquire a good horse to put under their forty-dollar saddles, they did. If they could round up a few horses worthy of sale, this added to their meager wages. If the boys of the Bar Z had nothing to do at some slack season of the year, there was nothing like a mustang chase to entertain them. J. C. Henderson, a cowman of Oklahoma, tells of chasing a herd in the Cimarron River country. This herd had apparently been run by every cow outfit, mustanger, and settler in the country, and even by the Pawnee Indians. In the fall of 1881, after the cattle had been sold, Henderson and his brother decided to catch the herd of horses. They first shot the stallion, then started to drive the horses to exhaustion. Riding in relays of four hours, and having six saddle horses to use, they followed the herd for three days and two nights, finally running them into a herd of saddle horses of a neighboring rancher. The rest was easy, for both wild and domestic herds were soon driven into the corrals of the ranch. All but one was sold in Arkansas City for pin money.[9]

To the cattlemen the wild horse herds were not only a nuisance but a menace. They consumed the range grass needed for profitable livestock, and drank the precious water of a country much in need of it. They made necessary night herders to guard the saddle stock of the cow camp. But the worst charge against them was what Theodore Roosevelt called their "propensity for driving off the ranch mares, and because of their incurable viciousness. . . . . "[10] There was nothing a herd liked better than to entice away a *remuda* of range mares into a life in which labor was unknown. There was an open season on stallions, to be shot with any weapon at any time. In the Southwest, the mere presence of so many non-profit producing livestock made the feral herd obnoxious. As early as 1824 this problem was so great that the government and the ranchers erected special corrals at the edge of towns, held great roundups to get them into the corrals, and as the horses were released one at a time, killed each one that was unclaimed or unbranded. Thousands were killed in this way. When cattle increased in value there due to the gold rush, more thousands of the wild horses were driven off the Santa Barbara cliffs into the sea, or boxed up in corrals to die.[11]

It was the rancher who had the closest contacts with the wild horse herds of America. While he shot and harried them, he also lost to them good saddle stock, even well-bred stallions and mares he had imported to improve his own herd. If one remembers that in the day of the open range the domestic horses grazed freely on the unfenced plains, then one easily sees how the "escapes" contributed to the remnants of the Spanish and Indian stock. Many of the wild herds were then not descendants of once wild stock, but estrays of the ranchers. This condition was probably more true in the North than in the South. As horse ranching increased after 1870, the prices of horses decreased. From 1870 to 1900, when horses were a drug on the market, the ranchers reduced the numbers by shooting, and at the same time increased the herds by no longer branding and caring for their own stock.[12]

The mustang was not "the cowboy's ideal of a horse..... For his work he took the best he could get, but as with many others of the concerns of his hard life, he had to be content and to get along with what was available....."[13] It is quite likely that the early cattlemen drew upon the wild herds as well as upon the Spanish range herds for their horses, while the cowboy spent many happy and dangerous afternoons trying to catch some good horse from a band. But it cannot be assumed that the cow horse of history was an animal caught from a wild herd. The early ranchers in Texas not only took good horses with them but they also purchased heavily from those Spanish ranchers who had developed good horses through careful selection. According to Frederic Remington, these horses "were not subjected to the fearful setbacks attendant on passing a winter on the cold plains, which is one of the reasons why all wild horses are stunted in size. Therefore we must look to the Spanish horse of northern Mexico for the nearest type to the progenitors of the American broncho."[14] This Texas pony with his "fine deerlike legs, a very long body, with a pronounced roach just forward of the coupling, and possibly a 'glass eye' and a pinto hide...." was small and shriveled and hard to break, but withal he was a fit ancestor of the Western pony.

Joseph G. McCoy in his significant volume, *Historic Sketches of the Cattle Trade*, published in 1874, speaks of the range horse problem as follows:

To supply a ranch, whereon a stock of ten thousand cattle are kept, with the necessary saddle-horses, a stock of at least one hundred and fifty brood mares should be kept. The geldings only are used for the saddle. This class of horses are small hardy animals, bordering on the pony closely, and are of Spanish origin. Their food is

grass exclusively, and many of them are as utterly un-
familiar with the use of grain as they are of Latin, and
will often, when kept in the north, starve to death before
they will eat grain. Almost everyone has to be taught to
eat corn or oats by placing a quantity in a small muzzle-
shaped sack and fastening it over the animal's nose..... [15]

The history of the well-known King Ranch in
Texas may be illustrative of the whole industry.
Soon after Richard King came to the frontier in

1853 he acquired cattle, horses, and sheep from
Mexico. The Texas longhorns, for all practical
purposes, may be said to have originated there. At
one time he had 100,000 cattle, 20,000 sheep, and
10,000 horses. Soon after the turn of the century
he had 2,000 brood mares and hundreds of horses. [16]
One of the earliest horse ranches in New Mexico,
established in 1877, was stocked with 500 Texas
horses, a few being true mustangs, most being
mixed. Other ranchers followed this attempt, raising "small wiry little beasts capable of strenuous

work day after day, but they were hard critters to look at. Their necks instead of bowing up like they should, bowed at the bottom, as though they were upside down..... "[17] Sturdy mares from Oregon and stallions from Kentucky built the herds of Arizona which found ready market in the Boer War. The breeders of California, developing fair mares from mustang herds, supplied the horse-ranchers with much basic stock. To Wyoming, Oregon, Colorado, and perhaps other states went these grade mares. A Wyoming example is typical:

[T. A. Kent, with 1300 head of horses, produces] what he calls American bronchos. They are small, tough animals, very cheap, and good for riding.....Mr. Kent's stallions weigh 1225 to 1640 pounds, and he expects the cross by them with California mares will reach the average size of American horses.....His mares cost him $28.50 each, [his stallions $690 each] and he considers his yearling colts worth $25 each, and his two-year-olds $50 each..... [18]

These horses probably were similar to the early range ponies of the Colorado frontier, which were described as "medium-sized, wiry, western-bred horses, a usual cross between a fairly well-bred horse and a broncho."[19] That horses moved in that direction is shown in the report from Topeka, Kansas, stating that in 1884 "about 7000" were shipped west to the range country.[20]

The general practice seems to have been for the ranchers to bring with them good mares, turn them out on the range to graze with the cattle, and

to place with them some well-bred stallions imported from Kentucky. Together with the Spanish
stock, this established the source for the early
ranches. Throughout the range country horse
ranches were established where scientific breeding
began to produce for a wide market.

When the settlers first arrived in the Pacific
Northwest there were few wild horse herds except
those of the Indians. The range horse industry
sprang into being soon after the gold discovery in
1862. The famous California mustang was introduced into Oregon by two early ranchers and was
crossed "with the best breeds of large hot blooded
lines. . . . . "[21] It was from these sources and the
Indian tribes that the great wild horse herds of
that country were to originate, and from which
also came a well-known Oregon pony.

This importation of good horses into the range
country, and the crossing with the Spanish mustang or the wild range horse, must have soon eliminated most of the small saddle stock found on the
ranches. Since it was the harness and not the saddle market in the period before 1900 that gave to
the range its chief commercial outlet, and since the
"whole situation was saved by a fortunate provision of nature which, in the average case while permitting the imported horse, on crossing with the
broncho, to pass down the former's qualities, nevertheless prevented it from also giving mere exag-
geration to qualities which the broncho alone

possessed. Thus a six-hundred-pound broncho, with say six hundred pounds of bucking force inside it, mated with a nine-hundred-pound non-bucker. Their colt would eventually weigh, say, seven hundred pounds and would have at most six hundred pounds of bucking force. Successive generations would tend to increase the figures for the animal's weights and to decrease those for their bucking force."[22]

This early Eastern demand for horses was responsible for the many horse ranches in the 1870's and '80's, and in turn restocked the Western range. The offspring became the Western pony. At what time this was achieved is uncertain, but the *Arizona Republic* stated that the mustang disappeared between 1880 and 1890 in that country, and that the offspring of the sturdy mares from Oregon and stallions from Kentucky had displaced them. Cattlemen were becoming horsemen, and probably before the days of the open range had passed the mustang blood was pretty well diluted.[23]

As the cattlemen went into the mountain country the desert blood was further chilled by the demand for a larger horse. "In meeting this demand, many strains were fused with the thinning blood of the old Mustang. It has seemed to me," writes a Westerner, "that, in this process, gains in weight and substance were, in most cases, more than offset by losses in endurance, hardiness, and cow-sense, which distinguished the original Texas broncho."[24]

J. Frank Dobie speaks admiringly of the old mustang cow pony. Described as not weighing over nine hundred pounds, with a thick barrel, bright eyes, ample nostrils, and having hard feet, he was capable of going in a gallop all day. Not so

sensitive as a thoroughbred but having "cow sense," endurance, alertness, and an instinct for direction, he was an ideal pony in most ways.[25]

The offshoots from the "breeding-up" process became in time true types. Oregon, through the use of Clydesdale sires and mustang mares, produced a "short-set, compact mount, with large bone and hairy legs, possessed of many admirable qualities ....," known as the "Oregon Lummox." In Montana and the Dakotas, through the use of the Percheron, was produced what some called the "Percheron Puddin'-Foots." By the early 1890's the ordinary cow horse in the North was a "rather nondescript animal, demonstrating only in rare instances the great ability of the old Mustang trail days..... The slower, more domestic, less primitive cattle did not offer the incentive for the development of finished horses that had prevailed in the earlier and more romantic period of the industry."[26]

Down in Texas was developed the "Quarter-Horse." It apparently had originated in Virginia and the Carolinas before the Revolution and had been used as a race horse for the quarter-mile track. One story explains that it originated in Texas through crossing a thoroughbred stallion and a black pony mare. Another tells that a thoroughbred stallion which had been imported from Kentucky became famous as a race horse, and consequently was used as a sire for cow ponies. Another story has it that a pair of horses was imported from Spain. The evidence seemed to point, however, to the conclusion that the "Quarter-Horse" was known before the development of the range business in Texas.[27] Regardless of origin, the "Quarter-Horse" became popular as a top cow horse and a polo pony, but was never recognized as a breed. Descendants were known as "Copper-Bottoms," "Cold-Decks," "Kentucky Whips," "Printers," "Steel Dusts," and "Billy Horses."

The "Colorado Ranger," developed from stallions and mares imported from Turkey and Spain, and bred under range conditions, was a 1,000 to 1,250 pound horse of no particular color but with preference for leopard markings.[28]

The Nez Perce Indians are accredited with developing the "Appaloosa" from mustang stock. Being one of the few tribes that did any breeding of horses, they mated horses for peculiar markings and for sturdiness. When they were placed on a reservation following the war of 1877, they surrendered 1,100 head to the white conquerors as the spoils of war. Thus the peculiarly marked horses were scattered and began to produce perhaps not a breed but a color type, having white spots on the croup, white in the eye, and pink or speckled skin on the nose, while the main body was roan, bay, or chestnut. They weighed from 800 to 1,150 pounds.[29]

The "Palomino," a golden-colored horse now recognized as a breed, was bred in California before 1848. The origin, as explained in one story the truth of which nobody can dispute, came around 1800 when a foreman at a mission offered a prize to the best horse in the country. When the range horses were brought in that fall to tramp grain, there appeared a yearling of cinnamon color with white mane and tail. This became the sire of that breed. Another story explains that the Indians stole a white stallion and a buckskin from the Spanish. After being loose on the range for a year, they returned with a golden-coated colt. Regardless of the stories, Professor John A. Gorman believes the "Palomino" came from Spanish horses which were the descendants of the Barb and the Arabian.[30] Americans soon developed a preference for this horse, as had the Spanish who gave them as gifts when a daughter was married. Arabians and thoroughbreds have been used in developing this colorful breed which is now perpetuated through the Palomino Breeders Association.

In 1937, in Stewart, Nebraska, an association was organized for the breeding of "Albino" horses. Legend has it that a stallion was bred to some yellow-skinned mares, descendants of "Yellow-Cat," a "Quarter-Horse," and this produced 50 per cent white, 25 per cent cream-colored, and 25 per cent golden-colored colts.[31]

The "cayuse" is a small horse, allegedly first developed by the Cayuse Indians. The term became applied to any small horse in the North and Northwest. The Indian always preferred a colored pony. The original mustang, though of various colors, was a *one* color horse. It may be that among the Indians there was a certain amount of selection in the color of the stallion they stole or caught. This may be the explanation of the emergence of the paint or pinto, never desired by the cattleman but still found in many *remudas*.

The conclusion seems warranted that the Spanish horse or his descendants on the open range was the forerunner of the Western cow pony. Evidence does not warrant the conclusion that the wild herds of mustangs were the accepted and preferred source of supply or that the mustang was the cattleman's ideal of a horse. He admired its intelligence and endurance, but he couldl not forgive it its size or its homely characteristics. The cattle barons wanted horses that looked as good as those originally ridden by the Spanish barons, not a run-down-at-the-heel range pony that had been starved by lack of forage and water, dwarfed by exposure and the cruelties of nature, and oftentimes made grotesque in appearance by peculiarly-shaped muzzles, bellies, or legs. Upon this mustang he built a horse more pleasing to the eye, larger and better proportioned. As he built his own herd he contributed to the mustang herds loose in the hills. By 1900 there was a new type of wild horse roaming the desert and mountain country. The mustang was largely engulfed in the process.

FOOTNOTES—CHAPTER FIVE

1. J. E. Haley, *Charles Goodnight, Cowman and Plainsman* (New York, 1936), pp. 11-12. Quoted by permission of Houghton Mifflin Company.

2. Theodore Roosevelt, *Hunting Trips of a Ranchman* (New York, 1927), p. 213.

3. H. H. Bancroft, *History of California* (San Francisco, 1890), VII, 58, footnote 4.

4. Z. M. Pike, *An Account of Expeditions....* (Philadelphia, 1910), Appendix to Part III, pp. 31-32.

5. C. A. Murray, *Travels in North America During the Years* 1834, 1835, & 1836 (London, 1841), II, 350-52.

6. Robert C. Notson, "Horses! Horses!" *Sunset Magazine*, LIX (1927), 29.

7. Prince Carl Solms-Braunsfels, *Texas 1844-1845* (Houston, 1936), p. 27.

8. Haley, *op. cit.*, p. 8.

9. J. C. Henderson, "Reminiscences of a Range Rider," *Chronicles of Oklahoma* (Oklahoma City, 1925), III, 253-88.

10. Roosevelt, *op. cit.*, p. 8. Quoted by permission of Charles Scribner's Sons.

11. Robert M. Denhardt, "The Role of the Horse in the Social History of Early California," *Agricultural History*, XIV (1940), 14 and 18.

12. W. C. Barnes, *Western Grazing Grounds and Forest Ranges* (Chicago, 1913), pp. 97-98.

13. National Live Stock Association, *Prose and Poetry of the Live Stock Industry* (Denver and Kansas City, 1905), I, 557.

14. Frederic Remington, "Horses of the Plains," *Century Magazine*, XXXVII (1888-89), 334.

15. *Ibid.*, p. 9.

16. National Live stock Association, *op cit.*, pp. 62 and 85.

17. Joseph H. Bursey, "Horses of the Southwest," *New Mexico Magazine*, September, 1933, pp. 36-37.

18. James S. Brisbin, *The Beef Bonanza; or How to Get Rich on the Plains* (Philadelphia, 1881), pp. 144-46.

19. Patrick Byrnes, *Wild Horses of Colorado* (pamphlet in Colorado State Historical Society Library, n. d.)

20. J. G. Nimmo, "The Range and Ranch Cattle Traffic," *House Executive Document* No. 267, 48th Congress, 2nd Session, Serial No. 2304.

21. Wayne Stewart, former mustanger, Dayville, Oregon, in a letter, August 30, 1939.

22. Philip Aston Rollins, *The Cowboy* (New York, 1930), p. 293. Quoted by permission of Charles Scribner's Sons.

23. Quoted in *Current Literature*, XXX (1901), 616.

24. Dan Casement, "The Western Cowhorse," *The Producer*, March, 1934, p. 3.

25. "The Spanish Cow Pony," *Saturday Evening Post*, November 24, 1934.

26. Casement, *op. cit.*, p. 4.

27. See the discussion of this by John A. Gorman, *The Western Horse* (Danville, Illinois, 1939), p. 192.

28. *Ibid.*, p. 187.

29. *Ibid.*, pp. 196-98.

30. *Ibid.*, p. 174.

31. *Ibid.*, p. 183.

Had the country over which they roamed remained unoccupied by the American frontiersman and settler, the Mustangs would eventually have vied in numbers with the buffalo, which roamed the prairies from Texas to Canada.

Major General W. H. Carter, "Story of the Horse," *National Geographic Magazine* XLIV (1923), 527. Quoted by permission of the National Geographic Society.

CHAPTER SIX

The Army and the Mustang

When Americans first entered the Great Plains in their mighty sweep toward the Pacific they came face to face with the horse Indians. Here in this dry area between the Spanish (or Mexican) and American frontiers mounted bands of redskins reigned supreme. Here on the cutting edge of civilization, where locks were unknown and honesty and honor were legendary, the Indians were regarded as the personification of all that was evil. Their position was of significance largely because they were an effective mounted cavalry, drawing their mounts from the plentiful sources of the wild bands and from the colonists on the opposing frontiers. The horse, ever the horse, was the cause of much of the trouble.

When early explorers entered this forbidding land they were impressed by the abundance of available horseflesh. Z. M. Pike, in telling of his expedition in 1807, says the wild horses were so

numerous in Texas that the herds supplied not only
the Indians and provinces of the present Mexico,
but were also sent to the United States.[1] To Pike's
men seeing the horse herds was an interesting diversion. They saw the first two wild ones near
Coon Creek, in present day Kansas, as they progressed up the Arkansas River. The men rode after
them but learned that the wild horses could easily
outrun them. At the lower crossing of the Arkansas
they encountered their first herd. With two men
Pike rode toward them. He says:

When within a quarter of a mile, they discovered us,
and came immediately up near us, making the earth
tremble under them (this brought up to my recollection a
charge of cavalry). They stopped and gave us an opportunity to view them, among them were some very beautiful bays, blacks and greys, and indeed all colours. We
fired at a black horse, with an idea of creasing him, but
did not succeed; they flourished round and returned
again to see us, when we returned to camp.

The next day, not being able to resist the tempta-
tion, they equipped six of their fastest horses with
riders and ropes, and sent them out on an unsuccessful expedition. Pike says that he has since
laughed at the folly of such inexperienced people
trying to capture wild horses.[2]

The army explorers who came after Pike never
failed to take notice of the wild horse bands on the
plains. Captain Nathan Boone, who made a trip
up the Arkansas and Canadian river valleys, makes
this entry in his *Journal:*

Started a wild horse to day, and one of the officers chasing it fell in with a herd of about 30, headed by a large white horse with black spots on his croup..... [3]

When Stephen Watts Kearny led his army overland to California in 1846, the Mexicans tried to cut off his entry into the San Diego country by driving a band of wild horses into them. The troops managed to turn aside the onrushing mustangs, and killed "two or three of the fattest on which the command feasted....." [4]

However, the Western troops became interested in the mustang for reasons other than diversion. They soon learned that a grain-fed horse of the Eastern thoroughbred variety did not have the stamina that the Indian pony had. The Texas Rangers apparently learned this fact before the army did. This police force, composed of daring men, operating as a fast-moving, hard-hitting cavalry, earned for itself an enviable reputation. Each man furnished his own horse in the early days. Webb, historian of these men, says they "always had good horses, and some of them had blooded race stock brought in from Kentucky or the other states that love the royal animal and the sport of kings....." [5] However, it is to be doubted if most of these young fellows in the period between the Texan Revolution and the Civil War possessed well-bred stock. Their horses perhaps were the type that had been caught on the open prairie or purchased from the ranches of the area.

James Pike, an early Ranger, tells of riding a fresh horse furnished him at Dobb's ranch, and starting for Fort Belknap. The horse was a "half wild mustang" that had never been thoroughly domesticated, and almost before he had touched the horse's back, it began to rear and plunge in a discouraging way.[6] He rode it out, however.

The evidence is not available to make any definite conclusions about the Ranger's horse other than that it is known that it was a Texas horse, raised on grass, so that it could operate on a par with the natives' horses and not be dependent on grains. This mount was a decisive factor in the Rangers' successful handling of the Indians.

The troops stationed on the Southwestern frontier in the 1830's showed considerable interest in the wild horses that roamed the area west of them. A former dragoon and Indian agent, Colonel H. C. Brish, wrote in 1833 that he had "never met with anything of the horse kind that possessed strength, action, and wind equal to the 'mustang' horse . . . . or any that could endure fatigue and hunger equal to them, or subsist on so little and retain their strength." He was "decidedly of [the] opinion that these horses are superior to any others *on the face of the earth for cavalry purposes.* . . . ."[7]

Major R. B. Mason of the dragoons, writing the next year, said he had just returned from a two months' excursion southwest from Fort Gibson and had had a good opportunity to observe the many

Wild horse bands supplied a few good cavalry mounts

wild horses roaming in that area. However, he was not impressed, having seen no more than four out of the thousands for which he would pay fifty dollars. The Indian ponies, he said, which are valued most by them and which can scarcely be bought at any price, have been stolen from the whites, "whilst those they have caught wild, they will sell for a blanket and a half a plug of tobacco."[8]

How long this quarrel continued in the officers' barracks and in the horse clubs of America is not known. It is known, however, that Major Mason set out to prove the worth of the wild horse as a cavalry horse. When he left with his dragoons in 1834 he was observed taking along his blooded stallion, a mare and a colt, "for the purpose," wrote a reporter from Fort Gibson, "of catching wild colts. . . . . "[9]

The results of this experiment were never reported, but the next year Lieutenant S. W. Moore brought to Fort Gibson a prairie stallion, named "Washita" after the river where he was caught. He was described as being white, having hard hoofs, fair legs and standing fourteen and one-half hands high. He had another stallion, but because it was injured he was obliged to leave it at a post on the Canadian. These two horses were purchased from the herds of the Osages, and judging from the height may be said to have had better blood in them than most of the wild mustangs.[10] A writer from Little Rock in 1835 still argued that the dragoons never saw the best wild horses. There "are some horses on the prairie," he said, "equal to any on earth—particularly for the purpose of crossing—and I am equally certain that the dragoons never got any but the very meanest of the species."[11]

According to Major General W. H. Carter it was around 1850 that the cavalry (and he mentions specifically that in Arizona, California, and Oregon) was mounted on the "hardy, sure-footed little horses . . . . " purchased from the ranges of the old Spanish grants in southern California. These animals, apparently reared from Spanish stock under conditions similar to those of the wild herds, were "gamier, hardier, and the more enduring animal for use in the desert and mountain region of the far West . . . . " than any other horse that could have been used.[12] As late as 1859, however, General Houston complained that the U. S. Cavalry could not chase the Indians a day without their horses getting sore feet, and that the horses could not be grain fed in a land that had no grain.[13]

The Comte of Paris paid the mounted troops and their horses this compliment after having observed them in the West:

All those who have gone through a campaign in the New World have often had occasion to admire the sagacity of the American horse and his sure footing in the middle of the darkest night. Able, though small, to carry a great weight; gentle and intelligent, enduring fatigue, rain, cold, neglect, and want of food, he seemed in every way adapted for the rough life of the prairie which man could not face without his aid.[14]

Horses for the army have been an ever present worry of the War Department. In the Mexican War each man in the cavalry had to furnish his own mount. Some came on thoroughbreds, others on Texas ponies, and some even on plough horses. The regular army at that time had Morgans and thoroughbreds. When the Civil War came, the demand for horses was greater than it had ever been

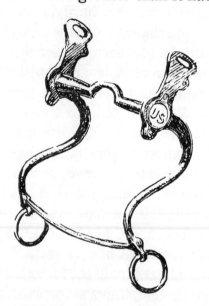

before. The Federal government was using 500 head daily in 1864, and in that year bought 188,-718 horses, and captured 20,388. The South was not a horse-breeding country, and had no surplus except in Texas where the mustangs roamed wild. As time went on General Robert E. Lee could not continue to operate due to lack of both forage and horses, but at no time did he propose the use of the mustang. Rather, he used fewer horses in the cavalry, obtained more mules, impressed farm horses, set up infirmaries for disabled horses, and talked of getting mules from Mexico.[15] Nevertheless, because of the cavalry demands of the Civil War, the price of mustangs advanced. One contemporary explains the situation in Colorado by saying that the "many California and Texas mustangs had not yet been driven into Colorado to supply the demand, as they were later..... "[16] Photographs showing light horses in use in both armies would indicate that the Western horse served the cavalry, but it is doubtful if the wild horse herds contributed much in that war.[17]

Before the Boer War broke out the price of the Western horse had dropped so low that the horse ranchers in many instances ceased branding their stock, consequently increasing the number of wild herds. This distant war caused them again to become horse breeders, and started a movement to capture the wild herds.

Export statistics show the growth of this new market and how America responded to it:[18]

1884	2,721
1894	5,246
1895	13,984
1896	25,126
1897	39,532
1898	51,150
1899	45,778

1900.. 64,722
1901.. 82,250
1902..103,020

The British government in this war used Cape ponies, artillery horses, English and Irish cavalry horses, North American, Hungarian, and Argentine horses. In this group the American animals were fourth in value, being made up of "Canadians and Texans," many of which were admittedly "raw and badly broken."[19]

When the U. S. Army had the task of mounting troops for the invasion of the Spanish possessions in 1898, the officials turned to the contractors and subcontractors who purchased horses from horse breeders all over the United States. It is probable that the mustangs made a greater contribution then than they did during the Civil War, although there is little evidence other than roundups on the Western ranges to prove it.

The government took a hand in horse breeding for the first time soon after the turn of the century, and this was for the Philippines. There the army found a native Spanish horse so small that in order to get a sufficient number of horses for cavalry and constabulary purposes, it sent one ship load of Morgans, Denmarks, and Arabians, both stallions and mares, to cross with native stock.[20] This shows again the war department's dislike for the Western pony. It was not his endurance nor his color that was responsible. It was not that horses were scarce, although there were fewer then than there had been ten or fifteen years before. It must have been their appearance. For chasing Indians, the mustang or his descendant served well. But in a day of military reviews, he made a poor showing. It is certain that many of the horses running wild or in a semi-wild condition on the Western ranges in 1910 were a nondescript lot.

World War I dipped deeply into the American horse reservoir. Exports jumped from 22,776 in 1914 to 357,553 in 1916. This looms large when compared to the exports preceding World War II, when between 1933 and 1938 the *total* exports were only 11,434.[21] The buyers in this period before mechanized forces became so important were:

France	130,296
England	83,829
Canada	52,036
Italy	20,634
Scotland	6,908
Greece	1,279

The effect of the demand of World War I upon the wild herds of the West was salutary. Ranchers began again to round up their unbranded stock and to turn good stallions and mares loose on the range. Mustangers who could make a fair living selling horses for thirty to forty dollars a head, sprang up everywhere in the Rocky Mountain country. The rancher had but little expense connected with this rebirth of the horse industry. The necessity of paying taxes on these animals was usually avoided by the simple fact that what the tax assessor could not see he could not tax. And in most instances there were no grazing fees for herds roaming the public domain.

Whether these feral horses made good cavalry horses is not established. Breaking them was a task great enough for any army of men. The *New York Times* commented on the Wild West scenes enacted daily at one division remount station where cowboys and farm recruits tried to convert these raw horses to the use of bit, saddle, and harness.[22]

Representatives of the Greek government who came here to buy horses for World War I showed little interest in the Western wild horse. These inspectors, who knew more about horses than they did about the English language, were offered upon one occasion 300 inferior horses for inspection. Of the first 200 paraded before them, only three were accepted. As the inspectors were leaving, the rancher, now desperate, instructed his cowboys to ride in circles, shooting their guns. The owner then explained the delicate situation by saying that the riders were displeased because the inspectors would not look at the rest of the horses. This caused the Greek representatives to reconsider, whereupon they returned, looked at the remaining 100, and gave every one a ticket of acceptance.[23]

Among these unbroken prairie horses purchased and sent to points of debarkation, the mortality was great. The climatic change, confinement in corrals, and the long haul to the Eastern seaboard perhaps explain this situation. The dean of one of the veterinary colleges suggested buying city horses that were older and had been broken. At a conference of veterinarians in 1918 the use as human food of the small Western ponies unfit for heavy draft work, was discussed, but no recommendations were made.[24]

It was the difficulty of getting horses for World War I that caused the army to turn its attention to the breeding of horses in America. The contract system of purchasing was never quite satisfactory. Consequently, about 1910 that system was supplemented by the establishment of three or more remount depots at which well-bred stallions and mares were kept.[25] Perhaps European experience finally caused Americans to go farther in this. Regardless, there was established in 1920 the Remount Service, a branch of the Quartermaster Corps, of the U. S. Army. Scattered throughout the country (including Puerto Rico and Hawaii) at remount stations in 1940 were over 700 thoroughbred, Arabian, and Morgan stallions which were maintained at the expense of the agent. The army reserved the right to purchase any colt, but did not guarantee to buy it.[26] The army still uses over 40,000 horses in the various branches of the service. Now its source of supply seems to be solved at a time when the demand will not be so great.

This effort shows a continuing distrust by the cavalry of the Western horse. In the 1920's the character of the horse herds was such as to cause lack of confidence. In 1940 there were no longer any horses available, other than strictly supervised range horses. The wild horse made his contribution to the army in the period after the Mexican War when he was worth something. After 1900 he no longer deserved the reputation his mustang ancestors made for him. Today he is headed for the cauldron.

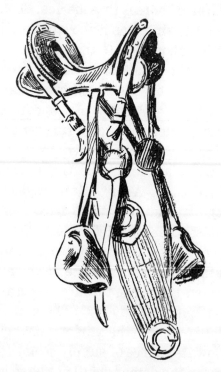

FOOTNOTES—CHAPTER SIX

1. Z. M. Pike, *An Account of Expeditions.* ... (Philadelphia. 1910). Appendix to Part III, pp. 31-32.

2. Stephen H. Hart and A. B. Hulbert, *Zebulon Pike's Arkansas Journal.* ... (Denver, 1932), pp. 110-13.

3. Louis Pelzer, *Marches of the Dragoons in the Mississippi Valley* (Iowa City, 1917), Appendix p. 215. Quoted by permission of the State Historical Society of Iowa.

4. *Ibid.*, p. 159.

5. Walter Prescott Webb, *The Texas Rangers* (New York, 1935), p. 83. Quoted by permission of Houghton Mifflin Company.

6. Carl L. Cannon, ed., *Scout and Ranger, Being the Personal Adventures of James Pike.* ... (Princeton, 1932), p. 70.

7. A letter, "On the Wild Horses of the South-West," *American Turf Register and Sporting Magazine*, V (1833-34), 463-64.

8. *American Turf Register and Sporting Magazine*, VI (1834-35), 166.

9. *Ibid.*, 30-31.

10. *Loc. cit.*

11. *Ibid.*, VII (1835-36), 205.

12. "Story of the Horse," *National Geographic Magazine*, XLIV (1923), 524.

13. Webb, *op. cit.*, pp. 201-202.

14. Quoted by William Walton, *The Army and Navy of the United States* .... (Boston, 1900), II, 45.

15. Charles M. Ramsdell, "General Robert E. Lee's Horse Supply, 1862-1865," *American Historical Review*, XXXV (1930), 758-777.

16. A. M. Strope, "Catching Wild Horses in the '60's," *Outdoor Life*, August, 1914. This clipping is in the Colorado State Historical Society Library.

17. G. M. Rommel says that even the "much-despised plains horse (the mustang cayuse, or broncho) .... doubtless contributed his share to remounting the cavalry of both Northern and Southern forces....." *Twenty-seventh Annual Report of the Bureau of Animal Industry for the Year 1910* (Washington, D. C., 1912), p. 113.

18. "The Horse Trade of the United States With Foreign Countries," *Scientific American Supplement*, LIII (1902), 22054.

19. Lord Denman, "The War Office and Remounts," *Nineteenth Century*, LII (1902), 747. One horse firm in Texas contracted to deliver 25,000 horses to the British. The animals were rounded up in the Rio Grande country and corralled near San Angelo, Texas. Since the Texas law prohibited the shipment of animals that carried no brand, it was necessary for cowhands to rope, tie, and brand a small "U" on the hips of 25,000 ponies. They were then shipped by train to Charleston, South Carolina, thence to Australia where eight American cowboys thrilled local audiences as they broke them to ride. These horses brought approximately twenty-five dollars each. See Oren Arnold and John P. Hale, *Hot Irons* (New York, 1940), p. 87.

20. J. G. Speed, "America's Horses for the Philippines," *World's Work*, VIII (1904), 5503.

21. *St. Paul Pioneer Press*, September 24, 1939.

22. "Dix Cowboys Shun Mule," *New York Times*, March 17, 1919.

23. C. P. Engel, "The War-Horse Business," *Colliers*, LV (1915), 34.

24. *New York Times*, January 27, 1918.

25. Rommel, *op. cit.*, p. 112.

26. Joseph A. Bursey, "Horses of the Southwest," *New Mexico Magazine*, September, 1933; John A. Gorman, *The Western Horse* (Danville, Illinois, 1939), pp. 202-15; Phil Strong, *Horses and Americans* (New York, 1939), p. 291; and the *St. Paul Pioneer Press*, February 23, 1941.

The real mustang . . . . vanished with the wild buffalo, whose doom he helped to seal, and with the wild Indian, whose comrade he became. He vanished for the same reason: the White man wanted his country and so had to go. . . . .

H. R. Sass, "Hoofs on the Prairie," *Country Gentleman*, July, 1936, p. 69. Quoted by permission of the *Country Gentleman*.

CHAPTER SEVEN

Disappearance of the Mustang

When the first cattlemen came into New Mexico and Arizona in the 1870's and 80's the mustang and the jack rabbit were two of the most common pests encountered. On every mesa and plain, in the shelter of sagebrush and mesquite, wherever there was a bit of green vegetation to be found, there also was the wild mustang, true descendant of the Spanish horse in America. A dusty rider across these arid wastes of the Southwest could have set into motion 200,000 of the critters.[1] Ten or fifteen years later the extermination had largely taken place except in the mountain country and barren desert areas.

The disappearance of a great proportion of the mustangs is a mystery. "Many stockmen attribute it merely to degeneration," said a contemporary, "but close observers assert that many thousands of these ponies were surreptitiously converted into canned beef and are even now being served over

Eastern tables and army messes as a select product of the cattle range..... "[2] But this could not explain the rapid disappearance of the mustang. He, no doubt, "intruded on the cattle ranges and was shot for his pains..... He ventured amid the sheep flocks and the coyotes feasted on his carcass. Everywhere he was a worthless reprobate, an interloper, and valuable only as a target for the revolver of the vaquero."[3] Those that were not shot or captured probably drifted to the inaccessible badlands. The lack of range grass may have caused the remainder to move on. When deer get too numerous the head bot and cougar reduce the herds. Partridge seem to propagate in cycles. Nature may have taken a hand in the reduction of these horse herds.

Strange as it may seem, in the years between the two elections of McKinley "no district had more wild horses on the ranges than northern Arizona. ....."[4] The stockmen who went into this area between 1878 and 1880 had found no wild horses—but they had brought in their own horses and had imported Oregon mares and a number of stallions from Kentucky and Indiana.[5] Turned out on the range that had never yet been enclosed with a fence, these horses truly followed the old commandment to breed and multiply. "Occasionally a young stallion, whipped out of the bunch by an older horse would 'cut out' some young mare for company, and eventually they would work back into the rough country, watering at some watering hole, hardly seeing a human being for months, and finally you had the nucleus of a wild bunch."[6] Within five years ranchers realized that a range problem existed. The wild horses—now of diluted quality—numbered tens of thousands in this area alone.

Cattlemen loathed the sight of feral horses. They drove the cattle away from the salt, broke up water troughs, milled around the springs, charged through herds, killing calves and knocking down cows. Will C. Barnes, then a rancher in that area, described the way the wild herds bothered at roundup time:

On round-ups, with twenty or thirty cow-boys scattered out "on circle" along a line six or seven miles wide, and with all the cattle moving in good shape ahead of the line of riders toward the round-up grounds, far off to one side some one would start up a band of "broomtails....." Away they would tear, picking up new bands here and there, until as many as two hundred head would sweep right through the cattle, throwing them back on the circle of drivers. When once a cattle drive of that kind is turned back on itself, it takes hours of hard riding to check the drift and get the herd again headed for the round-up ground. It was no uncommon thing for a day's work of a whole round-up outfit to be lost through such a wild-horse stampede.[7]

The worst nuisance of all, however, was the luring away of domestic stock. To turn these horses out on the range, even in the wintertime, was to lose them forever. Add to these indictments one more, and the horse would seem doomed. He

The white man wanted his country, and so he had to go

was a bad grazer. To mention a sheep to a cattleman is like waving a red flag in front of a bull. In
the West, where hard liquor is still the favorite
of many, it is not uncommon to hear that beer is
good only for sheep dip! However, the grazing of
the wild horse was more devastating than the
sheep's. He not only clipped the grass as closely or
more so than a sheep, but he traveled farther to
water and feed, often at high speeds, cutting the
range with sharp hoofs. Even when he was supposedly grazing peacefully in a grassy spot, his
playfulness would cause a milling around that did
considerable damage to the vegetation.[8] He was a
worse enemy than the sheep.

Not at all surprising is it that the cattleman
turned on his wild neighbors, even those which had
recently been valuable members of his saddle
string, and shot them on sight. Cowboys captured
many and sold them for what they would bring.
Mustangers devised methods of capturing them.
The first wire fences took their tolls, for a wire cut
meant screw worms.[9] War raged on this frontier
for many years. The only friend the horse had was
the Indian, and he offered him sanctuary, not a
hostler's care.

Farther north, in the middle range area, the
first cattlemen found a different situation. In the
Kansas country the settlers had captured, killed,
or run out most of the mustangs and Indian ponies
that had run wild there. By 1859 it was reported

that the wild bands still at large were in the Indian reserves and the unsettled portions of the territory. These herds were made up of Indian ponies and the escapes from the white settlers, the cross being in many instances a good horse. Organized parties were still trying to capture them alive, that failing they used the rifle. Only the flower of the flocks remained.[10]

No doubt early cattlemen not only found some of these herds but supplemented them with their estrays. There seems to be no evidence to indicate that the wild horse was ever a serious range problem in the middle plains states. Theodore Roosevelt wrote that in the 1880's in North Dakota wild horses or their descendants, being estrays from the ranches or Indian reservations, were found in most localities. Wild as the antelope were they, he wrote, but against whom unremitting warfare was carried on by the cattlemen who shot them at every opportunity.[11] These herds of the plains states were either destroyed by the rancher, pushed on to the mountain country, or finally engulfed by the "nesters" who crept across the frontier as the open range collapsed.

The situation in Nevada and Utah was different. Here the horse had a refuge. The early cattlemen in southern Utah found many horses, in one county alone there being probably 1,000 in 1898.[12] They were a serious menace to the public range, and everywhere the cattlemen organized to get rid of them. For a time they were hunted as wild game and noted big game hunters were said to have gone there to hunt horses for sport.[13] Hundreds were captured and shipped to livestock markets on the Missouri River. Zeke Johnson, old-time cattleman, tells how he organized the ranchers of San Juan County for the destruction of the herds there, many of which were good stock, being "escapes." To quote him:

At that time I bought a bunch of range cattle and began to talk to other cattlemen about getting them all killed off. So we started at shooting them down when ever we could. . . . . One winter . . . . after a snow fall 10 of us went out and run 250 over the ledge killing all as they fell 300 feet, got them to milling on edge of bluff till they got on sleek rocks covered with snow and all slid off we told all the Indians they could have all they could capture so they helped to get rid of many hundreds. early in the spring when they were poor we could take them of a good grainfed horse and we would kill and catch another none were ever shipped out but all killed by cattle men and now there is not one left to tell the tale. it took us about ten years to do the job.[14]

Thousands of wild horses were reported in Skull Valley, Utah, in 1920 when ranchers began a war of extermination. Before the plan of shooting them was tried, roundups were held, and the stock shipped to Eastern markets. The expense of the roundups and the freighting costs prevented any profits. Then the cattlemen invited the organization of parties for hunting expeditions. Guides and all necessary supplies were furnished. One outfit that was out a month reported a "bag" of

102 horses, largely made possible because of encountering two herds at a water hole where the stallions fought for supremacy.[15]

The horse problem faced in Nevada was a vastly greater one than that experienced by most residents above the Colorado River. Here was the perfect wild horse country. Here on the Eastern slope of the Sierra Nevadas lay one of the last real mustang countries outside the Indian reservations. Here in the bad lands embraced in the counties of Elko, White Pine, Nye, Lander, and Eureka were found as late as 1910 perhaps 100,000 "four legged reasons for believing that the popular obituary of the wild horse is premature..... "[16] There were more wild horses than citizens in Nevada, of a type that indicated that the dilutions by ranchers' horses had not yet completely engulfed the mustang strain. Rufus Steele, a literary mustanger of repute, thus described them:

.... they have the fine head, the slim legs, and the flowing mane and tail characteristic of the Arabian stock. They are bays, albinos, chestnuts, red and blue roans, pintos, sorrels, buckskins, and milk-whites. The mares average eight hundred pounds in weight, and the stallions frequently weigh three hundred pounds more than that; they stand from thirteen to fourteen hands high. Their endurance is phenomenal, and as for agility, the marks of their unshod hoofs are found at the summits of monumented boulder-piles which even a mountain goat might reasonably be expected to cut out of his itinerary. They keep to an elevation of from six to nine thousand feet, descending to the plains hardly at all. The water-holes are from twenty to fifty miles apart..... Bunch-grass is their sustenance in summer; then the first frosts cure the white sage, and that becomes palatable; they paw through the snow to reach it, and keep fat throughout the winter. .... [17]

Here where the wild horse decided to make one of his few last stands, the cattlemen had decided otherwise. Since in the Western states the voice of the stockman is as powerful in the state capitols as is the rural mail carrier's in Washington, the state legislature of Nevada passed a law about 1900, at the request of the Stock Association, allowing the killing of wild, unbranded horses on the range. Within a year or two about 15,000 horses had been shot, and the hides and bounties had more than paid for the efforts. As the supply became smaller, some of the hunters became careless and shot branded stock along with the unbranded. "An inspection of horse hides that had been purchased from the hunters and were in the hands of hide dealers [in Chicago] showed that a large percentage of the hides bore well-known brands belonging to stockmen all over the State. The farmers came to be afraid to turn old 'Dobbin' for a Sunday run on the plains about their ranches, lest some skulking hide-hunter pot him in a lonely ravine or cañon. .... "[18] Down to the legislature marched the stockmen to ask for repeal of the law, and they got it. They then quietly began to pay a bounty on each pair of horse ears brought in by their cowboys.

Not long after the repeal of this law the cattlemen made another request. Horses had rapidly increased until they were again pests. This time they adopted a resolution asking the next state legislature to pass a law giving to the U. S. Forest Service

the right to shoot all wild horses found on the public domain after a reasonable period had passed enabling the cattlemen to gather their stock[19]

Two months after the resolution was passed, February, 1908, the Associated Press carried two stories that brought the American public face to face with the wild horse problem:

Reno, Nev., Feb. 19, (1908).—A campaign to exterminate the wild horses in the Toyabe, Toquima, and Monito forest reserves in Lander County has been started, and it is believed that more than fifteen thousand wild horses now grazing on these preserves will be slaughtered before another year has passed.

The forest rangers report that there are more than 15,000 wild horses on these ranges and that they are attracting many domestic animals to the district. These horses destroy the vegetation and do much harm to the entire district, consequently a war of extermination will be waged against them.

Reno, Nev., Feb. 19. The forestry department at Washington has ordered the rangers to kill all wild horses on the government domain.[20]

A flood of letters from all over America began to pour into the Washington office of the Forest Service. Barnes, in describing them, said:

One tender-hearted individual called it an outrage to kill so valuable an animal when it could be used for the benefit of man.

A firm of hide dealers wrote asking to be given a contract for the sole handling of the hides taken from the slaughtered horse. A large manufacturing company wanted to purchase all the hides, for use in making certain kinds of leather goods. Another firm inquired if the animals were to be killed at some central point; if so, could they not arrange to utilize the flesh of these animals for canning purposes?

Dozens of men wrote offering to go to Nevada and capture the animals if the Government would pay their fare out and give them the horses in return for their work. One man wrote from Texas, "If the men who issued that order knew anything about the nature and habits of the Western mustang, they would know that it is a very easy matter to capture them. If the Government will employ me at a salary of $100 per month, I will agree to gather all in three months."

An excited individual from New York City declared with a confidence born of conviction, "I have a very simple system by which I can capture every wild horse in Nevada in a short time. If the Government will contract with me, I will enter into an agreement to gather and deliver them to the Government's representative as rapidly as possible at the agreed price of seven dollars a head."

Another group of correspondents, mostly Eastern lads with a desire for adventure, wrote to obtain employment as "horse killers," announcing themselves as dead shots with a rifle and expert hunters of game.

A member of the Humane Society demanded that a more humane method than shooting be employed.[21]

To all of these letters the Forestry Service dispatched a reply similar to the following:

Sir: Your letter of .... is received. No orders have been issued by the Forest Service for killing horses upon any of the National Forests. The report originated in an unwarranted press dispatch given out through the newspapers of the country.

The Federal government was not to be involved in the removal of wild horses from the public domain until the days of the Taylor Grazing Act, so the local stockmen and the mustangers had to solve Nevada's problem.

Between 1910 and 1918 large numbers were trapped and shipped from the country. Professor F. W. Wilson, of the University of Nevada, remembers observing a horse roundup in 1920 in which local ranchers captured between 1,800 to 2,000 head.[22] It is probably safe to say that in parts of Nevada the wild horse problem was not solved until the late 1930's.

The Oregon situation was much the same. Between 1895 and 1900 stockmen failed to brand or to take care of their range stock in any way. Thus began the wild horse herds that were to become so numerous in the southeastern part of that state in the 1920's.[23] Local stockmen seem to have taken no part in removing these horses until later, apparently, leaving the task to the professional horse hunters. Montana appears not to have had a range problem until the wheat farmers deserted their horses after the World War. No doubt individual ranchers and mustangers did their bit. A former cowhand who worked on the Montana range in 1905 tells of spending many happy Sunday afternoons sitting at the neck of a canyon, and from there as the horses came to water, shooting them with his Winchester.[24]

A unique experiment in the disposal of wild horses was attempted by a small group of Wyoming cowpunchers in 1897. They had heard that there was a demand for horses in the Klondike, that a horse could be sold for $400. They caught seventy-five, and after two years' struggle up the trail east of the Rockies, through Edmonton, arrived in the gold era with two mules and one horse![25]

Will James, well-known cowboy artist and writer, once wrote of his experiences when he worked for a cattle outfit catching mustangs.[26] They had been engaged in the semiannual roundup. One day the superintendent rode up and said he had instructions from the owners to offer a bounty of $2.00 to each cowboy for each horse shot. James says the owners, busy with their social life and taking champagne baths regularly, did not understand what they were condemning to die. The men "naturally" refused.

In this period between 1880 and 1920 when the American mustang was practically to disappear, and in his place there was to emerge in great numbers the "escape," when the price of a horse was to be at rock bottom most of the time, South America faced the same problem. In 1891, 700,000 horses were slaughtered in the Argentine for hides, and in Brazil, where the same destruction took place, a hide sold for $1.50.[27]

The whole history of the wild horse is tied up with the range and the price of horses. When the rancher went into open range country, he found in most instances few mustangs. As the horse market declined because of the increased horse population, and the use of the bicycle and the automobile, the rancher no longer cared for his own horses, and the wild herds grew. The prices were so low in the 1890's that railroads required freight and feeding charges en route prepaid before loading the stock. In 1898 several carloads of selected geldings were shipped out of Arizona to Kansas City, netting the owner twenty-five cents each.[28] The demand of the Boer War for Western horses caused cowmen and mustangers to clean up the herds in the accessible places. But the decline in prices after 1903, together with the fact that there were native herds that had never been captured, left the grazing problem again in the lap of the Westerner, where it reposed until a new market for horses arose in the Harding era.

By 1910 or so the public domain was overstocked in most places—ranges that could carry a cow on every one hundred acres had one on every ten.[29] The migratory sheepman expanded his activities. The "nester" kept crowding, aided by the reclamation work of the federal government. And all this time there was on most of the public domain no control over the use of the land. The unwanted and the useless horse merely aggravated a condition that was already bad. The World War horse market gave some relief, but the dog-food canneries and the Taylor Grazing Act were to provide the forces of control in another day.

FOOTNOTES—CHAPTER SEVEN

1. *Arizona Republican*, quoted in *Current Literature*, XXX (1901), 616.

2. *Loc. cit.*

3. *Loc cit.*

4. Will C. Barnes, "Wild Horses," *McClure's Magazine*, XXXII (1908-9), 291.

5. *Arizona Republican*, op. cit.*

6. Barnes, *op. cit.*

7. Barnes, *op. cit.*

8. *See* Will C. Barnes' discussion of this in his excellent study, *Western Grazing Lands and Forest Ranges* (Chicago, 1913), p. 77.

9. J. Frank Dobie, *A Vaquero of the Brush Country* (Dallas, 1929), p. 239.

10. *Leavenworth Herald*, quoted in the *Kansas Messenger* (Baldwin), January 1, 1859. This was made available through Lyle Miller, Kansas State Historical Society.

11. *Hunting Trips of a Ranchman* (New York, 1927), p. 303.

12. Zeke Johnson, old-time cattleman, now custodian of the Natural Bridges National Monument, Blanding, Utah, in a letter, August 26, 1939.

13. L. C. Montgomery, President of the Utah Cattle and Horse Growers Association, in a letter, August 29, 1939.

14. Johnson, *op. cit.*

15. *New York Times*, July 18, 1920, quoting *Popular Mechanics Magazine*.

16. Rufus Steele, "Mustangs, Busters and Outlaws of the Nevada Wild Horse Country," *American Magazine*, LXXII (1911), 757.

17. "Trapping Wild Horses in Nevada," *McClure's Magazine*, XXXIV (1909-10), 198.

18. Barnes, "Wild Horses," *McClure's Magazine*, XXXII (1908-9), 286. *Also see* Barnes, "The Passing of the Wild Horse," *American Forests and Forest Life*, November, 1924, p. 646. This method of control seems to have been tried in the Southwest years before. In 1827, the states of Coahuila and Texas required each captain of a mustanging crew to take out a license. This legally made provision for disposal of branded stock, set the season and area for operation, and levied a small charge for each animal taken. Texas is said to have passed similar acts again in 1852, 1854, and 1856. The reason for this would seem to have been to protect branded stock. It might have been to cover partially the cost of frontier defense. *See* J. W. Moser, "A Mustanger of 1850," and G. C. Robinson, "Mustangs and Mustangers in Southwest Texas," in *Mustangs and Cow Horses* (Austin, 1940), edited by J. Frank Dobie, Mody C. Boatright, and Henry H. Ransom.

19. Barnes, in *McClure's Magazine*, op. cit.*

20. *Ibid.*, p. 285.

21. *Loc. cit.*

22. Letter, September 26, 1939.

23. Letter from Tom Skinner, pioneer rancher of Jordan Valley, Oregon, dated September, 1939.

24. Statement of O. P. Sumner, former Montana cowhand, now of River Falls, Wisconsin.

25. Elizabeth Page, *Wild Horses and Gold* (New York, 1932).

26. "Piñon and the Wild Ones," *Saturday Evening Post*, May 19, 1923.

27. A. Livingstone, "Wild Steeds of the Pampas," *Outing*, XXVIII (1896), 130.

28. Barnes, in *American Forests and Forest Life*, op. cit.*, p. 646.

29. Barnes, *Western Grazing Grounds and Forest Ranges*, pp. 27-28.

The golden age of the broncho was ended some twenty years ago when the great tidal wave of Saxonism reached his grassy plains. He was rounded up and brought under the yoke by the thousand, and his glories departed. Here and there [in 1888] a small band fled before man, but their freedom was hopeless. The act of subjugation was more implied than real. . . . . Of course the wild stallion is always eliminated, and he alone was responsible for the awe which a wild horse inspired.

Frederic Remington, "Horses of the Plains," *Century Magazine* (1888-89), XXXVII, 337.

CHAPTER EIGHT

The Ranchers' Revolt

The number of feral horses in the West has always been a matter of conjecture. Estimates have run from five to seven million in the day of the mustang, before the cattlemen and the "nester" had occupied the public domain. That number was gradually reduced, but to what point nobody had the temerity to estimate, due to the fact that a horse census has always been a difficult task in the mountain area of the West. By 1925 the number had increased again, no doubt, due to various factors, there probably being at that time no less than 1,000,000.[1]

Following World War I wild horse bands became numerous again, especially on the Northern ranges. The farm horses, replaced by tractors, were left to forage for themselves. Then when the collapse came and the wheat farmers moved out, the feral herds had more draft horse additions. Even the range horse, which had at least been worth something most of the years, could no longer be sold. The range, long overstocked, now had to bear the increasing burden of unwanted and unclaimed horses. The final blow came as the price of beef began to advance. The rancher's problem was to have two spears of grass instead of one. Of the 160,000,000 acres of the public domain which could be grazed, most of it had little value other than "holding the rest of the country together. . . . . It may well be called," wrote a range expert, "a shining example of our national trait of spoliation and destruction and stands to-day [1925] a monument to our lack of foresight and happy-go-lucky methods of managing these resources."[2] The horse had to go. Fortunately a new market, the dog and cat food industry, rose to serve as an outlet for these "fuzztails." State legislatures wheeled into action to authorize the removal, just as had Nevada fifteen years before. Even Arizona had protected the wild horse by its game laws.[3] Horse thieves had never been tenderly dealt with in the West. Now the common law of the range permitted any man to lay claim to or to shoot any unbranded horse. The horse was a natural resource unwanted by all. So the roundup and the rifle, the canning plant and the cauldron, started the beginning of the end.

The wild burro deserves his niche in the story of the removal of the horse. As early as 1884 small herds of these Spanish imports had been seen in the vicinity of Grand Canyon, apparently being the estrays of the prospectors. When Grand Canyon was created into a national park, it was estimated that there were a thousand within the boundaries which served as a tourist attraction as well as being a nuisance. Federal officials quietly put out poison-

ed grain and salt for them and shot them with silencers on their guns. The burro disappeared there,[4] but was to be found in several national forests and on the public domain in the Southwestern states. In the Sitgreaves National Forest, where they were a pest to the sheepmen because they lured away pack animals, a burro roundup was organized in the early 1920's. By the use of the corral and rope about four hundred were captured "at a cost in time and horseflesh far above their market value....."[5] The burro was still present in the mining states and was not destroyed in the removal process that took so many horses. He is still with us.

The Bureau of Animal Industry was called into action in the 1920's to eradicate the tick from some wild horse herds in unexpected areas. On the coast islands of South Carolina the feral herds, called the "marsh tackies," probably descendants of the military horses once stationed there, were destroyed. The "banker ponies" on Hatteras Banks at Chincoteague, Virginia, which tradition explains as being descendants of the horses introduced by a wrecked Spanish ship and by Sir Walter Raleigh, were removed to make way for a park.[6] Down in the Little Missouri River Valley in Arkansas roamed several hundred head of tick-infested wild horses, the estrays from farmers. These were being removed with great difficulty in the spring and summer of 1931.[7] The *New York Times Magazine* gave this description of the Arkansas roundup:

Wild horses are being hunted in the remote bottoms of Southwestern Arkansas, where 100 square miles of open range country in the meandering valley of the Little Missouri River provide a permanent retreat for an untamed herd. The animals are thought to be the descendants of domesticated beasts that were left behind by pioneer farmers and timbermen driven out of the area by floods. They have been pursued by occasional parties for a quarter of a century, but are being sought now with increased energy in line with a State-wide campaign against carriers and spreaders of the deadly fever tick.

Dogs are used to spot and trail the animals and the pursuers ride horseback, in relays, in an attempt to drive them into rail corrals built beforehand at Creek or trail

In the Grand Canyon the burro was a tourist attraction as well as a nuisance

crossings. The hunts are long, frequently requiring as many as twelve long hard hours in the saddle.

The chases are begun as near the centre of the open range area as possible in an effort to head the prey toward the corrals at the outer margins, when the animals can be roped or run down by relays of fresh mounts.[8]

Farmers in western Kansas complained in 1929 about the unclaimed horses running loose, tearing down fences, and trampling the spring wheat. Because they thought that life would be simpler without these estrays a bill was introduced into the state legislature giving the right to the hard-pressed wheat farmers of acquiring legal possession by capture.[9]

But all of this was minor as compared to the difficulty of the rancher in the range areas. Even up in Alberta, Canada, a delegation of sheepmen declared to the provincial government that the wild horses were driving their sheep from streams, and demanded legislative action for the destruction of the beasts.[10] Montana and Wyoming in the Western states seem to have had the greatest estray horse population.

The pre-war development had brought thousands of immigrants to these states, each bringing horses, many of which were soon retired by the tractor. When the dry years and the agricultural deflation caused a great exodus to the East, their horses, being mortgaged for more than they were worth, were turned loose to forage. One hundred thousand unclaimed horses wandered over the public domain, encroached on cultivated lands, and sought the bad lands and the inaccessible breaks of the Missouri River.[11] When these animals became a real menace to the livestock industry, the revenue producing cattle and sheep, the cattlemen of Montana were the first to do something about it. The legislature of Montana was the first in the 1920's to authorize the gathering and destruction of the herds by the stockmen through county roundups. The employees were to be paid out of the receipts of the sale of the horses.[12] In the subsequent years, roundups were held in twenty-six of the fifty-six counties in Montana.

These roundups, beginning in 1925, came as welcome drama to America in the jazz era. Feature writers wrote volubly of the thousands of horses for which the state legislature had signed a "death warrant." The *New York Times* carried several stories written from the horse camps. One of their correspondents wrote from a camp near Great Falls about this drama during its later days:

[By June 5, 1929, the] first chapter has been written in the greatest wild horse roundup ever held in the West and today hundreds of horses—large and small, vicious and indifferent, mustangs, "fuzz-tails" and bronchos— are in pastures ready for the first sale and elimination check.

The roundup will continue through most of the Summer, with the hardest of the work still ahead, for the horses are retreating from the more open range into the wildest of the "bad lands" known as the Missouri River Breaks where coulees and gorges flanked with towering rock buttes offer the wild range ponies more than an equal chance to elude the pursuing cowpunchers.

Thousands of the wild horses have taken to the Breaks and though the riders are bringing in many, they are reporting big bands sighted at a distance.....

One of the fiercest wind and rain-storms of the year swept across the range during the week end, flattening out the roundup camp [near Great Falls], which is in the open range beside a large watering hole, like an army camp. In the midst of the storm, a bunch of riders came racing through the gumbo mud with forty-two horses, gone mad from the flashing lightning and crashing thunder.

Headed by a mustang stallion as black as night, the band broke past the camp, brushed into the watering hole which is like a lake only shallow. Plowed through it and vanished with the storm—back to freedom which they had so nearly forfeited.[13]

These county roundups, each in charge of a competent foreman of the type of Carl Skelton so lionized by the press, gathered thousands of horses between 1925 and 1929 or after. Each roundup was advertised so that any horse owner could appear to lay claim to horses bearing his brand when he had paid his proportionate share of the cost of gathering them. The remainder were sold to horse buyers who disposed of them as light work horse stock or shipped them to the reduction plants.

Following the lead of Montana, the state legislature of Wyoming in 1927 authorized county commissioners to conduct horse roundups.[14] They were to select a foreman whose responsibility it was to organize and execute the drive for the "range-robbers." Several counties organized and succeeded in ridding the range in "pretty short order." That the removal was still going on in the early 1930's is evident from the report that one buyer shipped from the Big Horn Basin 22,000 horses in 1933 and 1934. In the subsequent years he shipped 13,000[15] The number removed and sold for a few dollars was not recorded, but "undoubtedly it ran into several thousand."[16] Thus the desperate stockmen, when faced with a challenge to the revenue-producing range business, achieved in a few years what the few mustangers had been unable to do over a longer period.

Across the Rockies, in the eastern part of Washington and Oregon, the abandoned horse became a nuisance in the 1920's. In Washington, near the Yakima Indian Reservation, the problem was reported to be worse than in any other section of the state. These herds were largely "escapes" from the reservation.[17] There seems to have been no legislative action, the cattlemen merely organizing locally as they had done in other states about 1900, and proceeding to remove these pests without the fanfare of large roundups. Buyers from a Yakima dog food packing plant quietly purchased most of the horses that were removed.[18]

In eastern Oregon range conditions were much more serious. The mustangers and cattlemen had never been able to remove many of the wild animals in the rough country bordering the Nevada and

Idaho boundaries. World War I prices had encouraged mustangers to operate here, as elsewhere, and horse breeders kept close watch on their herds for a few years. But when the World War price levels declined, the ranchers permitted their herds to go unbranded and to join the other feral horses. In 1928 there were "at least ten thousand head of wild horses on the Oregon desert in the southern part of Malheur County. These horses," explains a range expert of that area, "had been run so much and let get away that they were just about as hard to handle as so many antelopes. . . . . "[19] At this time Archie Meyers, veteran Pacific coast horseman, came into the area. After he had rented a ranch, he set out to earn a few dollars catching horses. He first bought from the owners of the horses on this desert the right to all horses caught. Within two years he had caught 3,000 head, about one third being unbranded. In 1930 he engaged an airplane to run horses but this ended in a complete failure. From 1930 to 1935 he ran them on cow ponies and succeeded in capturing 5,000. Between 1936 and 1938 an airplane was again used, this time proving highly successful. Thus within one decade one man removed 10,000 horses from the Oregon range.[20]

This movement for removal apparently was general, but was much greater in the North. The evidence to show its extent in Colorado, Nevada, and Utah, is not available. Regional Grazier T. R.

Brooks, located at Reno, Nevada, is of the opinion that there was no "unusual activity along this line in Nevada."[21] Apparently the mustangers who had operated here in the period 1900 to 1910 had done a thorough job. It may be, as Mr. Brooks points out, that in Nevada the state law governing the removal of wild or unbranded horses from the ranges prevented much action in the 1920's. The removal by interested stockmen and individuals in isolated cases was done in violation of this law. In the broken country of southern Utah, between Cedar City and the northern rim of Grand Canyon, horses were plentiful as late as 1925, when it was estimated that fifteen thousand still ran loose.[22] They were a major tourist attraction. However, it would seem that the middle tier of range states did not have the wild horse problem that existed elsewhere.

Texas, long famed as a mustang country, had succeeded in decimating its herds by about 1930. The *Dallas News* told in 1933 of a herd numbering about forty horses near Fort McKavelt, that at that time were being trailed by cowboys intent on eventual capture.[23] Across the line in New Mexico, largely due to the presence of the Indian reservations which were constant feeders of the feral horse herds, and because of the drought, the range problem became acute by 1925. In that year the ranchers began their organized, voluntary onslaught against this robber of the range.[24] The Forest

Service joined with them and started to remove the pests from the forest preserves. A representative of New Mexico writes of this episode as follows:

Thousands of head of the stock were rounded up and sold to reduction plants in El Paso and Gallup where they were ground into fertilizer, dog, cat and fish food, and used for many other purposes.

Some ranchers could not afford to drive their horses to reduction plants, since the prevailing price of from two to three dollars would not pay the cost of transportation.

Thousands of horses have been shot on the ranges where their carcasses provided feasts for coyotes and other range scavangers. Other thousands have been killed and fed to hogs. The Ladder Ranch in Southwestern New Mexico kills scores of horses every year for this purpose.[25]

These voluntary efforts of ranchers to rid their ranges of the animals apparently did much to solve the problem, but it did not eliminate it.

Overgrazing and drought forced Arizona stockmen to dispose of great numbers of their wild herds after 1920. Interested ranchers would organize a roundup from various points of the compass and would converge at an agreed central point where the horses would be corralled.[26] G. R. Parry, a veteran mustanger, recalls a roundup in the vicinity of Fredonia, Arizona, in which 600 horses were captured and all of them killed.[27] This was common practice before a dog-food market developed for the horses. Mustangers, who had operated in northern Arizona and southern Utah ever since the days Zane Grey wrote about, apparently were not so successful as those in the Nevada country. But the success of the ranchers cannot be measured accurately anywhere, although 8,000 were reported taken in 1929, and officials expected the destruction of 15,000 in 1930. It was estimated that one half million were still at large.[28]

Before the passage of the Taylor Grazing Act in 1934, the wild horse was on the wane largely because of the determined efforts of the men who made their living from the range. In 1930 the estimated number of horses still at large on the public domain was between 50,000 and 150,000.[29] These figures are exclusive of those on the Indian reservations. The "broomtails" were either feeling harness in Southern cotton fields or were being processed into smoked hams or dog food on the Pacific. Even though the Taylor Grazing Act, with its rigid control over the range, was enacted in 1934, it is likely that the horse had seen the beginning of the end.

FOOTNOTES—CHAPTER EIGHT

1. This estimate, probably by the Forest Service, is given by R. L. Neuberger, "Wild Horses of the West are Vanishing," *New York Times Magazine*, February 10, 1935.

2. Will C. Barnes, *Story of the Range* (Washington, D. C., 1925), p. 15.

3. Editorial in the *New York Times*, June 9, 1929.

4. Will C. Barnes, "Wild Burros," *American Forests and Forest Life*, XXXVI (1930), 641-42. Barnes gives no date for this disappearance. The Biological Survey in 1923 reported Tonto Plateau in Grand Canyon National Park to be "considerably overgrazed....." See the *Annual Report of the Department of Agriculture for the Year Ended June 30, 1923* (Washington, D. C., 1924), p. 443.

5. Barnes, *op. cit.*

6. H. R. Sass, "Hoofs on the Prairie," *Country Gentleman*, July, 1936.

7. *New York Times*, May 19, 1931.

8. August 9, 1931. Quoted by permission of *New York Times Magazine*.

9. Editorial in *New York Times*, February 18, 1929, based on *Lyons* (Kansas) *Daily News*.

10. *New York Times*, May 8, 1931, quoting the *Canadian Press*, Calgary, Alberta.

11. The *New York Times*, July 7, 1929, gives the estimated number as 400,000. The figures used above were given by Professor Henry Murray, Montana State College, Bozeman, Montana, in a letter, August 30, 1939.

12. Letter of S. A. Phillips, Secretary of the Montana Stockgrowers Association, August 9, 1939.

13. Russell Bankson in the June 23, 1939, issue. Quoted by permission of the *New York Times*.

14. *New York Times*, February 6, 1927.

15. Harold J. Burback, Regional Grazier, Grazing Service, Rawlins, Wyoming, in a letter, February 9, 1940.

16. Letter, September 28, 1939, from Russell Thorp, Secretary-Chief Inspector, Wyoming Stock Growers Association, Cheyenne, Wyoming.

17. Professor H. Hackedorn, State College of Washington, Pullman, Washington, in a letter, September 1, 1939.

18. *Ibid.*, and Robert C. Notson, "Horses! Horses!" *Sunset Magazine*, LIX (1927), 29.

19. Given in an enclosure (written by a regional grazier) by Nic W. Monte, Acting Regional Grazier, Burns, Oregon, in a letter of January 23, 1940.

20. *Ibid.*

21. Letter, September 29, 1939.

22. Rufus Steele, "Wild Horses as Scenery," *Outlook*, CXLI (1925), 85.

23. Quoted by the *New York Times*, July 23, 1933.

24. *New York Times*, July 7, 1929.

25. Joseph A. Bursey, "Horses of the Southwest," *New Mexico Magazine*, September, 1933, p. 37.

26. G. R. Parry, Superintendent of Motor Transportation, Utah Parks Company, Cedar City, Utah, in a letter, October 5, 1939; Mrs. J. M. Kieth, Secretary, Arizona Cattle Growers' Association, in a letter of August 17, 1939; and Professor E. B. Stanley, University of Arizona, in a letter of September 18, 1939.

27. Letter of October 5, 1939.

28. *New York Times*, July 14, 1929, quoting the Arizona Industrial Congress.

29. The *New York Times*, November 21, 1930, gives 50,000. Archie Ryan, Director of the Division of Grazing (now Grazing Service), estimated the number at 150,000. Letter of July 7, 1939.

A wild horse consumes forage needed by domestic livestock, brings in no return, and serves no useful purpose.

Archie D. Ryan, Grazing Service, Department of Interior, letter of July 7, 1939.

CHAPTER NINE

The End of the Horse on the Public Domain

On June 28, 1934, the "Magna Charta" of the Western range became a law. This act of Congress, known as the Taylor Grazing Act, set up in the Department of Interior a system of controls that sought to save the range from the continuous misuse to which it had been subjected since 1890. The act carried the name of a veteran spokesman of the stock and irrigation farmer interests, the late Edward Taylor, of the western slope in Colorado. Regional offices, each in charge of a trained grazier, were established in key cities of the West: Salt Lake City, Utah; Reno, Nevada; Burns, Oregon; Boise, Idaho; Grand Junction, Colorado; Albuquerque, New Mexico; and Phoenix, Arizona. Grazing districts were drawn up, and the use of the range therein was granted by licenses under carefully prescribed conditions which assured the officials that the range was not to be overgrazed. This act was aimed at migratory sheep, unclaimed horses, and irresponsible stockmen who refused even to put up hay for winter feeding. Through the Civilian Conservation Corps and the use of part of the grazing fees, range improvements such as reservoirs and rodent control were to be made. This heralded a new day in the West.[1] The policy of the Grazing Service, formerly the Division of Grazing, as given by the director was set down as follows:

[The Service is] interested in the removal of wild horses from the public ranges but the population of these animals in grazing districts is localized and for this reason the Division has not attempted removal on a general scale but has relied on efforts made by individuals who have worked in cooperation with the Division.[2]

This general approach to the question should not obscure the position of range experts. They regarded the wild horse as a menace to the range as well as a pest to stockmen. A horse consumes enough grass to keep two cows, lures away domestic stock, tramples the water holes, destroys the protective vegetative growth on the watershed, and withal, as one of the officials wrote, "brings in no return, and serves no useful purpose."[3]

In the early days of the act the mustangers and cattlemen continued in home areas to operate without authority or knowledge of the Grazing Service. As the administration was tightened, the system of issuing permits for the gathering of wild horses was devised. The general procedure has been for

the officials to co-operate with voluntary stockmen's associations and thereby to free the range
of the robber. It has, however, required the rancher
to pay fees for his stock's use of the range, usually
a monthly charge of five cents a head, thus establishing a control over the feral additions to the
already present herds.

In the state of Montana that was so bothered in
the 1920's with feral horses, the horse problem is
solved. One competent Montanan states that he
believes "it imposible to obtain any authentic cases
of mustangs at large. . . . . ."[4] Certain it is that
there are few unclaimed or abandoned horses, or
descendants of the mustang there. The Grazing
Service reported in 1940 that it had a few horses
"in trespass in two or three areas in eastern Montana, but these horses are all branded and are
claimed by someone. . . . . "[5] Apparently, the county
roundup law and the rise of new horse markets had
eliminated a bad situation. The Grazing Service
had merely served trespass notice upon the owners
of the horses, threatening arrest unless they were
removed. This method had worked everywhere except in northern Montana.

Conditions in Wyoming are nearly the same. The
heavy loss of horses because of the drought of 1934
did much to supplement the work of the roundup
crews authorized under the law of 1927. In 1939
the Grazing Service, in co-operation with cattlemen, made an unsuccessful attempt to round up

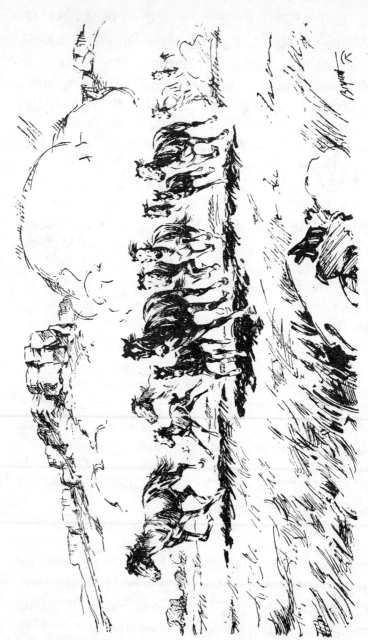

On the public domain they were constantly harried and hunted

horses by air'plane. In other sections of the state
the few horse runners and the stockmen succeeded
at their task. About four thousand head were removed between 1936 and 1940. In February, 1940,
the official number of horses whose ownership was
not known was given as about fourteen thousand.[6]

The Grazing Service co-operated with local
stockmen in the removal of the horse in Idaho
where in certain areas they have entirely disappeared. No estimate of the number in the state is
given but it is "not so numerous as it was fifteen
years ago. . . . . Yet there is no evidence that they
will ever eliminate them."[7]

When the Federal government forced the ranchers to pay a grazing fee and to get a permit to keep
their horses on the public domain for seven months
of the year and on private pasture or on feed the
other five months, the death blow against feral
horses was struck in Oregon. In 1940, when there
were 11,682 head of horses licensed to run on the
11,500 acres in southeastern Oregon, there were
only 1,000 unbranded wild horses running the
range in scattered herds. Prior to the creation of
grazing districts, approximately 25,000 horses ran
on the public domain, 40 per cent being unbranded.[8]
Federal regulations had encouraged the local stockmen to organize as they never had done before. It
must be said that Archie Myers who operated with
saddle horses here from 1929 to 1935 must be given
considerable credit for the removal of 8,000 head.[9]

Others like him likewise ridded the range of a number. It is not clear whether the local stockmen or Myers financed the use of the plane piloted by Floyd Hanson which succeeded in driving about two thousand out of the bad lands in Malheur County. It is known that the ranchers did hire the men for the other roundups. Mr. Tom Skinner, veteran cowman of Jordan Valley, says that in the latter part of 1939, the Grazing Service had "taken over the job of ridding the range of wild horses, hiring men and shooting horses that can not be taken otherwise. . . . . ."[10] Regarding this policy, one old Westerner noted:

> A good many range horses being wild you could not gather just what you wanted to, they were ordered shot or disposed of. There is a lot of this in Malheur County that is good for nothing but horses it seems a shame.[11]

There were still wild bands in the inaccessible range country in Utah in 1939. Apparently local stock associations had used the airplane "to a very great extent"[12] and were also trying to improve the quality of these herds by releasing well-bred stallions among them. It had long been a practice for anyone to claim any unbranded animals they could capture. County commissioners were authorized to issue permits to mustangers.[13] In November of 1939 a project was then being set up by the Grazing Service to rid the range of these horses unless licensed.[14]

The mustanger did the range a great service in

Nevada in the years between 1900 and the World War. Native stockmen, through the use of the Winchester, the trap corral, and the roundup were responsible for the disappearance of many horses during all the years. Cowboys made small dents in the herds when they captured a few head to sell at eight or ten dollars each. The Federal Bureau of Animal Husbandry removed about five hundred head in 1935 because of the presence of dourine. Severe winters and deep snows also took their toll. The better price of horses, and the grazing restric-

tions caused ranchers to improve the quality of small herds.[15] But the Grazing Service could report in 1940 that in district 1 (Elko County principally) "only a small percentage of the wild horses have been removed...." after individual cowmen and professional horse runners were through; in district 2 (Humboldt, Pershing, and Washoe counties) there were between one thousand and fifteen hundred left; in district 3 (Churchill, Douglas, Lyon, Mineral, Ormsby, Storey, and part of Washoe counties) "little has been done to remove the wild horses .... "; in district 4 (White Pine, parts of Nye and Lincoln counties) the removal was "fairly complete and .... they are no longer a range problem ...."; and in district 5 (Clark County), 50 per cent of the un-branded stock had been removed.[16] The days of the range pest were nearing an end for the stock associations, and the Federal government was making further plans for its destruction.

In Colorado the stockmen had never had the horse problem that several other range states had. In the period 1935 to 1940 in several sections of the state roundups in co-operation with the Grazing Service were held for the purpose of branding colts. The estrays captured were sold and the money placed in the state's estray fund.[17] In north-western Colorado the wild horse hunters were of much assistance. But the Grazing Service con-tracted in only one area for the gathering of un-branded horses.

The status of the feral herds in the spring of 1940 was precarious. In northern Colorado, in the White River Country, there were only 200 un-branded horses left, although there was "a con-siderable number of branded horses that have gone wild and are not worth gathering ...."; in the

southern part of the state the removal was practically complete, there being only 150 left; in the
southwestern area 200 had been captured and 200
remained; while north of the Yampa River to the
Wyoming line there were approximately 225 still
roaming at large.[18]

By 1940 New Mexico had succeeded in bringing
under control a great part of the public range, exclusive of the Indian reservations. Individual cattlemen and a few horse runners, through the use
of the trap corral, the roundup, and the rifle had
largely done this before the establishment of the
grazing districts. The regional grazier could report early in 1940 that "practically all of the unclaimed or abandoned horses had been removed.
. . . ."[19] There still remained at large a considerable number on the waste lands outside of the
grazing districts and fenced areas.

Co-operating cattlemen and lone-wolf mustangers took their toll for years among the wild herds
in Arizona. The situation was still acute, particularly in the "Arizona Strip," when the Federal government tightened its control over the range following the passage of the Taylor Act. These thousands of wild horses followed the feed and water of
the season. By 1939 the solution was in sight. The
airplane had been used on one occasion, rounding
up 350 horses. About 95 per cent of the users of
the ranges had co-operated with the Grazing Service.[20] When corralled, the unbranded horses were

turned over to the State Livestock Sanitary Board, pastured for thirty days, advertised for claim through a local justice of the peace office; those unclaimed were sold at auction, the proceeds going to the Sanitary Board.[21] The market for these horses among the California cat and dog food packers did much to aid in disposing of the animals. However, in southwestern Arizona in spite of several wild horse and burro roundups, the district was still overrun with wild horses and burros, the elimination of which proved quite a problem. In the Gila River area in the eastern part of the state, the Grazing Service has removed more than seven hundred.[22] In other areas the removal was more complete, yet Arizona could not look forward to complete elimination of the herds for some time.

The conditions affecting the range of the United States, which were responsible for mass removal of wild horses, also existed in parts of Canada. There their last great roundup was held in 1925, when animals were sold for five dollars each, and the "leftovers"—thousands of them—were shot. The government then tried the bounty system, which was the method used for awhile by Nevada stockmen and which is widely used as an instrument of fox and cougar control in counties and states. Between 1925 and 1940 professional hunters and cowboys gathered more than 10,000 "in the vast ranges of the Cariboo, chiefly in the land west of the Fraser river."[23] The bounty system was permitted to lapse, perhaps because of abuses. British Columbia then placed the public domain under strict control. In 1940 horse hunters were allowed to get a permit for $2.50 to dispose of horses at large. The owner of a horse carrying a registered brand could redeem his horse on payment of $2.50. Roundups in progress in 1940 promised to bring to that section of the Canadian range as complete a removal of horses as had been achieved in the United States.

Even Hawaii, a possession which has considerable ranching interests, has a problem in pigs, goats, and sheep that have gone wild. The Park Service killed over five thousand wild goats in 1939. It was estimated that, in spite of many roundups in which thousands had been killed, there were still forty thousand sheep and goats at large.[24]

In the United States in scattered and remote mountain areas, particularly in the states of Arizona, California, Colorado, Idaho, Montana, Nevada, New Mexico, Wyoming, and Utah, there were approximately twenty-five thousand wild horses, most of them unbranded, in 1939. A few hundred burros were still to be found in Arizona, California, Nevada, and New Mexico.

The wild horse of today, in most areas, is not a competitor of the sheep and the cow. It is not likely that he will ever be completely removed, for there are places in the West where a horse can go that a man with a Winchester cannot or will not unless there is more remuneration than the income from a horse hide. When the horse does not compete with the stock interests, the Grazing Service will probably not be vitally concerned about its elimination. The wild horse will always be found in the West.

FOOTNOTES—CHAPTER NINE

1. *See The Grazing Bulletin*, published by the Division of Grazing (now Grazing Service), April and June, 1939.

2. R. H. Rutledge, Director of the Division of Grazing, letter, August 25, 1939.

3. Archie D. Ryan, Acting Director, Division of Grazing, in a letter, July 7, 1939. Andrew R. Boone, in his article, "The Wild Horse Passes," *Travel*, LX (1939), 23, quotes a survey revealing that range horses waste one-twelfth of the water by destroying the vegetation of the watershed.

4. Professor Henry Murray, Montana State College, Bozeman, in a letter, August 30, 1939.

5. R. E. Morgan, Regional Grazier, Billings, Montana, letter of January 31, 1941.

6. Harold J. Burback, Regional Grazier, Rawlins, Wyoming, letter of February 9, 1940.

7. Professor E. F. Rinehart, University of Idaho, Boise, letter of September 11, 1939. The Regional Grazier, J. E. Stablein, gives no statistical evidence in his letter of February 7, 1940.

8. Letter of Nic W. Monte, Acting Regional Grazier, Burns, Oregon, dated January 23, 1940.

9. From an enclosure written by a district grazier, in a letter of Monte, *op. cit.*

10. Letter of September, 1937.

11. Murray Morton, Assessor, Malheur County, Oregon, letter of August 22, 1939.

12. G. R. Parry, Superintendent of Motor Transportation, Utah Parks Company, Cedar City, Utah, in a letter dated October 5, 1939.

13. John H. Gorman, *The Western Horse* (Danville, Illinois, 1939), p. 222.

14. Chester P. Seeley, Regional Grazier, Salt Lake City, Utah, letter of November 10, 1939.

15. Letter of Joseph W. Wilson, County Agent of Elko County, Nevada, August 2, 1939.

16. Letter of Regional Grazier, T. R. Brooks, Reno, Nevada, March 30, 1940.

17. B. F. Davis, Secretary, Colorado Stock Growers and Feeders Association, in a letter of August 15, 1939.

18. Letter of Regional Grazier, Chas. F. Moore, Grand Junction, Colorado, April 3, 1940.

19. Ed Pierson, Acting Regional Grazier, Albuquerque, New Mexico, in a letter of January 23, 1940.

20. *The Grazing Bulletin*, June 28, 1939.

21. John Ray Painter, Acting Regional Grazier, Phoenix, Arizona, letter of January 29, 1940.

22. *The Grazing Bulletin*, June 28, 1939.

23. *St. Paul Dispatch*, February 4, 1940. Quoted by permission of the *St. Paul Dispatch*.

24. *The Grazing Bulletin*, April, 1939.

The wild horse, in short, has become as great a nuisance as the Australian rabbit. He is hard to catch, almost impossible to tame, and so undersized and scrubby as to be worth little when you get him.

"Horse Nobody Wants," *Literary Digest* LXXXIV (1925), 20-21.

CHAPTER TEN

The Indian Submits to Civilization

Ever since the Indian first acquired the horse from the Spanish, stole it from other tribes, or captured it from the mustang herds roaming the plains, it has been a symbol of Indian culture. In the days before the buffalo disappeared and when the red man still held his own in the West, the horse was the instrument with which he gained his living and preserved his life. A chief showed his position by the number of ponies he possessed. That cultural trait has stayed by him during most of the years of reservation life. Even in 1940 success and social position were still demonstrated in the same way. Just as the white man keeps up with the Jones's by driving a respectable automobile, so does the ambitious Indian seek to gain the respect of the community by the number of ponies he possesses. Ambition, then, is revealed by the number of horses, not by the energy shown in providing a standard of health and decency for the family.

The horse has long been a symbol of Indian culture

It is not surprising that the Indian horse herds, after they were boxed up on reservations, continued to grow. When the rancher declared war on the horse, chiefly in the 1880's and '90's, the Indian was not interested. He harbored them because to destroy a horse was like wrecking an expensive automobile, even though the more he possessed, the less range there was available for cattle and sheep. Soon after the turn of the century the agents of the Federal government began to show some concern. The Indian pony apparently was still a fair cow pony and readily found a market, though at a low price. Agents encouraged the sale of these animals in order that overgrazing could be prevented. According to the reports of the Department of Interior, the Flathead Agency in Montana sold 4,000 in 1905, which with the abnormal loss during the winter, considerably reduced the pressure on the range.[1] The Klamath Reservation, having a population of 1,200, had 2,500 horses, 100 mules, 3,000 cattle, 175 hogs, 12 burros, and 5 goats, which were devastating the range. The Nez Perces had 3,000 cattle and as many horses, only a few of which were genuine cayuses, most of them being scabby little things showing their neglect. There was a considerable surplus still in evidence at the Warm Springs, Oregon, Agency, even though $5,000 worth of horses, or close to 1,000, were sold in 1906.

Conditions were worse in the reservations to the

south. At the Western Shoshoni Agency, Owyhee, Nevada, where the wild horse has been such a problem in recent years, the 516 Indians there possessed 2,500 horses as compared to 550 cattle. In 1905 they submitted to selling 1,000, for which $5.00 each was paid. The superintendent at the Southern Ute Agency at Ignacio, Colorado, felt relief when his wards sold 300 head for $6.00 or $7.00 each, but he said he "would be glad if they would sell most of them. They spend most of their time after these ponies. . . . ." Among the Navajo the drought of 1905 which killed "thousands of worthless ponies" was regarded by the government as not "an unmixed evil," for it promised to transfer the standard of wealth from the pony to the sheep. The Indians of the Fort Apache Reservation were willing to sell 2,000 or more of their 14,000, yet the sales were few. The superintendent recommended purchase by the government of thirty good stallions to improve the quality of the herds. Among the Jicarilla in New Mexico it was believed that sale at any price of the many ponies would be advisable. Five hundred head were sold in 1906.

Apparently failing to get the Indian to part with a sufficient number of his ponies, the Federal government turned its attention to improving the quality of the herds, reasoning that if the price were better the Indian would sell more horses, and thus have fewer. As early as 1905 the Office of Indian Affairs had given blooded cattle for breeding purposes. In 1913, tribal herds of cattle and good horses for breeding purposes were established at a cost to the government of $1,500,000. It was thought the Indian would thus learn scientific management and that the good blood would improve his stock. The costs were to be repaid by the Indians. Among the Western tribes the following horses were distributed: Blackfeet, 44 stallions; Colville, 125 stallions; Crow, 200 stallions; Cheyenne, 46 mares; Crow Creek, 74 mares; Lower Brûlé, 12 stallions; Navajo, 4 stallions; Navajo Springs, 20 stallions and 12 mares; Pine Ridge, 25 stallions; Standing Rock, 2 stallions; and Tongue River, 4 stallions.[2] This attack on the problem has been continued up to the present time, with success in more than a few instances. In 1919 the Northern Cheyenne Indians, it was reported, had "a pretty good class of horses. Due to the introduction of those stallions the horses have been bred up until now the majority of them find a good market."[3] With the 75,000 horses estimated on the reservations, the difficulty of catching prevented much scientific breeding. Most of the ponies continued to inbreed, die of old age, disease, or the lack of winter feed.[4] The drought from 1917 to 1920 reduced somewhat the 75,000 wild and worthless horse population, but the Indian Office was still having its troubles there. Before the House Committee on Indian Affairs in 1919 an official reported:

We have made a practice for several years to castrate the pony stallions all over the country. We are' selling those ponies for what we can get for them. We regard them as a nuisance.

We try not to use compulsion at any time. We use strong moral persuasion. We even go so far as to lasso the stallions on our motion and castrate them..... We have purchased with the reimbursable funds, and induced them to purchase with individual funds, medium-weight Percheron stallions all over the country. The stock of the Indians' horses had been very much increased and the pony stock greatly increased.[5]

The basic problem of the Indian, as far as the Federal government was concerned, was that of making a living. This had to be done in the main with sheep, goats, and cattle. Horses were desirable only insofar as there was a market for surplus stock. When drought came the range problem was aggravated further, the Indian becoming more dependent on his guardian. The sheep industry was looked upon as the salvation of the Indians of the Southwest, and the success of this movement, begun about 1920, was dependent upon range conditions.[6] The Indian Office was hopeful in 1922 that the dawn was beginning to break, for that year had seen the Indian largely self-supporting again.

The heart of the Indian problem lay in the wild bands of useless ponies, most of which a white breeder would have destroyed through the use of the roundup and the rifle. The attempts to improve the quality of these herds have largely failed. The use of the tribal herd—horses owned collectively by the tribe and scientifically managed—was discontinued in 1927. Attempts made to interest the army in this source of horses for the cavalry seem to have failed. When the United States entered World War I, the Board of Indian Affairs, at a special meeting in California in 1917, recommended to the Indian Office the substitution of grade Morgan stallions for the Percherons then generally used, hoping to produce a better cavalry horse. In 1926 the War Department was making a survey

to learn what horses were suitable. There is no evidence to indicate that the army was enthusiastic over its discoveries.[7] Yet the Indian Office continues to make available stallions to those who will bring their mares to a central point, while other experiments are being conducted with native horses.[8]

The surplus horse seems to have been eliminated in the northern agencies at about the time the ranchers were busy removing them from the public domain. On the Crow Reservation in 1924 cattlemen who leased Indian lands for range purposes were tormented by an abundance of wild Indian ponies. They not only offered the red man $5.00 for each horse brought in to be killed, but offered to replace each horse so removed with a steer upon which grazing fees would be paid.[9] In the interval between 1924 and 1940 "thousands of head of horses" were gathered by the Crow and sold for a few dollars each. Today they are buying horses for farming and range use.[10] On other reservations in the North the problem had similarly reversed itself. The cayuse was gone.

Thousands of horses still range the arid reservations of Arizona and New Mexico where it may be said it is still a major problem despite all the efforts made in the last few years. At the Mescalero Agency in 1930 it was estimated that there were 3,500 head of wild horses. Enterprising Indians trapped most of them which, being of a better type, sold for an average price of twelve dollars. The tribal treasury received 20 per cent of the proceeds which were to be spent for improvement of the remaining herd which numbered approximately three hundred.[11]

Conditions at the San Carlos Agency of the Apaches about fifteen years ago were getting desperate. In this area having one and one-half million acres of range, there were approximately seven thousand horses and two thousand head of cattle. Efforts made to get the Indians to destroy these feral horses failed, for they did not appreciate the possibilities of the cattle industry and "the absolute necessity, especially in dry years, of having every acre available for their cattle."[12]

Meetings were held continuously for about two or three years and in about 1926 a determined effort was made to remove a number of these ponies. The work was started on the Ash Flat area, which is a large pasture of approximately 60,000 acres and which contained according to the best estimate at that time three or four thousand head of horses. Wing traps of barbed wire were constructed at points of advantage and many weeks were spent in an effort to gather this stock. About three hundred head were finally caught, casterated [sic] and turned over to the Indians for saddle stock. A few head of colts was reserved for tribal usage in connection with the care of the tribal herd. Many of these ponies either died in being brought down by the Indians to whom they were individually issued or totally failed in the purpose of becoming saddle stock.....

During the latter part of 1929 and 1930 several carloads were again removed, being sold for chicken feed at $3.00 a head. When the depression hit the processing business, the price dropped to $1.00 a head, making capture of these inbred horses, too small for saddle stock, an economic impossibility. Approximately eight thousand still remained at large, most of them being in the mountain country.

When the Bureau of Animal Industry made sample tests among these wild ponies of the San Carlos Agency in 1930, they found 17 per cent affected with the dreaded horse disease, dourine. Later tests indicated that as high as 80 per cent of these horses in the high country had this disease. The Bureau of Animal Industry and the Indian Office arranged for the death blow. The recommended program of *complete* removal was adopted by the Apaches after several meetings. Apparently these Indian cattlemen, who now were branding 5,000 calves each year, saw the light. This vast removal program of 1930, costing over $25,000, destroyed nearly 2,000 branded and 6,000 unbranded horses. For the branded horses destroyed, the Indian was given $3.00 each, payable in cattle from the tribal herd. Congress appropriated $20,-000 in 1935 to purchase geldings for replacing the good saddle stock removed because of dourine or by shooting.[13] The superintendent of the Agency claimed that this eradication campaign increased the range capacity by close to 15,000 head of cattle.

On the Fort Apache Reservation at Whitewater, Arizona, about the only progress in the removal of the wild herds has been made by cattlemen who lease grazing lands from the tribe. Of the several methods, shooting has been the most practical, but even that costs $2.00 a head, thirty cents going for ammunition. The agency at one time "promoted a horse elimination project that depended upon the use of tribal funds, but so many of the owners insisted upon turning their horses back on the range after they had been gathered that the number actually sold was so disappointing that the project has not been repeated....."[14] The wild horse problem in 1939 was growing "increasingly more serious" since the practice of moving cattle to winter range had been adopted. This gave the horse better conditions under which to propagate since he no longer had to compete all year with the cattle. Although there was some evidence of a changed attitude on the part of the Indian, the 2,000 (that being a "wild guess") descendants of the ancient mustang continued to multiply.[15]

Of all the Indian reservations, that of the Navajo has presented the gravest horse problem. Seventy-five per cent of these Indians were dependent for their livelihood on sheep, cattle, and goats, and about that number owned the 45,000 horses, which made 50 per cent too many mouths to feed.[16] In May, 1939, at a meeting of the Navajo Tribal Council, a resolution was passed promising co-operation with the Indian Office in a removal program. This was a break with the past. At long last a majority of the Indian leaders realized that their range was in serious condition and that sheep and cows brought money while worthless horses did not. The superintendent said, "Hope and optimism are replacing despair and misunderstanding. . . . . ."[17] The offer of five sheep to replace every horse removed may have encouraged this new attitude. Previous attempts had failed, but in 1939 was to be organized a program that worked.

As described by Superintendent E. F. Freyer, this was a revolution:

A great horse round-up, one of the largest in the history of the Southwest, is now under way over the vast country of the Navajo Indians. To save the disappearing grass more than 10,000 surplus and useless horses have been sold by the Navajos. . . . . [18]

The actual roundup was carried out by Indians, aided by range riders employed by the agency. The reservation was divided into eighteen districts, each of which had been assigned a maximum number of horses as a permanent range load and each owner was given a quota, based on individual needs.

When the horses were gathered in the central corrals, the colorful owners began to do considerable trading among themselves. This completed, the horses were herded into chutes where they were branded with the searing iron so characteristic of the Western cattle industry. Surplus horses not branded were marked with paint, "A" for fair saddle stock, "B" for a barely usable horse, and "C" for "killer," those to be sold to packing plants to be converted into dog or cat food. Following the classification, auctions were then held, being attended by buyers from all over the country. Each buyer was required to bid on the whole herd of each classification. If the bid was too low, the horses were then purchased by the Navajo Livestock Disposition Fund, a special fund used for the purpose of removing undesirable stock. These horses were then driven to the railroad for shipment and sale unless purchased by individual buyers through private negotiations.[19] Many horses died en route to the shipping point. The price range was from fifty cents to $18 a head, the average being $3.00.

These roundups of 1939, being not the first but the largest, reduced the Navajo herds by more than 11,000. That the Indians are still not quite attuned to the new order is shown in a petition sent to the White House in August, 1940. Allegedly signed by 1,670 persons, this complaint stated that "the Indians were unjustly accused of crimes, and that a large number have been arrested and jailed for failure to comply with range regulations and stock reduction programs. . . . ."[20] Another rumbling came from the southern Utah Navajos in July, 1941, when 300 of them voted to "take the warpath in protest against the government's range conservation and stock reduction program." Officials of the Indian Office were reported to have "smiled at the action but, nevertheless are keeping a wary eye on the Indians."[21]

It is doubtful if there has been any injustice done the American Indian on any reservation by the horse removal program. On the Navajo Reservation, after each family had been allotted a given number of branded horses, hearings were held at which individual Indians appeared to request an increase in the number of horses allowed them. This is not the work of an arbitrary government bureau persecuting the wards of the Federal government. When one reviews the whole process of removal, not yet complete but on its way, the student is inclined to marvel at the patience of the Indian Office. Why should the relief agencies pour out money to indigent wards when they could be self-sufficient if they did not possess the cultural "hang-over," the love of a worthless horse?

FOOTNOTES—CHAPTER TEN

1. The following material on conditions in 1905 and 1906 are compiled from the *Annual Reports* of the Department of Agriculture for those years.

2. U. S. Department of Interior, *Annual Report* . . . . 1914 (Washington, D. C., 1915), II, 18.

3. U. S. Congress, House Committee on Indian Affairs, *Indians of the United States*. Hearings before the Committee on Indian Affairs, II, 537. House of Representatives, 66th Congress, 1st Session.

4. U. S. Department of Interior, *Annual Report* . . . . 1918 (Washington. D. C., 1919), II, 45.

5. *Indians of the United States, loc. cit.*

6. U. S. Department of Interior, *Annual Reports of the Commissioner of Indian Affairs* for 1922 and 1923 (Washington, D. C., 1923-24).

7. U. S. Department of Interior, *Annual Report* . . . . 1917 (Washington, D. C., 1918), p. 337, and the *Annual Report of the Commissioner of Indian Affairs* . . . . 1926 (Washington, D. C., 1926), p. 14.

8. Letter of T. D. Holloway, Agricultural Extension Agent, Fort Apache Indian Agency, Whitewater, Arizona, September 14, 1939.

9. Will C. Barnes, "The Passing of the Wild Horse," *American Forests and Forest Life*, November, 1924, p. 648.

10. Superintendent Robert Yellowtail, Crow Agency, Montana, in a letter, February 26, 1940.

11. H. L. Newman, Superintendent, Mescalero Agency, Mescalero, New Mexico, letter of August 22, 1939.

12. Copy of a report to the Commissioner of Indian Affairs, dated May, 1934, enclosed in a letter from Superintendent Ernest R. McCray of San Carlos Agency. The following quotation is taken from that report.

13. Letter of Ernest R. McCray, Superintendent of San Carlos Agency, November 27, 1939.

14. Letter of T. E. Holloway, *op. cit.*

15. *Ibid.*

16. E. K. Douglass, Assistant Range Examiner, Navajo Service, Soil Conservation Service, Window Rock, Arizona, letter of July 2, 1940. They had in 1935, 92,222 goats and 548,848 sheep. W. G. McGinnies and others, *The Agricultural and Range Resources of the Navajo Reservation in Relation to the Subsistence Needs of the Navajo Indians* (Washington, D. C., 1936), *passim.*

17. E. R. Freyer, Superintendent, in a four-page statement, sent by Walter V. Woehlke, Assistant to the Commissioner of Indian Affairs, September 14, 1939.

18. *Ibid.*

19. Compiled from the same, and a letter from E. K. Douglas, *op. cit.*

20. Grand Junction, Colorado, *Daily Sentinel*, August 2, 1940. Quoted by permission of the *Daily Sentinel.*

21. *St. Paul Pioneer Press*, July 13, 1941. Quoted by permission of the *St. Paul Pioneer Press.*

It was a picturesque period in the history of the southwest which brought the mustang and it was a picturesque period which saw his decline and fall.....

The mustang reached the height of his worth and usefulness after the Civil War when cattle barons were building up the West and he faded from the picture before advancing civilization, until now it is doubtful, according to old ranchmen, if the true mustang can be found anywhere.

He played his part in the winning of the West and now doubtless would be happy to know that his breed had not tarried too long upon the face of the world, if he could be told in equine Valhalla, the fate that awaits the range horse of today.

Joseph A. Bursey, "Horses of the Southwest," *New Mexico Magazine*, September, 1933. Quoted by permission of *New Mexico Magazine*.

CHAPTER ELEVEN

From Cow Pony to Cauldron

The Western mustang, seen by the first Americans in the trans-Mississippi West, was in most instances far from a noble animal, but there were many in the herds that m a d e desirable cow ponies. The feral horse on the public domain today may be anything from a small, awkward - appearing animal showing some inbreeding and a hard life, or it may be a good horse with not a little thoroughbred blood. Many of the Indian ponies in their semiwild state show little breeding of the Percheron and Morgan strains that have been introduced into the reservation herds for many years, but have the earmarks of degenerate mustangs that have not had enough to eat.

The early traders found a ready market for these mustangs on the Allegheny side of the country. Even Patrick Henry owned a horse of Spanish origin. The late A. B. Hulbert, in seeking to explain the origin of the American cow pony, points out the existence among the farmers and the cattlemen of the old Southwest and Northwest of a small horse, being a cross, so he thought, of the Indian pony from New Spain and the "American" stock.[1] More than likely these ponies were the descendants of stock imported from the Spanish frontier. Even in the post-Civil War period Texas mustangers found a ready market for these horses in the horse lots of San Antonio, New Orleans, and Kansas City. One California emigrant who made the back trek drove 150 mustangs to the Missouri frontier to help pay the cost of his trip.[2]

There seems to have been a good market available to horse catchers until about 1900. A good living could be made when a broken horse sold for from $35 on up to $100 or more. The demands of the Boer War came as a godsend to those men who gathered horses. "Agents came to the West and shipped out many thousands of them, taking their choice from the herds rounded up, at from $2.00 to $5.00 a head. The shipping losses were tremendous and fairly appalling, for the agents admitted that three out of every four horses shipped to that far-off land from New Orleans died on the voyage out.... These shipments took many thousands of horses from the ranges, but as a result of the hazing they received while being captured, the remainder became wilder and harder than ever to round up, if that were possible."[3]

At this time the domestic market seems to have been at a low ebb. First-class, well-broken cow horses sold in the range areas for $20, and unbroken mares and colts could hardly be marketed. Railroads refused to load horses bound for midwestern sales barns unless freight and feed costs en route were prepaid. It was not unusual for the horse runners to get only twenty-five cents to $1.25 for each horse after the transportation and commission fees were paid.[4]

Despite the fact that mares were not salable at any price and that a large percentage of the horses were killed being captured or died en route, mustangers continued to make a living on the ranges of the Southwest. The rise in prices in 1902 and 1903 encouraged more of these men to capture horses for the Midwest market. The reconstruction of San Francisco after the earthquake in 1906 took thousands of horses from the ranges of California, Oregon, Nevada, and some of the states farther east. More than fourteen thousand were used in cleaning up the debris.[5] And the needs of the orchard farmers for small horses also kept a flow of horses in that direction.

Shipment of range stock and the wild horses from Southwestern ranges continued to the Missouri River where they were used for light farm work, milk wagons, boys' ponies, and even for racing purposes. "Geronimo," a race horse of the period, was once a wild horse. It was reported that hundreds of these were being processed and canned, but the evidence seems lacking.[6] The rise of the mustang for meat is likewise shrouded in mystery. Charles T. McNichols, who grew up on the Indian reservations of the West, believes the use of horse-flesh for meat was more common than is supposed. He states:

> When I was a boy (1900-1910) there were a lot of old coffee-coolers around yet (in Arizona, New Mexico, and California) who had been buffalo-hunters back on the Plains and this fact [that mustang meat was sold for buffalo meat] was a standard joke with them. Evidently in the earlier days, buffalo were killed for hides only, but later, after the railroads came through there was a market for jerky and smoked meat, but as the buffalo were already gone, mustang meat was substituted because it was easier to get. . . . . I have no way of knowing how general this practice was other than this.
>
> In my day both Mojaves and Apaches shot horses and jerked their meat. . . . . I know that this jerky was sometimes sold as beef to prospectors, who didn't seem to know the difference.[7]

When 375 wild burros, removed from the Sitgreaves National Forest in the 1920's, were sold to an Arizona butcher, local residents with good memories had reason to suspect that they were used for making hot tamales instead of being used for hog feed.

The wild horse herds of the West might still number several hundred thousands were it not for the development of new markets. The horse population needed in the gasoline era is much less even

He had played his part in the winning of the West

than before the days of the bicycle. While the Taylor Grazing Act deserves much credit for removing the unbranded horse from the range, it was these new markets arising soon after 1920 that effected the major revolution. These major markets arose among the chicken feed processors, dog and cat food canners, and among the Southern cotton farmers who foresook the tractor as cotton prices declined.

The use of horse meat for chicken feed was instituted on the Pacific coast. These concerns, mostly in Vernon, Petaluma, and Hayward, California, began to buy wild horses about 1920.[8] The railroads co-operated in this venture, offering for a period at least, a special "chicken feed rate" on horse shipments. By designating a carload of horses as "chicken feed," the railroad was under no legal obligations to give humane treatment to the cargo. Under this rate thousands of horses, purchased for one cent a pound or less on ranges as far east as the Dakotas, were transported to California. This was almost the only market for scrub horses caught by co-operating cattlemen, mustangers, and one or two government bureaus in the 1920's. This industry is still in existence, but the shortage of horses will cause a rapid decline in the number of firms within a few years. Local domestic stock, retired through age, and a few Indian ponies will enable some to keep in business.

Supplementing the chicken feed industry was the

rise around 1923 of the canned dog and cat food business. This has become a $25,000,000 industry, and has been one of the chief outlets for the wild horses of the period of the "great removal." In the United States there is about one dog for every ten people, while the number of cats is unknown. When the country was agricultural, food for the dog was not a problem—scraps, left-overs, and rodents constituted the diet. But as the urban population increased, the delicatessen came into its own, and the knowledge of balanced diets became common property. The dog then entered the discussion. When this country spent $40,000,000 on canned and dry dog food in 1935, it revealed a consciousness of the existence of its pets.[9] Obviously here was an industry that needed meat.

The canned "balanced ration" for dogs seems to have originated in 1923 in Rockford, Illinois, where about half the 1,446 horses processed under federal jurisdiction that year were canned. This is disputed, however. Mr. P. M. Chappel, who claims to have been the originator, shipped horses to Europe during World War I. In the postwar period when the herds increased in Montana and Wyoming because of the general use of the tractor, the agricultural deflation, and the consequent low price of Western horses, he began buying those unwanted horses from the cowboys for about $3.00 each. Thousands went to Rockford, where some of the flesh was used in the manufacture of dog food. The better cuts were shipped to Scandinavian markets for human consumption. As the wild herds decreased, Mr. Chappel purchased range lands, bought good mares and stallions, and tried to produce a perpetuating supply of horse-flesh.[10]

The Ross Dog and Cat Food Company of Los Alamitos, California, claims to have been the pioneer on the West coast, having been established in 1924. When Ross started operating, he bought most of his horses from the Indian reservations in New Mexico, Utah, Arizona, Nevada, and Mexico, paying approximately two cents a pound in Los Alamitos, using 180,000 pounds between 1924 and 1939.[11] Among the competitors of Ross in California, only one or two used horse meat, the rest using by-products of packing plants. A small business could not buy whole herds of horses as was required by the Indian Office officials, since the cost of building corrals and paying feed costs would have been too great. In 1935 there were about two hundred firms in the United States engaged in the making of canned and dry dog food.[12] The records of the U. S. Department of Agriculture since 1923 show the growth and decline of the business, a business that parallels the destruction of the degenerate herds of the West. Of course, it cannot be assumed that all horses processed into dog food came from wild herds, but it is certain that a greater part was thus derived. The following tabulation is significant:[13]

	Pounds Canned
1923	149,906
1926	457,858
1927	673,922
1929	4,065,232
1930	22,932,265
1933	29,610,381
1934	20,889,215
1935	9,171,348
1936	14,432,577
1937	2,849,157

The future of horse meat as a source of dog food is not bright. Of necessity, as the "chicken feed" horses disappeared from the range, packing plant by-products, old ewes and rabbits, began to play a larger role than ever before.[14] Dr. W. F. Ross, proprietor of the Ross Dog and Cat Food Company, who can see no promising future for his business on the Pacific coast, believes he will have to turn to marine products when the final roundup of the Indian ponies takes place. From the plains of Mexico were still coming in 1940 "a large number" which were postponing *der Tag*.[15] They may continue to provide the Pacific firms for awhile, but there is a limit to this supply.

Scattered through the range country have been processing plants that rose either to deal with horses and then closed, or which converted their plants temporarily for that purpose. Utah, Texas, Arizona, Montana, and Washington had one or two each, most of which are now closed. These plants made soap, glue, or bone fertilizer of the carcasses, and from the hides baseball gloves, shoes, and buttons, or even ladies' coats.[16] Serum for biological laboratories, fish food for hatcheries, and hair for mattresses are among the other uses of this product.

Between 1926 and 1932 there developed a new industry that did more to clean the ranges of the Northwest than either the dog food or rendering plants. This was the processing of horses for human consumption. There was a belief, as mentioned before, that horses shipped east at the turn of the century were being canned for export. According to one popular writer, speaking of the organized efforts at large scale removal of Pacific Northwest horses, a market in Europe for horseflesh developed and flourished about 1900, but ultimately died out. "A plant for slaughtering and pickling the range horses was operated for a number of years in Portland, Oregon, but finally failed because of the cost of shipping horses from Eastern Oregon points and for lack of a market."[17]

The use of horseflesh is an ancient practice in Europe. Horse meat was probably used by European primitives. The early Christian Church issued a decree against it "for the reason that horse meat was sacrificed and eaten by the Germans in honor of Odin and Freya. The present prejudice against the consumption of horse meat is a remarkable example of the change of taste brought about by a church order against a belief which has been forgotten. . . . . ."[18]

The Danes were the first Europeans to return to the use of horseflesh. When they seized Copenhagen in 1807 they authorized the sale of horse meat, and from this time the practice has become general among the north Europeans. Germany publicly used it as early as 1847, and within a year there were eleven slaughter houses for horses in Berlin. Since 1886 horse meat has been an item of importance in the diet of many Frenchmen. A horseflesh banquet was given in London in 1868, but the practice presumably never became as widespread as on the continent.[19] Except among a few tribes of Indians and perhaps a few whites unwittingly, the practice was not popular in the United States.

Yet during most of the years of this century horses have been processed in this country for the export market. The number of horse slaughtering and processing establishments under Federal jurisdiction since 1920 shows a gradual rise from 1923 to 1930, the period when thousands of wild horses disappeared from Western ranges.[20]

1920........3	1925........2	1930........8	1935........2
1921........3	1926........3	1931........6	1936........2
1922........3	1927........4	1932........5	1937........2
1923........1	1928........5	1933........4	1938........2
1924........2	1929........5	1934........4	1939........2

The export figures indicate the same trend. In the first available report of the Bureau of Animal Industry of the U. S. Department of Commerce, that of 1918, the inspection of horse meat for export is not shown. The record starting in 1920 indicates the rise of the export business:[21]

	Pounds		Pounds
1920	23,124	1930	10,075,324
1922	325,781	1933	3,263,640
1923	183,484	1934	2,175,102
1926	5,402,652	1935	1,238,712
1927	5,116,704	1936	1,276,095
1928	9,646,975	1937	1,517,130
1929	8,712,602	1938	1,626,689

Most of these exports were in the nature of cured meats, chopped and smoked meats, sausages, and edible oil, while mixtures of horse meat, mutton, and beef constituted a small part of the total business.

Of the several firms engaged in this aspect of the packing plant industry the better known were the Butte Horse Products Company of Butte, Montana; Chappel Brothers of Rockford, Illinois; and Schlesser Brothers of Portland, Oregon. These firms built either a new plant used only for horses, or in the case of the Portland firm, converted their plant formerly used for cattle, sheep, and hogs into one used solely for horses.

The story of Schlesser Brothers probably is typical of the industry. At the time when the wild horse became an unbearable nuisance on the Northern ranges they conceived the idea of using these horses commercially. No doubt they were familiar with the early attempts to export horse meat for human consumption, and with the small export business existing at the time they turned to horses in 1926. The stockmen were canvassed and found to be sympathetic. Consequently, cowboys were hired to start the roundup, being paid one cent a pound at the shipping point. Local cattlemen cooperated, as in Montana, in authorizing country-wide projects. Between 1926 and 1933, when this plant was converted again, over 375,000 animals were processed. The meat was exported for use on the tables in Holland and the Scandinavian countries, the hides and hair went to Germany for mattresses, and the casings for sausage, and the other by-products were disposed of in the domestic market—ground bones and scraps for chicken feed, blood for fertilizer, and hooves, tails, and ears for glue. According to Schlesser Brothers, the business "represented a fine source of revenue, and we brought into the State of Oregon at least two millions of European money, which never would have come into this state."[22]

The processors of horseflesh apparently had the idea that the buffalo butchers had in an earlier era, that the supply was unlimited. It was a good business. To pay one cent a pound for the horse, then to sell the cured meat for eight to twelve cents a pound, provided a fair margin. Stockmen looked upon this outlet, even if the monetary rewards were few to them, as the savior of the range industry. Before the movement largely spent itself, thousands of horses had been corralled in the Western states. From the Northern states—Oregon, Nevada, Montana, and even Wyoming—went thousands of horses to Portland, Butte, and Rockford firms. Other thousands were drained from the rest of the states to California. The packing plant came as a fitting development in the history of the use of the wild horses—at least, human beings instead of chickens ate him. That shows some evolution. If the ranges had continued to pour forth their undernourished and often deformed little horses, and if the price of beef had not declined, these distant descendants of the mustang and range ponies might well have continued to compete in European markets with the lord of the West, the "Whiteface."

The processing business has not been the only outlet for wild horses. In the roundups of the last few years there have usually been some animals that would serve the purpose of saddle horses or light work stock. Many of these have been sold locally at auction, or have been shipped to the Southern cotton market. Many of the cotton farmers purchased tractors in a period when cotton brought a good price, but had to get horses again when deflation struck their principal product. In the days of the New Deal the rehabilitation loans have been responsible for an increased demand. The better wild horse, when domesticated, fits well in this economic picture, since a light-weight horse is what is needed to pull the cotton harrow. The *Miami Herald* stated in 1933:

It is said that not since the early days of the world war has there been such a demand for horses as has now developed in the Western states..... Purchasers take them eagerly broken or unbroken. Almost any kind of horse, even a burro, is in demand. Wild bronchos, retired saddle horses, mules, and mustangs are all wanted..... And it all comes about because the farmer, in the South and West, is abandoning the use of the tractor and is going back to the old animal motor power.[23]

A popular book of the 1930's tells of a group of Oklahomans, who, having heard there was money in the sale of "broomtails," went to New Mexico in 1932 and drove back 110 of the animals to sell in

Oklahoma.[24] The railroad and the truck did most of the shifting of these horses to the cotton belt, youthful adventurers on horse did very little of it.

Reports of the Grazing Service in 1939 and 1940 indicate that the usable horses captured in every state in the roundups at that time were going south.[25] In Montana nearly one half of the horses caught were shipped south, while the rest went to the "chicken feed" trade. The few mustangers still operating, being largely in the Southwest, were mostly motivated by the cotton market. One range expert is of the opinion that the Southern demand "had done more to remove the horses from the Western ranges than any other factor."[26] This viewpoint has validity when it is considered that with the rise in prices of range horses, ranchers are again in the horse business and keep the domestic stock branded and in control. However, the cotton trade has not been the chief outlet for the wild horse of the Western range, only for the better horse and the range-bred domestic pony.

The polo field formerly created a demand for a limited number of these range robbers. It has been said that the best polo horse was seven eighths thoroughbred with a dash of the Western pony. An Arizona mustanger captured a few years ago a yearling stallion which was first sold to a Utah cattleman for $250, next to a polo pony dealer for $400, and later to a polo expert for $1,200. A recent writer recommends to polo players the few good wild horses having bottom, speed, intelligence, and movement.

The rodeos and Hollywood may take a limited number of the good horses caught by the mustangers, but it is the zoo and the fox farms that seem to be the destiny of most of the horses that will be caught in the future. The day of the good wild horse had largely passed before the range had been violated by too many cattle and sheep. The only horses worth catching in the day of range control will be the exception, not the rule. That "mighty monarch of the plains," often referred to by the popular writers, is fox food in the future, if anybody goes to the trouble to catch him.

FOOTNOTES—CHAPTER ELEVEN

1. Quoted by Phil Stong, *Horses and Americans* (New York, 1939), p. 176.

2. Mentioned by Carl Detzer, "Portraits of a Pioneer," *Reader's Digest*, June, 1939.

3. Will C. Barnes, "The Passing of the Wild Horse," *American Forests and Forest Life*, XXX (1924), 646. Quoted by permission of the American Forestry Association.

4. *Ibid.;* also Barnes, "Wild Horses," *McClure's Magazine*, XXXII (1908-9), 291-92.

5. R. M. Steele, "Killing an Army of Horses to Rebuild San Francisco," *Harper's Weekly*, LI (1907), 580.

6. Letter of L. C. Montgomery, President of the Utah Cattle and Horse Growers Association, Heber City, August 29, 1939.

7. Letter of August 25, 1939.

8. Letter of C. U. Duckworth, Chief of the Division of Animal Industry, Department of Agriculture of the State of California, August 22, 1939, and Don C. Brandt, Acme Products Company, Hayward, California, November 2, 1939.

9. L. I. Becker, "Verily, This Product Goes to the Dogs," *Printer's Ink Monthly*, January, 1935.

10. F. R. Whaley, for Chappel Brothers, Inc., letter of August 29, 1939.

11. Letter of Dr. W. J. Ross, October 5, 1939.

12. L. I. Becker, *op. cit.*

13. Compiled from the *Annual Reports* of the Bureau of Animal Industry. There is a discrepancy in the figures for 1930. In the statistics for the fiscal year of 1935, 79,164 pounds were horse meat and beef, 1,394,740 pounds were horse meat and mutton.

14. *Business Week*, August 17, 1936.

15. A. R. Zumwalt, Bureau of Animal Industry, U. S. Department of Agriculture, Phoenix, Arizona, in a letter of January 27, 1940. "The only incentive that dealers have to buy our horses in preference to the Mexican horse is that they are free to top the best of ours for other than slaughter purposes. . . . ."

16. The *New York Times*, July 14, 1929, in an Associated Press article from Phoenix, Arizona, mentioned that a "demand for young hides has developed from fashion centers, where they are made into ladies coats."

17. Robert C. Notson "Horses! Horses!" *Sunset Magazine*, LIX (1927), 80.

18. Dr. Robert Ostertag, *Handbook of Meat Inspection* (Chicago, 1919), p. 123. Quoted by permission of the American Veterinary Medical Association.

19. Compiled from *ibid.*, pp. 123-24, and Lees Knowles, "Horseflesh," *Nineteenth Century*, LII (1890), 592-607.

20. Letter of E. C. Ross, Chief, Meat Inspection Service, U. S. Department of Agriculture, August 11, 1939.

21. Taken from the *Annual Reports* of that bureau. The exports for 1930 are given at two different figures in the report.

22. Letter of Albin Naugler, Secretary, Schlesser Brothers, Portland, Oregon, August 7, 1939.

23. Quoted by Joseph A. Bursey, "Horses of the Southwest," *New Mexico Magazine*, September, 1933.

24. Forrester Blake, *Riding the Mustang Trail* (New York, 1935). An article by Blake on his experiences appeared in *Scribner's Magazine*, XCVII (1935), 248-51.

25. Based on letters from regional graziers cited in chapter IX.

26. R. E. Morgan, Regional Grazier, Billings, Montana, letter of January 31, 1940.

With every man's hand against them, these wild horses will eventually be exterminated. In the meantime any red-blooded man thirsting for adventure, excitement, and some Wild West riding can get plenty of it chasing these unwelcome residents of the western ranges. There is no closed season on them at any time in the whole year, for they are classed with the wolves and coyotes, as predatory animals marked for slaughter.

Will C. Barnes, "The Passing of the Wild Horse," *American Forests and Forest Life,* November, 1924, p. 648. Quoted by permission of the American Forestry Association.

CHAPTER TWELVE

Methods of the Mustangers

Around the running and catching of wild horses has been woven much romance. It was Zane Grey's favorite line of action in his books on the Southwest. Even Hollywood has found some profit in exploiting this interest of people, both young and old. On the magazine shelves in the drug stores where are found the "action" publications for the inhibited or wistful American, will be seen those having as one of their recurring themes the capture of wild horses.

The practice is as old as white man's first contact with the horses of the plains, or the Indian's interest in keeping a herd. It is being carried on today in the windswept mesa country. Doubtless there are some individuals who will continue this vocation or avocation as long as there are any horses left that do not carry a brand. The original mustanger was one who in the early days of Texas stole horses from the Mexicans. However, horse running was practiced before then, not only by a few Americans but by the Spanish. Indians might be called the original pursuers of the wild horse. In the late 1840's and '50's it is recorded that "many Mexicans" whose families resided in the Rio Grande watershed supported themselves by capturing mustangs and wild cattle. Some of the Mexican ranchers would drive into the horse country in April, and there encamp with families, milk cows, and other possessions, and run horses until fall came. There might be as high as two hundred men in a single group, led by a *capitán*. "To see these mustangers in full chase was to behold one of the most exciting scenes presented by the wild sports and occupations of Texas frontier life....."[1] Some of these groups specialized in catching colts, getting as many as a hundred in one season.

Since then the term has applied to one who made a vocation, at least part of the year, of chasing horses for profit. The buffalo hunter, who became the victim of technological unemployment in the 1870's, became the first professional mustanger of the modern era. However, most of those who ran horses, or most of the horses were run, it would seem, by those who engaged in the practice as an avocation. Most cowboys, not only during the days of the open range but down to the present, have at one time or another seen horses they wanted and gone after them. Before the days of commercialized recreation, the automobile, and good roads, the young man of the small towns as well as some of the ranchers spent many days of adventure riding the mustang trail. In western Kansas in 1880 there were ten horse runners for every wild horse, some riding horses, some on foot, some in wagons. During the past twenty years, it is not the professional horse catcher who has ridden the range, so much, but it has been the stockman with his cowboys, or the officials of a Federal agency. When prices are good and the horses are fair the mustanger comes back. When the quality of the wild horse gets so poor that he is not salable to other than a packing plant for two or three dollars, the mustanger retires from the scene.

Some of these men have become famous. In the 1870's, according to "Buffalo" Jones, the bravest and most daring of all the mustangers on the middle plains was "Wild Horse Bill" who captured over a thousand horses and lost but one herd in his career. He usually worked alone. To James R. Fulton of west Kansas goes the credit for the biggest catch in his area—seventy-two horses at one time.[2] Nevada produced two in the heyday there around 1910 in "Pete" Barnum and Rufus Steele. It was Barnum, a thirty-two-year-old native of South Dakota with a college education, who revolutionized the methods used in Nevada and succeeded in capturing 7,000 horses in a six-year period. Rufus Steele, a literary man who left in magazines of this period several excel-

Chasing wild ones was a favorite cowboy sport

lent accounts of his experiences in the same country, ranks as an enterprising mustanger. Ike Hill, noted in the Texas country as one who caught more horses than any other man, had a unique method of deception. G. R. Parry, now superintendent of motor transportation at Cedar City, Utah, gained fame on the southern Utah horse plateaus. In the modern "chicken feed" period the name of the "aerial cowboy," Floyd Hanson, is known to many boys. Less familiar are Archie Meyers of Oregon, who engineered the capture of 10,000 horses; Carl Skelton, of Montana, who was in charge of one of the large county roundups; and hundreds of others who lived in the last century.[3] These professionals or semiprofessionals led hard, dangerous lives. They were the only men who could make a living at this game, and even when horses were only one or two dollars a head a few kept going largely for the adventure and the love of the life. One who has left the business as a vocation said in 1939:

I can say without question there is only one thing to me that has the thrill that chasing mustangs has, and that is playing polo. There are men in Southern Utah who have done more wild horse chasing than I have, but in years past, as I look back over the thrills I have experienced, I can truthfully say that chasing "stangs" as we call it is really a lot of fun.[4]

The capture of the wild herds was done by two types of individuals—amateurs and professionals —and it was the professionals who removed most of the horses in the "Zane Grey" era. These men sat around "all winter planning campaigns against them in the hope of making big profits, and all summer in proving that most of these plans have flaws in them,"[5] while the amateur used only some of the methods improvised by the professional to catch a few saddle horses. The mustanger used the effective methods profitably while the amateur often used the same methods unprofitably. Shooting has always been a proper method of ridding the range of horses if one did not care for the horses. Ranchmen long have relied on the Winchester for this task. Texas settlers were known to ride a horse out on the range until they saw a stallion, then get off and stand behind the horse. When the stallion approached to satisfy his curiosity, he was shot dead.[6] This was not the method of the mustangers, needless to say.

The methods of the horse catcher include creasing, snaring, roping, and running into some type of corral.[7] The first three get individual horses, the corral technique gets numbers and has been the most often used. To crease a horse was to shoot him in the upper part of the neck, in front of the withers, one inch deep, close to the spinal column. This shock stunned the horse for a sufficient length of time for the rider to approach, tie the feet, put on a halter or rope, and snub the rope to the saddle. Where the method originated is not certain but it came into practice quite early. Even Zebulon Pike, who went across the plains in 1807, unsuccessfully tried to use this method on an appealing black horse. This method was not frequently used by professionals. Sometimes after days spent unsuccessfully running a herd, they had to use it or lose a horse they wanted. One time a father and son decided to "nick" a beautiful blue stallion that roamed the Texas range. They hid at a water hole and waited for the thirsty animal to come for water. Finally the mustang came to drink. The father shot, the horse fell, and the boy ran up to tie its legs, only to learn that the shot had been too low. Apparently the animal had raised its head at the moment of the shot. On another occasion some Kansas horse runners creased a stallion as he ran, which caused the animal to run with head down but did not affect his speed. They ran him into the village of Itasca, but in spite of the fact that every able-bodied male pursued him, he escaped to the prairies.[8] The difficulty in this case as in all such attempts was in making an accurate shot. If the bullet struck too low, the horse was killed. For every one caught, fifty were killed. One old mustanger says to "talk of going out to catch horses this way is pure bunk. I have tried it many times and have broken their necks scores of times and never caught a horse that way and never knew anyone else who did."[9]

The trail trap or snare was also used in the attempt to catch single horses. This use of a sapling or a limb with some spring in it, and a rope, was an improvision on the old trap used for many years by farm boys to catch rabbits, and by trappers to get various fur-bearing animals. This snare would be secreted on a trail familiar to a herd, and the horses either were driven down the mountain path or else the trapper waited until they came to water. When trapped by the foot or the neck the horse made a new arrangement of the mountain scenery. If the end of the rope were tied to a log the animal took the whole trap for a long ride. Usually an old mare was caught using this method, she being the leader of the herd. The "fuzz-tails" became wise and would use cattle as leaders. Consequently, if a trap caught anything, it often was a steer. "The leading horse would back and nicker, seeing if her foals were all present and accounted for. And they would be."[10] The mortality among animals snared was high, a great majority being choked to death. Some amateurs out after individual horses would tie a domestic horse to a tree. After a large loop had been made in a lariat and placed near the tied animal, the participants would hide themselves near by. When the wild animals came near to see the tied horse, the rope was pulled, closing the noose. After much threshing around, there might be a snared horse. One rancher, who lost a splendid saddle horse to a band of wild ones, decided to use a lasso on the narrow canyon trail used by the animals when going to water. He tied the end of the rope to a tree in which he secreted himself, and as the horse came from the water hole, he dropped the noose over its neck. The animal lunged, bent the tree, the snap throwing the rancher twenty or thirty feet. When he regained consciousness the horse was standing there as unconcerned "as if being caught was an everyday occurrence."[11]

On another occasion, a group intent on roping a mare on a narrow trail in southern Utah, saw her push ahead on a small ledge above the canyon, and then fall. The "horror-stricken watchers heard a thud that came faintly from a rocky canyon floor, fifteen hundred feet below."[12]

Chasing "broomtails" with the expectation of roping a good horse from the herd was a favorite outdoor sport of many amateurs, especially in the spring when the wild horses were poor. If the rider's animal were fast, it was no problem to overtake a band in a country permitting a race. The first ones overtaken would be the colts and the decrepit which were passed up for better horses. In the Southwest this was popular among some of the Indian tribes, the early settlers, and even the army. There were two practices in the use of the lasso: one by throwing the loop around a foot or neck, the end fastened to the pommel of the saddle, or tied to the neck of the horse; the other, by placing the noose at the end of an eight-foot stick, thereby making the capture easy if the rider could approach the side of the mustang. The Spaniards, being adept at the use of the rope, probably originated both practices, although the Indian exploited the latter method. A soldier of 1833 describes the unsuccessful use of the latter equipment by a group of amateurs in the Canadian River country:

Having equipped ourselves with a noose and stick, tightened our girths, and tied up our heads, we rode forth into the prairie, and soon discovered a large herd of about one hundred quietly grazing and unaware of our approach. As soon as we approached near enough to be seen by them, and were gradually recognized, the whole body began to nicker, and was soon in commotion, stamping the ground with their fore feet; while a few of the bolder spirits moved up toward us, slowly and doubtingly, eager to ascertain our character. Each rider now stopped on his horse, laying close to his horse's neck; and in this manner we silently advanced, watching closely the movements of the herd, and making each a selection of such a fine animal as pleased his fancy. This part of the sport was very fine; and, in the present instance, so many elegant forms of both sexes, and all colors and sizes, presented themselves, that it required not a little promptitude to form a decision. We had not long to deliberate; for, by the time we were within one hundred yards, the increased nickering and confusion showed they had winded us; and the whole herd suddenly wheeled round, and dashed off over the plain..... We ran them about two miles; but the rocky nature of the country, and the number of deep ravines crossing our track in every direction prevented our coming up with such as were desirable..... On our return towards the main body of troops, we saw a large stallion, whose fore leg had been broken in the chase, yet in spite of this, he managed to hobble off on the remaining three very cleverly.[13]

The Indians, apparently following the lead of the Spanish, were never users of much guile in hunting horses. Their methods called for the use of the Spanish lasso and for groups of varying sizes for pursuit. The Osages, according to an observer in 1835, started out on horseback, each man supplied with a noose at the end of a pole. When the herd had been surrounded, the riders started pursuit, soon being able to place the noose on the necks of the poorer horses and colts.[14]

The Mandans, of the Northern Great Plains, became skilled in the use of the lasso, being able to drop the noose over the head of a horse running at full speed. When the horse was caught, the Indian dismounted and choked the wild one until he could be handled.[15] Pictograph records show the Dakota Indians of the upper Missouri using the lasso. The rope became the conventional sign of the wild horse.[16] The usual method of the Comanches of the Southern plains was the lasso. After years of horse running they learned to run the animals in a ravine where comrades lay in ambush. The lariat was then used to advantage. The unfortunate experience of a Pawnee is told by an old range rider. A party of the Indians had run a herd all day. In the evening one Pawnee took a short cut and came up to the wild herd, roped a horse, and held it for awhile. When the other Indians came up, "the wild horse became so badly scared that he jerked his captor's horse down and in the mix-up, the Pawnee's neck was broken."[17]

The use of the "grand circle hunt" by the Anadarkos and perhaps other Indians is an interesting example of early techniques that show some progress in the art. In the 1860's James Pike, frontier scout and ranger, accompanied the Anadarko Indians on such a chase in the Texas Panhandle. He states that this method was the only one that could be called effective.

A column of hunters, consisting of two or three hundred men—sometimes even more—is formed in the same order as if on the war path, with an advance guard, and numerous flankers, to look out for horses. As soon as a herd is discovered, the column is notified, by some preconcerted signal, which instantly halts, and awaits the orders of the Chief, who always rides in the direction indicated and reconnoitres, accompanied by four or five of the principal men of the tribe. This done, they ascertain the course of the wind; and taking advantage of that, march their forces toward the herd, keeping at a great distance away, so as not to excite alarm.

At intervals of a mile or so, a band of twenty-five or thirty men will be posted, until the game is entirely surrounded. These squads again deploy, to right and left, as the movements of the herd, or the nature of the ground require. When the circle has been completed, another signal is given, and the ring is contracted as much as is possible to do, without alarming the herd. As soon as the wild horses scent the hunters, the chase begins. Off go the animals, in the vain hope of escaping the enemy, which they suppose to be approaching only from one side; but no sooner do they approach the circle, than several hunters show themselves, and turn the frightened herd back again; and thus they are kept galloping across, and around the sac formed for their reception, for hours, and until they are so wearied that they are readily taken, by the contracting, and closing up of the circle. Occasionally these horses, over frightened, make a desperate charge upon some single spot in the line by which they are surrounded, and thus make their escape; but this is not usual. . . . . [18]

Roping a horse in the open country presented a special problem. The Anadarko Indians, who used the "grand circle" method described above, would place ropes on the feet of the captives, and turn them loose in the ring in order to cause greater confusion. A mustanger of the modern era, when confronted with a wild horse on the end of his lasso, realizes the difficulties ahead. Probably the saddle horse used in the chase is worn out after the run. The mustang may throw both rider and horse before it is thrown. When it is down, and perhaps choked, the rider leaps to the ground, and ties a front and hind foot together. If the saddle horse permits the taut lariat to loosen, the captured animal may strike the rider with the front foot or head. In this position the horse is left to thresh around until a burro or old mare is brought, to which the mustang is tied and taken in to camp. When the horses are left to thresh around on the ground all night, three out of four will be found dead in the morning.[19]

A unique story of holding a wild horse is told about an army officer stationed in Texas in 1839. After roping the stallion, he held him until his companion shot another, skinned him, and made a thong from the hide with which to tie the feet.[20]

The use of the rope after a hard run was never a profitable pastime, and it is not surprising that it was little practiced by those who were catching horses for money or who were trying to rid the range of the grass eaters. Certain pioneers who had the patience tried to improve on this method by tying domestic mares out on the prairie, and then when the band of wild ones came in, they rushed forth from concealment and hurriedly roped one without a long run. Cowboys often hid near water holes to which the bands came at the end of the day. After the horses had drunk their fill, they rushed forward on their fast horses, with ropes swinging, and splitting the night with blood-curdling yells. A horse that has just quenched his thirst after a day or two on the desert cannot run far before slowing up, therefore is more easily caught. The herd is prevented from slackening its speed so that it may get its "second wind." Will C. Barnes, who has seen many horses caught in this way, described the usual scene:

Logy with water, the wild horses ahead begin to slacken a bit. Perhaps a very young colt falls behind, whinnying pitifully as his dam crowds forward from the nameless terror behind.

With manes and tails streaming in the wind, dripping with sweat and covered with lather, the clouds of dust sometimes completely hiding them from view, they plunge ahead until out from a hill or from behind a sheltering tree or rock tears the third mustanger on his fresh horse.

The band swings aside and sweeps around in a broad curve, as the third man, riding to one side, turns them slowly. Finally they double back upon the other two riders, and by this time the horses in the band begin to show their weariness, and their speed slackens very perceptibly.

Crowding close in upon the band, which is by this time greatly distressed, each rider picks out the horse he wants and works along beside it; and as it is a very short throw, the roping is an easy matter. A quick jerk draws the noose up about the captive's neck; the bight of the rope is thrown over the horse's withers and down so that his front feet step over it. At this instant the riding horse is swinging suddenly out at right angles.... if he regains his feet, as he sometimes does, the poor saddle-horse gets a pretty rough deal before the animal is finally thrown and tied.[21]

The "walk down" method, used with and without corrals and either on foot or horseback, or in some cases in a buckboard, is an adaptation of the water-

hole technique. It exploits the practice of wild herds, using but one range. An early fur trader in the Pacific Northwest, who hunted horses for two summers about 1807, before they had been made wild by the constant efforts to catch them, could find no way to capture them without running them down. He and his partner ran a small herd of fat animals for two days. On the second day two fell dead and two were captured.[22] This was too hard on saddle horses to be used by lovers of horse-flesh.

Cowboys often tried this technique, not as the two fur traders did—for that usually meant the death of the riding horses—but either in relays or by constant following of the animals. Its use was widespread in the period when horses were numerous on the Great Plains. The practice of the wild horse of staying on its familiar range made possible the changing of mounts by the pursuers, or the stationing of riders at strategic points in the big circle. When the moon was full, so that one could keep the herd moving at night, these animals could be driven for three or four days and nights, at a slow speed, until they were finally exhausted and crazy for water. One old horse catcher does not believe that exhaustion is the sole explanation of why the horses, after being "walked down," no longer feared man. He believes that because of the former association of the mustang or his ancestors with man, he felt secure in man's presence again.[23] Regardless of the season, the exhausted horse could be roped or driven into a corral. Feeling ashamed of his conduct, one cowpuncher who helped "walk down" a herd of eighty in four days wrote:

Some would lie down; then the stinging rawhide end of a lariat would be snapped at them and strike unerringly where the vaquero intended it to. Up they would get, and reel ahead. It was night when the men got them to camp, and they kept those that were not literally fagged out on the move nearly all night—moving backward and forward.[24]

There is on record a case of horse catchers pursuing a band of two hundred for nine days and nights. Even the men were thirty-six hours without water. Just when they were ready to give up, they struck the Arkansas River where the men quenched their thirst and forty-eight head of animals were corralled.[25]

A Texan in the Nueces country, and his Negro hand, alternately ran and walked a herd of thirty-five for ten days before capturing them. In this group was a mule that was finally shot, since it constantly tried to lead the herd in the wrong direction. The Texan killed his saddle horse and was left afoot twenty-five miles from home.[26]

A former slave turned cowhand used a unique adaptation of the "walk down." After depositing food at strategic places on the horse range, he rode his horse in a walk toward the herd. He never changed horses or clothes, but relentlessly walked on. After days the horses no longer minded him. If they would "spook," he would "spook." Sometimes he would "scare" and run away first, and the wild ones would follow. When ready to corral, he ran in first and the herd came after him.[27]

Tradition has it that the "walk down" originated among the forty-niners who, when they lost horses, walked after them until they were captured. More likely, it originated among the Indians. Regardless of the origin, there seems to be some evidence of its use in a modified form long before the California gold rush. There is no doubt that it was a popular method among the amateurs in the time of the open range. It was not foolproof, for if the plan was to run the animals into a corral, they oftentimes would break and run to near-by cover as they approached the gate. The riders' horses being exhausted, the men could do nothing but watch the mustangs disappear.

The use of the circular corral with wings is a Spanish contribution to the horse country of the West. In the place where the mustangs were numerous they built a large enclosure with a door opposite the entrance leading into a smaller one. From the opening of the large pens were built wings of brush which served as the sides of a funnel which deflected the horses into the corral gate. No corral was considered complete until it had been dedicated to some saint and a cross erected at the entrance. If hundreds were forced in on one drive, the enclosure was either burst open or the milling and trampling killed a considerable number. In this case, according to Pike, the camp had to be moved.

The party are obliged to leave the place, as the stench from the putrid carcasses would be insupportable; and, in addition to this, the pen would not receive others. Should they, however, succeed in driving in a few, say two or three hundred, they select the handsomest and youngest, noose them, and take them into the small enclosure, then turn out the remainder.....[28]

The Indian apparently did not borrow this technique from the Spanish. In addition to the running use of the lasso, he used pits on the trails (the pits having sloping sides), and blind canyons.[29] Early Texas settlers built fences of brush in the prairies to serve as enclosures.[30] Others used wings of sod, logs, and even stone. Some plowed a furrow from the end of the wing out on the prairie. Horses were afraid to cross this. Pioneers in Kansas located in the timber near a stream where the horses crossed, a corral with wings on each side of the trail.[31] When woven wire came to the plains, it was used as the substitute for brush and poles. However, none of these early groups seem to have found necessary the finesse that has been required most of the time in the last quarter century.

The canvas corral, developed by Pete Barnum about 1910, was hailed as a revolutionary device at that time. The noise of the stockade building often caused the remnants of the great herds to leave the range. Woven wire was not only difficult to move into the horse country, since most of it had to be done by pack horse, but was brutal in the effect upon frenzied horses as they plunged into it. In order to eliminate these objections, Barnum obtained two pieces of heavy canvas long enough and wide enough to make a corral fifty feet in diameter and eight feet high, the canvas being placed one foot above the ground. To the wildest parts of Nevada, where horse runners had never successfully operated before, this equipment was taken.

When horses became wary after having dodged the trap once or twice, it was moved to a new area where an hour's work was sufficient to put it up again. After some experience he learned where to set the trap most advantageously so the horses would suspect nothing until it was too late. To quote Barnum's historian:

> Everything ready, the starter would slip away and start the nearest bunch of horses. If he saw them running toward the trap and into the hands of the outlying men, he would go farther back to start another bunch, and still another. I have seen separate bunches totaling thirty head coming into the corral within a hundred yards of each other. They were all corraled and held, though the riders had a very busy time of it.[32]

It is not true that this type of corral revolutionized horse catching. Will James, writing in 1923 about his experiences in the piñon country (probably after Barnum's time), tells of using woven wire pens eight feet high laced with juniper or cottonwood poles, with wings running a mile on both sides of the gate. A month or more was required to build this equipment which, he said, was a "humdinger of a place" in which to run a horse thief.[33] W. R. Leigh, who has had considerable experience in the mustang country, saw used in the Southwest only the mesh wire netting corral ten feet high with wings of two strands, on which were hung gunny sacks and saddle blankets.[34] There seems to be no evidence that cattlemen and mus-

tangers of the past fifteen years have used other
than the pole corral or box canyon.

The use of the corral, regardless of composition,
at a water hole, has long been a technique widely
used. The Spanish seem not to have used it in
that way. A form of it was in use in Kansas as
early as 1859. Will James says that the blind
corral was unknown in the Southwest when he
was a mustanger, so it may be a Northern innova-
tion.[35] Yet that seems unlikely because of the presence of more water in the North. Its first use apparently has not been recorded.

The usual method was to find some water hole
that was visited by wild horses. A large circular
corral of poles, boards, or wire then was built
around it. A light-weight gate, opening inward,
was placed on the side from which the animals usually approached. Perhaps a smaller corral was
attached to a side. For some time the mustangs
would be permitted to water here, until the fear
of human scent had gone. In the summer when
most of the water holes were dry and the horses
desperate for water, they returned. When it came
time to use the trap one man secreted himself on the
"off-wind" side, holding a rope with which to
spring the trap closing the doors.[36]

Will James once graphically described his experience in the "pit":

While I was in the hole familiar snorts warned me a
bunch was coming. I could tell they were suspicious of man

scent even though I was quite a distance from the gate. They'd come up a few steps, then go back; the lead mare would start ahead and the stud would circle around, his head up and taking in all he could see. At times he'd turn the lead mare back, but he wasn't sure—just instinctively suspicious..... Finally, half of them went in, only to come out again, snorting at every jump and shying at nothing. I knew they'd come back, and they did after a good hour's wait. I had my doubts that I could catch the whole bunch, but when they came again they seemed to throw caution to the winds, crowding in and around the water. While the stud was circling nervously around his bunch I pulled the trigger and the gate closed with a bang. The bunch leaped at the noise and struck out in panic for the other side of the corral, the earth shaking with the thunder of the hoofs. As they hit the wire it yielded a little and kicked them back off their feet. Those mustangs tested the whole corral—every inch of it—but it was built for such assaults..... [37]

The water hole trap represents the most scientific method used by man. As the horses became wise to the ways of the horse runner they left for the high country where roundups were difficult if not impossible. However, they had to have water— so even many of these fell to the ingenuity of man. The water hole trap was still in use in 1940. For many years tame horses placed inside the trap have been employed as "bait." Salt has also been used.

The driving of horses from the hills and desert into a box canyon or corral was a task of no small dimension. Riders stationed themselves along the radial lines of the wings of the pen or the hills leading into that central place. Back farther went other riders who started the herd toward the pen. If the herd had been chased before, or if there were domestic horses in it that had gone wild, trouble was to be expected. One rider says the best approach was to let the mustangs think they were getting away, try to run them in the opposite direction, and nine times out of ten they would double back toward the trap. The presence of dead stock or even the squawk of a crow can frighten the thundering horses from the trail. A mustanger operating east of Denver in 1864 tells of chasing a herd led by a small, scarred, white stallion:

[They came] from concealment with a whoop, and at full speed we were after them, and with a wild rush they were off down the draw [where the corral had been built]. We had arranged that two of us would take the left side, as we counted they would try to swing back to the north, and one rider take the right side and one follow the wild bunch. Just what reason that wild stallion had for not wanting to go through that gap, we know not, but certainly it was he whipped down the left side of that running band, and with ears back and using his teeth in a very business-like way, he crowded the leaders right up the steep bluff .... and escaped..... The little white stud had out-generalled us..... [38]

The stallion was often the cause of much trouble. He had been known to attack his pursuers as he and his band attempted a break. With ears back, teeth bared, and hooves flashing, he charged. The mustanger often settled the argument with a six-shooter. These difficulties made horse running uncertain for professionals. The amateur was likely to learn that he had nothing in the corral except the old and the young, and had ruined several good saddle horses in the attempt. For every ten horses captured and broken, two or three saddle horses were either killed, wind-broken, or crippled. "Cowboys have been seen to sit down beside their horse thus used up and cry like babies at their loss, although in their eagerness to catch the wild ones and their excitement in the chase they had spurred the horse until there was a raw place on either side as big as a dollar."[39] Will James once saw a man whose horse had collapsed under him, pull out his Winchester, shoot into the escaping band of mustangs, then throw his arms about his pony's neck and sob in remorse for what he had done.

A snowshoe roundup staged in the Modoc National Forest a number of years ago is of interest, not because it was widely used but because of its novelty. At that time when there were more than ten thousand wild horses there, rangers and ranchers on snowshoes, by shouting and shooting drove a herd through the deep snow until some of the animals died where they last floundered. The remainder were forced on through the deep snow to a cattle corral. If not rounded up, they would have died before spring, so the act was one of kindness, not of cruelty.[40]

In southeastern Oregon, the Big Horn Basin in Wyoming, and possibly Utah, the airplane was introduced in the "chicken feed" era as a supplement to the old-time method of the corral drive. The horse country in Oregon is an area that is difficult to negotiate even on horseback. Into these breaks of the Owyhee River had gone thousands of horses, driven there by competition of cattle and sheep and by the mustangers. Here could be found all the strays from ranches, horses that had never carried a saddle, a few good horses, but most of them the seven-hundred-pound descendants of once good stock.

In 1930, Archie Meyers, who was responsible for much of the removal work on this range, engaged an airplane for the sum of $1,000, to use in driving the herds from the inaccessible to the accessible places where cowboys could run them into a corral. The venture failed. In 1936, along came Floyd Hanson who, employed by ranchers, used the plane there for two years successfully. His method was to leave camp before sunup and fly over the horse country until he saw a herd. As he zoomed down on them from a high altitude, with siren shrieking and wind screaming through the struts, the panic-stricken horses ran in wild alarm. If they went the wrong direction, down the one-motored plane roared again to turn them. As the horses fled in the direction of the corral, Hanson would repeatedly circle behind them, running them until they were in the canyon or until the riders had swooped down upon them on their fresh horses from behind rocks or hills. If they threatened to break back, down would come the shrieking airplane again. If individual animals broke, the riders would either shoot them or rope them, leaving them until later. The horses were driven then into a blind canyon or corral, and that part of the hunt was over. Hanson was on his way back for more. Back on the desert he would fly over the old horses that had been left behind in this mad chase. There would also be the colts that could not keep up with their terror-stricken mothers. They were left here to die. It was as impractical to gather these colts when using the airplane as it was for mustangers, wildly chasing a herd toward a box canyon, to turn back to get them. This was one of the unmerciful aspects of the game.[41]

Hanson quit this business after two years of it. His life will probably be longer because of this decision, for he took many chances. He flew in a one-motored plane over a rough country that had no landing fields. The air currents in the mountain areas are treacherous. He constantly power-dived to within a few feet of the ground, at one time hitting a horse and knocking off the plane's landing-gear. A spectator once saw him dive within a few feet of the rim of the canyon and turn a loop before straightening out. It is small wonder that Hanson decided to quit, or that others less daring than he failed in their use of the plane.

To get a horse into a corral far back in the hills was not the end of the mustanger's task. The "critter" had to be marketed. That meant either breaking it to ride, or getting it to the railroad station and loaded, or both. The Spaniards, when once they had corralled a herd, kept them going until they were worn out, then rode them.[42] Kansans were reported to have "starved them for some time, in order to render them gentle, then lassoed and taken [them] out, easily broken to the saddle or harness. . . . . ."[43] Most mustangers, when once the horses were corralled, hobbled them or in some way made it impossible for them to run when released. Mexican runners were reported to have taken a knife and "cut each front knee-cap. This severed a ligament and let the joint-water out at the same time. Then they would brand them and turn them loose." With both front legs stiff, there was no trouble in driving them to the point of shipment.[44]

"Forefooting" was another method used. After roping the front feet and throwing the animal, a rope, tightly knotted around the neck of one, was tied to the tail of another, with a short space between. With the herd tied together in groups of four or five, no trouble was faced after the initial threshing around was done.

Some horse catchers would put a rope around a horse's neck, run it between the front and back legs and tie it to the tail. This prevented the mustang from raising its head, making it impossible for it to run. Sometimes the horse's head was tied to the front foot, holding the head halfway down. This caused the horse to fall when he attempted to run. The "side-winder" technique was a modification of the above. In this case the rope around the horse's neck was drawn tightly along the side of the animal and tied to the tail. This prevented the horse from walking in a straight line, forcing it to move in a circle.

The clog chain seems to have been widely used. A light log chain cut into two- or three-foot lengths, with an iron band attached to one end, was fastened to the ankle. The chain dragging along did not impede the horse if he walked slowly. If he ran, the loose end of the chain would wrap itself around the forelegs and throw the horse. Even forked branches of trees were used.

Other methods include "side-lining" or tying a front foot to a back foot three feet apart; "necking-up" one horse to another, having four or five abreast; tying one foot up so that the horse had to walk on three feet; and sewing up the nostrils so that the breathing was hard.[45] In any instance the horse thus treated reached the home base "somewhat the worse for wear," but there was no other practical way to deal with these wild animals. A mustanger was in the business for money. He probably had as great a love for a horse as any one. But he had the practical problem of getting that horse-flesh to market or to the home ranch. To do that, something drastic was necessary in the case of the obstreperous ones.

The "broncho buster" of the old school was not often a believer in the methods of kindness. Seldom was there one who, after having lassoed the horse in the corral, first accustomed it to the halter, then to the saddle. There were some in 1940 who still used the old method and starved them into submission before riding. It is no wonder that for every horse captured and broken out of a wild horse roundup three or four were accidentally killed, or cut by the rope so that they had to be shot or turned loose.[46]

Pete Barnum, who occupied such an important position in Nevada horse country, had canvas corrals at the home ranch. This, he claimed, prevented terror-stricken horses from impaling themselves on a pole or lacerating themselves on wire. When the breaking process began, the men threw a horse, put on a hackamore, and saddled it. A rider sprang on as the rope was removed from the feet. Then the spur and quirt were applied unmercifully to the bewildered animal. The next day the same process was repeated, with a bridle instead of a hackamore being used. The third day the "buster" went for a little ride.[47] Some outlaws refused to be broken, others bucked some in the morning just to "limber up." Probably not over 50 per cent of the horses caught in a corral were finally broken and domesticated.

The Blackfeet Indians had an interesting method

of breaking wild horses. While four men held the lariat, one approached, talking to the animal in low grunts. Then he would wave a blanket and hiss. After awhile, he could get close enough to rub the nose of the entranced animal. A halter was put on, and as he continued to hiss, he rubbed its head, neck, and flank. The blanket was then thrown against the horse. The rider-to-be treated the other side the same way. The conclusion of this long ritual was reached when the blanket was thrown on the pony's back, and the Indian mounted and rode away.[48]

George Catlin tells of the Comanche Indian, who after a horse was choked and hobbled, placed his hand on the animal's nose, over its eyes, and finally breathed in the nostrils. This caused the horse to become docile. Leading or riding was then in order.[49]

The Cayuse Indians of the Columbia River choked the animal into insensibility before tying the hind and forefeet together. When the animal regained consciousness and began to struggle, bear skins, wolf skins, and blankets were thrown at its head until it became exhausted. The ropes on the feet were then loosened; but the horse was kept snubbed to the saddle of his captor's pony. The skins were again thrown at it until it was more exhausted. This continued until the animal was docile enough to be saddled and ridden.[50]

The Spanish ranchers in California used a much longer process in breaking horses. When the young stock roaming the open range reached the age of four or five, they were corralled, and one at a time, thrown and blindfolded. When the animal was allowed to rise, the blind was lifted. After so much plunging he gave out, finding himself still at the end of the rope. He was then blindfolded again, and saddled. Then the blind was raised and he was permitted to buck. After this procedure which took several days, the horse was considered ready for domestic use.[51]

A fitting climax to the ways and means of breaking wild horses is the story told beside a campfire, no doubt, to one of America's leading artists. A cowboy, so the story goes, when riding a borrowed horse in the horse country, roped a wild stallion, threw him, and transferred the saddle and bridle from the riding horse to the captive. His own mount, now relieved of his responsibilities, left the country, leaving the cowboy with his prostrate stallion. After loosening the ropes about the feet and mounting him, this adventurer found himself in the saddle of a bolt of lightning. After running through his repertoire of tricks the horse reached the stage of exhaustion but still was not conquered. The cowboy, having lost his gun, was afraid to get off and was too tired to stay on. The broncho tried to bite, only to have his eyes punched out by the spurs of the rider. Still the cowboy was afraid to get off. After twenty-four hours, so the story ends, when a "searching-party found the pair, the stallion was quivering in agony and weakness, doomed but still defiant, and the man was a maniac."[52]

FOOTNOTES—CHAPTER TWELVE

1. *See* Frank Collinson, "Fifty Thousand Mustangs," and Thomas A. Dryer, "From Mustangs to Mules," in J. Frank Dobie, Mody C. Boatright, and Henry H. Ransom, *Mustangs and Cow Horses* (Austin, 1940).

2. C. J. Jones, *Buffalo Jones' Forty Years of Adventure* (Topeka, 1899), pp. 173-75.

3. Texas mustangers were running horses as early as 1839 and probably before. C. A. Gulick, ed., *Lamar Papers* (Austin, 1922), II, 406.

4. G. R. Parry, Superintendent of Motor Transportation, Utah Parks Company, Cedar City, Utah, in a letter, October 5, 1939.

5. Rufus Steele, "Trapping Wild Horses in Nevada," *McClure's Magazine*, XXXIV (1909-10), 198.

6. G. C. Robinson, "Mustangs and Mustanging in Southwest Texas," in Dobie, Boatright, and Ransom, *op. cit.*

7. Creasing and two types of corralling are discussed by Will C. Barnes, "Wild Horses," *McClure's Magazine*, XXXII (1908-9), 285-94.

8. *Sherman County Republican* (Itasca, Kansas), December 10, 1886.

9. Quoted by Dobie, Boatright, and Ransom, *op. cit.*, p. 75. Quoted by permission of the Texas Folk-Lore Society.

10. Will James describes this method in "Piñon and the Wild Ones," *Saturday Evening Post*, May 19, 1923.

11. Barnes, *op. cit.*, pp. 293-94.

12. Rufus Steele, "Wild Horses as Scenery," *Outlook* CXLI (1925), 86.

13. Letter from a member of the 380th Infantry, Ft. Gibson, Arkansas Territory, appearing in the *American Turf Register and Sporting Magazine*, V (1833-34), 73-74.

14. *American Turf Register and Sporting Magazine*, VII (1835-36), 204-5.

15. George Catlin, *North American Indians* .... (Edinburgh, 1926), I, 160.

16. Garrick Mallery, "Picture-Writing of the American Indians," *Tenth Annual Report of the Bureau of Ethnology* (Washington, D. C., 1893), pp. 656-57.

17. C. Henderson, "Reminiscences of a Range Rider," *Chronicles of Oklahoma* (Oklahoma City, 1925), III, 284.

18. Carl L. Canon, ed., *Scout and Ranger* .... (Princeton, 1932), pp. 96-97. Quoted by permission of Princeton University Press.

19. Will C. Barnes, "Wild Horses," *Atlantic Monthly*, CXXXIV (1924), 618-19.

20. Given in a letter of J. W. Robinson, February 24, 1839, published in *Lamar Papers*, II, 468.

21. Barnes in *McClure's Magazine*, *op. cit.*, pp. 288-89.

22. J. B. Tyrell, ed., *David Thompson's Narrative of His Explorations in Western America, 1784-1812* (Toronto, 1916), pp. 377-88.

23. Robinson, *op. cit.*

24. John R. Cook, *The Border and the Buffalo* (Topeka, 1907), p. 255.

25. R. M. Wright, *Dodge City* .... (Wichita, 1913), pp. 82-83.

26. J. Frank Dobie, *A Vaquero of the Brush Country* (Dallas, 1929), pp. 243-44.

27. Florence Fenley, "The Mustanger Who Turned Mustang," in Dobie, Boatright, and Ransom, *op. cit.*, pp. 61-66.

28. Z. M. Pike, *An Account of Expeditions* .... (Philadelphia, 1910), Appendix to Part III, p. 32.

29. John Warrington, "Wild Horses of the Old Frontier," *Travel*, November, 1939, p. 6.

30. Referred to by E. E. Dale, *The Range Cattle Industry* (Norman, 1930), p. 27.

31. *Leavenworth Herald*, quoted in the *Kansas Messenger* (Baldwin, Kansas), January 1, 1859.

32. Rufus Steele, telling Barnum's story, in "Trapping Wild Horses in Nevada," *McClure's Magazine*, XXXIV (1909-10), 206-7.

33. James, *op. cit.*

34. W. R. Leigh, *The Western Pony* (New York, 1933), pp. 29-30.

35. James, *op. cit.*

36. This type of trap is described by James. *See also* Barnes in *McClure's Magazine*, *op. cit.*, and his article in *American Forests and Forest Life*, November 24, 1924, p. 647.

37. James, *op. cit.*

38. A. M. Strope, "Catching Wild Horses in the '60's," *Outdoor Life*, August, 1914.

39. Barnes in *American Forests and Forest Life, op. cit.*, p. 646.

40. *Ibid.*, p. 647.

41. Tom Skinner, rancher of southeastern Oregon, says that he rescued one of these colts and that at the time of his letter (September, 1939), his son was riding it. It was two years old and made a good pony. The details on the use of the airplane have been compiled from letters by Skinner, Nic W. Monte, of Burns, Oregon, and Professor R. G. Johnson, of the Oregon State Agricultural College at Corvallis. *See also Life,* July 4, 1938, in which pictures of the operation are shown, and the article, "Wild Horses Corralled from the Air," by Jeff Sparks in *Popular Mechanics,* October, 1938.

42. Pike, *op. cit.*, p. 32.

43. *Leavenworth Herald, op. cit.*

44. Described by Cook, *op. cit.*, p. 255.

45. Most of these methods are described by Barnes in *American Forests and Forest Life, op. cit.*

46. Barnes in *McClure's, op. cit.*

47. Steele, *op. cit.*, p. 759.

48. Chief Buffalo Long Lance, *Long Lance,* quoted by Dobie, Boatright, and Ransom, *op. cit.*, pp. 165-68.

49. Quoted in the same.

50. Described by T. J. Farnham, *Travels in the Great Western Prairies, the Anahuac and Rocky Mountains, and the Oregon Country* (New York, 1843), p. 82.

51. Robert C. Denhardt, "The Role of the Horse in the Social History of Early California," *Agricultural History*, XIV (1940), 18-19.

52. Leigh, *op. cit.*, p. 37. Quoted by permission of Harper and Brothers, publishers of the 1935 edition.

The mustang can hold his own with natural enemies, but let the entire white race ally itself against him, and he's doomed, just as his one-time neighbor of the plains, the American bison, was doomed.

Charles B. Roth, "Intelligence, Plus Speed, Plus Bottom, Equals Mustang," *The Horse,* November-December, 1937, p. 18. Quoted by permission of the American Remount Association.

CHAPTER THIRTEEN

The Herd and the Horse

There has been much romancing on the subject of the wild horse, and with much of this the mustanger would not be in agreement. About most wild animals legends have risen that make even the believing somewhat incredulous. Early chroniclers of the buffalo told tall tales about his size and prowess.[1] The Indian, hoping to capture many of the traits of the wild creatures of his land, wore or used various parts of the animal or bird so that some of those qualities might be transmitted to him. Even the very human cowboy has been raised to the realms of the superman by the magic tales woven around him.

The wild horse and the buffalo shared the Western range for many years. Particularly in the Texas country the horse was an ever-recurring part of the scenery. A Spanish judge reported, after a trip of inspection on the Nueces River, that mustangs were so thick that settlers could not raise domestic horses on the open range, and that the "only improvements of any character on the land were some old mustang pens in bad condition."[2] One observer spoke of horses in "such multitudes between the Columbia River and the high desert country that sometimes a single band traveled from dawn until dusk in passing a given point!"[3] In parts of South America the same held true. An English Jesuit, writing in 1754 about a trip made on the plains told of great numbers passing him, at full speed, "for two or three hours together, during which time it was with greatest difficulty that I and four Indians who accompanied me on this occasion, preserved ourselves from being trampled to pieces by them!"[4]

An American explorer wrote of the great horse herd he encountered in the plains and desert country of the Southwest.

A few hours after leaving, the prairie near the horizon seemed to be moving, with long undulations, like the waves of the ocean. Unable to account for this singular appearance, I looked with my telescope, when, to my surprise, I discovered the whole prairie towards the horizon alive with mustangs. Soon afterwards they could be seen moving toward the [wagon] train.

Major Emory at this time was in advance of me about half a mile with his portion of the wagons. We saw the long line of mustangs approach him, and soon after pass before, the whole herd following after, and extending as far as the eye could reach across the prairie. . . . . On went the great stream, and the next moment one of the mule teams in advance sprang from the train and dashed off at full speed after and among the wild horses. The teamster in vain tried to restrain them. It was all to no purpose. Away they went.... followed by all the loose animals that were driven with the train.....The herdsmen, in order to check the runaways, left the train and went in pursuit, making altogether the most exciting spectacle we had yet witnessed. The chase continued for a mile; for the mules in the wagon had become perfectly frantic with fear.....The men of the other party fired at the herd, which had the effect of breaking the line, and turned it in another direction.

The frightened herd made directly for us, in the same long line, the termination of which we could not see, as it lost itself far in the distance. I now became alarmed, fearing a general stampede among our mules.....Our first precaution was to close up the wagons, so that only those in the first one could see the mustangs. The mules of the second were placed alongside of the foremost wagon, the next by the side of the second, and so on.....We now locked the wheels of all, and men stood by the leaders to restrain and quiet them. As I had no inclination to be carried off against my will among a herd of frantic wild horses.... I dismounted and hitched my mule to a wagon, and with several others ran with my fire-arms to meet the advancing steeds.....We discharged our arms at them as they approached and fortunately with good effect. The leader was turned, and the avalanche of wild animals swept by us like a tornado, much to our relief.....[5]

Traveling in great herds was not characteristic of the mustang except in the densely populated areas, even then it is doubtful that the thousands constituted a horse herd, mastered and led by one stallion. In the stampede described above, a stallion was in the lead, but it cannot be concluded that this was usually the case. It is said, however, that among the Tarpans of Asia, the leader stallion controlled many minor families.[6] The American buffalo migrated in great herds which on close scrutiny might have revealed many small units. The mustang did little migrating, if one thinks of going from the Northern to the Southern plains with the seasons. His range was seldom over ten or fifteen miles, and when run by horse catchers, he would circle and return to the old stamping ground. Food, water, and protection determined the location of this grazing area. Years ago the presence of an abundance of prairie grass may have affected the practice of many small herds forming a single large mass of animals.

The social unit of the wild horse was a band of mares under the command of a stallion. This *manada* was "as well defined as the tribal unit among the Indians."[7] The bands, from two or three to twenty or thirty in number, often had a similar appearance and color because most of them were sired by the same stallion. Groups of young stallions were often seen, they being the cast-off members of a band that had been driven out by the stallion at the age of one or two years before they successfully challenged his leadership.

Occasionally in the horse country two bands of horses meet. The stallions, at a distance, weigh the proposition of whether to have a fight to the finish for the other's mares and colts. If the decision is made to fight it out, action soon begins. With his tail held at a forty-five degree angle, he starts circling his herd. His head is lowered to the ground, his nose turned up. When his mares are rounded up into a compact group, away goes the master toward the challenger. One horse-hunter thus described such a struggle:

They approach each other walking on their hind feet, with eyes which simulate balls of molten metal, or the electric light. Their great mouths are already open, exposing their sharp teeth, with which they inflict most terrible punishment, and in a few seconds the impending shock comes, for which each enraged animal has been preparing himself. Now their keenly cutting hoofs are flying in every direction over their adversary's body, and their powerful jaws grasp neck, shoulders, or any portion they can get hold of. They fight with all the desperation of bulldogs, throwing their whole force against each other; consequently the weaker "goes to the wall" a terribly mutilated brute. If he is not equal in strength, or lacks in endurance to withstand the awful shock of his adversary, he is at last hurled to the ground—kicked, stamped on, and torn by the teeth of his mad antagonist; and if by chance he can rise again, he rushes off, glad to escape with his life. Unlike the contests between buffalo bulls .... wherein no blood is drawn, those between the wild stallions of the Plains are fraught with sanguinary results. Wherever their cruel teeth are fastened in each other's flesh, their bodies are lacerated in the most terrible manner. When these instruments of warfare slip off the hide where they have taken hold, they snap together, sounding like the report of a firecracker..... [8]

When a stallion lost a battle but kept his life, he retreated to the solitude of the range where time healed wounds and a broken spirit. Later he might challenge another field general, but he probably wisely drove out of a small herd a two- or three-year-old stallion that was not strong or wise

The most powerful stallion ruled the herd

enough to hold his ground. He might raid the domestic herds of some rancher and there lure away
a few mares with which he could run the range
again, with head up and hooves flashing. These
failing, there was little for the horse to do but run
the range alone. The fact that he could not make
a "come back" would indicate that he was nearly
ready to die or his wounds were a serious handicap
for normal living. A young stallion ultimately
sent him to his eternity.

The stallion was without doubt a vicious creature. Even the high-pitched, shrill whistle made by
the nostrils when he went into battle would send a
chill of terror through almost anyone. Horse
catchers testify that such an animal was one of the
most vicious creatures on four legs, whose leadership could successfully be challenged only by a
jackass.

It was not at all unusual to find asses and burros
in a wild horse herd. A stallion seemed to accept a
jack with a consideration which he did not show
for any other living thing. A jack burro often became the leader of a band of horses, a leader more
cunning and vicious than a horse. In a Montana
roundup of 1929, two such animals seen leading
large herds caused the riders to swear that "before
the Summer is over they will capture the mules."[9]
When a stallion and a jack met, a fight ensued. W.
C. Barnes, an Arizona mustanger who became
well known, described such a struggle as follows:

Once a jack burro with a small harem of mares at his heels entered the gate of a trap corral set to catch wild cattle. Inside this particular trap corral was a young stallion with a bunch of wild mares..... For an hour or more the sturdy little jack and that active young stallion fought like nothing else can fight. With their teeth they tore great pieces of flesh from each other's forelegs, necks and breasts and often were locked in a deadly grip for five minutes at a time, the teeth of each sunk deep into the flesh of his enemy. The throat is the main point of attack and when the burro finally managed to seize his enemy on the under side of his neck where the throat joins the head he hung on with a bull-dog grip from which the horse could not free himself. Ten minutes later the horse sank slowly to the ground, soaked with the blood of both, gave one groan and was gone. The burro, bleeding from a dozen frightful wounds, staggered back to his little family that had watched the terrible combat with idle interest, gave one exultant but somewhat uncertain "hee-haw" and followed his late enemy up the long trail.[10]

Teddy Roosevelt tells the story of a Dakota rancher who saw a jack enter a corral in which two stallions were milling around. The jack took hold of one horse and held on, and the other horse attacked the jack. Intervention by the rancher prevented another massacre by a jack.[11] Charles Moore, who grew up on the western slope of Colorado, tells of a jackass coming to his horse camp near Moab, Utah, and attacking the saddle mares at night. This stud was tearing the skin from the hobbled mares when a bullet stopped him short.[12]

It is not true that a stallion, or a jack "led" a band of horses. It is true that each group was in command of the male who fought for its leadership and was the sire of the colts born therein. An old

mare, however, was also of much importance in the
struggle of a wild band for its existence. The stallion stood guard while the herd grazed. At the first
sight of man the sentinel commenced neighing,
which sent the herd off at breakneck speed toward
safety. The sentinel lingered to get the lay of the
land, then dashed away to serve as rear guard of
the band. Even while the group was fleeing, the
stallion might circle at full speed, nipping the lag-
gards, and if a mare were tarrying for her colt,
he might seize the colt by the neck and dash it to
the ground, then drive the mare on with the herd.
When all this was going on it was a wise old mare

who led the band toward freedom, surrendering
the leadership at the head only if the stallion decided danger was past. Should he see that the rider
was on a tired horse he might circle around, with
head high and tail up, teasing the rider to come on.

If they were pushed by mustangers it was the stallion who led the break to freedom, and who might turn to fight the pursuers. Horse runners generally hesitated to shoot a stallion under the circumstances, because the mares might scatter if such a leader were gone.

The stallion has been known to desert his herd, escape his pursuers, and enjoy his freedom alone. The mare, apparently more crafty than the male, was the field marshal who led the band up the horse trails of the last frontier. Experience had taught her how to avoid the pitfalls, traps, and ropes. The fact that trail snares seldom caught a stallion is evidence that the stallion, unless leading the band to a water hole or grassland, usually brought up the rear. It is possible that this pattern was not always followed, that the mountain country to which the horses have retreated in recent years has put upon the mare greater responsibilities than in days when they wandered in the flat grasslands. It would seem a fair conclusion to call her the brains and the stallion the brawn (as well as the "front") of the wild horse herd.[18]

Another trait of the range herds has been their ability to do without water. Ordinarily the stallion led the herd to water every evening. This practice has been exploited by the horse hunter, for he has lain in wait at the water hole in order that he might give chase when the horses had drunk their fill, or where he has built a trap-corral, the gates of which were sprung when the herd entered in its desperate search for water. Once when Hollywood was trying to film some horses in Utah, they waited at a water hole with the camera. Finally a palomino led his thirty-eight mares to the spring. He halted the herd, circled for approximately an hour, then flew at the *manada* and led them away without drinking. Five days later, over a hundred miles away, the band finally filled their gaunt sides with water.[14]

One old cowpuncher saw horses so desperate for water that they fought for the opportunity of pawing holes and knocking out rocks so they could have a water hole.[15] Mustangers found that in "walking down" horses, giving them water occasionally was necessary, otherwise they would become unmanageable. Speaking from South American evidence, one writer speaks of the disposition to become so frantic from thirst that "when chance or instinct has at last conducted them to a pool or river, [the mustangs would] rush forward to the brink, trampling each other under foot, others sticking in the clay .... causing a destruction of their numbers beyond belief. Thousands of skeletons are said to blanche the borders of some localities where they resort. ....."[16]

One observer who shot a horse in the Pacific Northwest in 1807, spoke of the disagreeable odor which came from the animal, so bad, he said, that "washing my hand for two days with soap barely took it away. . . . . . "[17] He did not notice this among those horses when domesticated. This, if true (and it is not recorded by others), might be explained by what he conceived to be a bad odor or by the vegetation of the region upon which the horses in wild state lived.

Gaited horses were often found among the wild ones in the post-Civil War period. A number, possibly "escapes" from domestic herds, were natural pacers. Buffalo Jones occasionally came across a whole herd of pacers. At one time on the headwaters of the Smoky Hill River in western Kansas, he saw a beautiful stallion which was a pacer. He frequently ran that herd, but failed ever to break the gait of the pacing leader.[18] Others were seen which could outrun the fastest horse pitted against them. More frequently, it must be said, the horse in the wild state lacked any of the graces possessed by the gaited horse. In the words of one from Arizona, "these mustangs are born running. It's all they know. It's run, run, run from the day they are foaled, and a gallop is as natural a gait to them as a walk is to a stall-raised animal!"[19]

That the mustang had speed and endurance could be testified by everyone who has run one. Well-bred horses imported from the East to run wild horses were known to be able to out-distance them in the open country and for a short period of time. But it was a truism in the West that no Eastern-bred horse, carrying a saddle and a man, could catch a "broomtail" in fair condition on his own range. The story is told of "Concha," a thoroughbred that had won some money on the oval track, that was imported into Arizona to outrun some good horses among the wild herds. "The result was ludicrous..... He never put any rider close enough to a mustang to make it interesting."[20]

Of all the traits of this range animal, endurance was recognized as the most important. Mustangers who ran them by the relay method testified to the reality of this possession. It was this trait which largely gave the mustang its respectability. In 1929, just to test the native horses of the Argentine, one man set out riding a true descendant of the Spanish horse, the *criolla*, and with one for a pack horse, made a trip from Buenos Aires to Washington, D. C., 9,600 miles, in two and one half years.[21] The Spanish cow pony was used to deliver mail between El Paso, Texas, and Chihuahua City, Mexico, a distance of 300 miles in a waterless country. The trip was regularly made in three nights. Upon numerous occasions this horse was ridden 100 miles between sunup and sundown, apparently without ill effect upon it.[22]

Sure-footedness was another trait that had been acquired by the Western horse living for so many generations on the open prairies and desert. The constant contact with rocks gave to the hoof a flint-like hardness not possessed by other horses. These animals were as dexterous as the cutting pony on the modern ranch, hopping up and down ledges, crossing streams, serenely walking on precipices that man would not approach, running up mountain trails with the ease that equalled if not surpassed the mountain goat. This was another quality that endeared him to the Westerner.

This horse perhaps lacked the intelligence of a well-bred animal, yet what he lacked in brains he made up for in matured instincts. His enemies were chiefly the elements, the puma, and man. To the lack of water he adjusted himself. To find water his olfactory sense (or was it something else?) was developed to the point of being able to detect water many miles away. To get food in the days when he was driven from the Great Plains, he went to the high land in the summer and to the valleys in the winter. He learned to paw through the snow, eat bark, and break ice. That the elements destroyed many horses is certain, but the adjustment was made even if they ravaged not only the numbers but also the general physique of the horse.

In dealing with the puma the wild horse seemed never to develop an olfactory sense that could detect danger in time. Many a mustang, as well as other animals, has served as a meal for such beasts. Man, however, was the greatest enemy. It was he who in a large measure destroyed the wild horse herds. The poorer animals were first captured, leaving the fast and crafty to serve as lodestones to the horse hunter. This horse had one habit that was a fundamental weakness and showed lack of intelligence, that of staying on or returning to his old range. If a wild one should escape from captivity, back to the old range he went, even if it were two hundred miles away. Seldom would a herd leave its own circle of ten to twenty miles even when pushed by man. The rancher's domestic stock, after joining a wild band, seemed readily to acquire some of the traits of the wild ones. A fur trader on the Columbia River in 1809 testifies further on this trait in telling of his experiences with an "escape":

A dull mere pack Horse was missing, with a man I went to look for him, and found him among a dozen wild Horses, when we approached, this dull Horse took to himself all the gestures of the wild Horses, his nostrils distended, mane erect, and tail straight out.[23]

The "escape" not only learned the new tricks but used his intelligence and training to advantage. When run by man, he would not always run in the same direction or stay on the same range. "It is a well-known fact," states a mustanger, "that the hardest one to 'cut-out,' the leader of them all in a mad race across the prairie, is the old, gentle, well-broken saddle or work horse, once he gets a taste of freedom."[24] When captured, however, this "escape" will fall into the routine of domestic life without any trouble, whereas the wild one (as long as the animal lives) will have to be mastered step by step and probably will buck some each time the rider mounts. It might be said that among the mountain bands, the wild instinct is more fully developed, while among the "escapes," the intelligence is more fully recognizable.[25] Generally speaking, the animal of Northern bunch grass country was larger, better proportioned, possibly smarter than the Southern desert horse.

The horse of the mesa and "breaks" today, with a much greater percentage of branded stock in the herds than ever before, is a more difficult animal to catch than was the mustang of a century ago. The elements and lack of forage have produced worse effects upon his body—but withal he is still capable of shifting for himself, is adroit and resourceful, and is more wily than the former occupants of the winding trails. He may be smarter, but he still has great need for habit and instinct in order that he may live the life of the free.

FOOTNOTES—CHAPTER THIRTEEN

1. E. Douglas Branch, *Hunting the Buffalo* (New York, 1929).

2. G. C. Robinson, "Mustangs and Mustanging in Southwest Texas," in J. Frank Dobie, Mody C. Boatright, and Harry H. Ransom, eds., *Mustangs and Cow Horses* (Austin, 1940), p. 4.

3. Victor Shawe, quoted by H. R. Sass in "Hoofs on the Prairie," *Country Gentleman*, CVI (1936), 68.

4. Quoted by R. B. Cunninghame Graham, *The Horses of the Conquest* (London, 1930), p. 11.

5. J. R. Bartlett, *Personal Narrative of Exploration and Incidents in Texas, New Mexico, California, Sonora, and Chihuahua* . . . . (New York, 1854), pp. 522-24.

6. Lieutenant Colonel Charles Hamilton Smith, *Horses* (Edinburgh, 1841), p. 177.

7. J. Frank Dobie, *A Vaquero in the Brush Country* (Dallas, 1929), p. 242.

8. C. J. Jones, *Buffalo Jones' Forty Years of Adventure* (Topeka, 1899), pp. 170-71.

9. Russell A. Bankson, *New York Times*, June 23, 1929.

10. Will C. Barnes, "Wild Burros," *American Forests and Forest Life*, XXXVI (1930), 642. Quoted by permission of the American Forestry Association.

11. Theodore Roosevelt, *Hunting Trips of a Ranchman* (New York, 1927), pp 303-4.

12. Interview, Grand Junction, Colorado, August 2, 1940.

13. This leadership material has been gathered from correspondence with rangemen and from these articles and books: Will James, "Piñon and the Wild Ones," *Saturday Evening Post*, May 19, 1923; Rufus Steele, "Mustangs, Busters and Outlaws of the Nevada Wild Horse Country," *American Magazine*, LXXXII (1911), 756-65, *passim;* Dobie, Boatright, and Ransom, *op. cit., passim;* John R. Cook, *The Border and the Buffalo* (Topeka, 1907), *passim;* J. Frank Dobie, "The Spanish Cow Pony," *Saturday Evening Post*, November 24, 1924; and the *New York Times*, June 23, 1929.

14. Told by Rufus Steele, "Wild Horses as Scenery," *Outlook*, CXLI (1925), 86, quoting G. R. Parry.

15. Earl Haley, quoted by Andrew R. Boone, "The Wild Herd Passes," *Travel*, LX (1923), 23.

16. Smith, *op. cit.*, p. 178.

17. J. B. Tyrrell, ed., *David Thompson's Narrative of His Explorations in Western America, 1784-1812* (Toronto, 1916), pp. 377-78. Quoted by permission of The Champlain Society.

18. Jones, *op. cit.*, p. 176. *See also* Robinson, *op. cit.*, and *Leavenworth Herald* (Kansas Territory), quoted in Kansas Messenger (Baldwin, Kansas), January 1, 1859. One mustanger wrote that he had never seen a pacer stallion. Homer Hoyt, "Catching Wild Horses," *Colorado Magazine*, XI (1934), 41.

19. Quoted by Charles B. Roth, "Intelligence, Plus Speed, Plus Bottom, Equals Mustang," *The Horse*, November-December, 1937, p. 17. Permission to quote given by the American Remount Society.

20. *Loc. cit.*

21. A. F. Tschiffley, "Buenos Aires to Washington by Horse," *National Geographic Magazine*, LV (1929), 135-96.

22. *See* John Warrington, "Wild Horses of the Old Frontier," *Travel*, November, 1939, and Dobie, *op. cit.*

23. Tyrrell, *op. cit.*, p. 401.

24. Will C. Barnes, "Wild Horses," *McClure's Magazine*, XXXII (1908-9), 286.

25. Smith, *op. cit.*, pp. 177-78, speaks of the stallions, after being caught, domesticated, then escaping, as having their wild instincts confused and says a "tendency to obedience and domestication remains impressed on their tempers. . . . ."

The time is not perhaps far distant, when they will be gradually again absorbed by domestication, excepting those which will retreat towards the two poles; and as the species is not restricted by the rigour of climate, but solely by the extent of available food, the wilds of Patagonia and the latitudes of the northern deserts will continue to maintain them in freedom, and render them migratory like the deer and the bison of the same climate.

Lieutenant Colonel Chas. Hamilton Smith, *Horses* (Edinburgh, 1841), pp. 174-75.

CHAPTER FOURTEEN

From Mustang to "Broomtail"

The history of the wild or feral horses from the time when they were mustangs to the present when they are "broomtails" and "fuzztails" is more the story of dilution than deterioration. The "escapes" among the rancher's stock oftentimes improved the quality of a wild herd. Selective breeding in the state of nature likewise improved the quality, and early horse hunters, both red and white, who first captured the poorer members of the herds, likewise influenced the character of the wild horse for the better. In the final stages, when both starvation and inbreeding have taken place, the "broomtail," an ill-proportioned and homely animal, became the Western wild horse. Both the forces of selection and deterioration have operated upon them since the white man first encroached upon the public domain.

The term mustang has been misused by many to refer to the wild horse, whether in the seventeenth or the twentieth century, to the cow pony of today, and to all other stock that has been used in the West. The word is said to have come from the Spanish *mesteño* which came from *mesta*, meaning a group of stockmen. Horses which escaped from a *mesta* and ran wild were *mesteños*, the "eno" suffix meaning "belonging to."[1] Regardless of the exact origin of the word, the term mustang was applied to the original wild horse that came from the Spanish herds. In the Northwest, where the Cayuse Indians bred a pony, the term cayuse came to be accepted for practically any small horse, especially if it were in possession of Indians. Broncho, the Spanish word for rough, originally meant a horse that could not be broken or a mustang that had an "unsavory reputation," but later came to be applied to almost any Western horse.[2]

The original wild bands of the Southwest, as has been shown, were descendants of the Spanish horses which, in turn, traced their ancestry back to North Africa and to Arabia. While the Spanish in the Rio Grande country were much interested in the horse, it is doubtful if more than a few could be called horse breeders. Their practice of making their "best and likeliest colts into geldings for saddle or harness" and leaving the inferior stallions on the range, did nothing to improve the quality of the herds that became the wild mustangs.[3] Since there was little market for horses, it seems probable that like Topsy, mustangs just grew by them-

selves. When the estrays or "escapes" lost contact
with the home ranch, they became in a true sense
mustangs. As they multiplied, and no longer wore
brands, their degeneration is not likely to have
proceeded as fast as when they were owned by
some *mesta*. The Spanish practice of breaking their
horses to ride at an early age and the attempt to
keep them on a scanty range surely had an ill effect
upon the animals that was not present in the wild
state. It is idle to speak of these ponies as being
of pure-bred Arabian stock or as representing in
any way the best of South Europe and North Africa. One authority speaks of the mustang in this un-
complimentary way:

A small-boned inbred, undersized pony, generally of an
"off" color, mean of temper and narrow between the eyes.
Nor is there anything in existence to prove that because
he came over with the Cohquistadores he was of royal,
Arabian descent. The Spanish people as a race have
never been noted for possession or raising horses of very
good blood, and there is nothing to show that the animals
Cortez, Coronado and the rest of the early explorers
brought over with them were anything but the small,
common-bred horses such as the Spanish then generally
used.[4]

These horses were neither large nor beautiful.
As one described them, they were "descendants of
strays and castaways . . . . medium in size, wiry,
hardy beasts, with a very decided tendency toward
horse-ugliness."[5] The Conquistadores' horses may
have been larger than the prairie mustang, even
ranging from fourteen hands three to fifteen two

in height, but it is doubtful if the others imported into Mexico were of that size. When the first Americans saw the mustang, they invariably spoke of his small stature and homely appearance. It may be that there was a certain evolution in the wild state toward smaller hooves, rougher coats, bushier manes, and stronger legs.[6] There probably was an atavistic tendency, in that many showed some of the markings of the early historic horse, having a black stripe down the back and black bands around the legs.

On the open range the little pony had many enemies that gave support to Darwin's thesis that there was a natural selection of the species. The rattlesnake, wolf, and mountain lion, blizzards, droughts, and quicksand helped remove the weak, the old, and the unfit. The process of breeding itself was selective. The most powerful stallions ruled a herd and sired the colts as long as they could hold their position in combat with others on the prairie. Instinct itself caused the stallion to drive out of the herd the young fillies, thus preventing inbreeding. The young stallions soon left the herd to gather up their own mares. Inbreeding could not have affected the quality of the mustang under normal conditions.[7] The size of these horses might have been adversely affected by the breeding of mares at an early age, but if true, and there is much evidence to show the ill effects of early breeding, the same held true of the horses existing in a half wild state among the Spanish ranchers.[8] The effect of hard winters has been offered as an explanation of supposed degeneracy.[9] The winter snows are heavier and the temperatures are more severe in the North, yet it was here in places that white men found larger horses than in the South. The only factor left is that of inadequate forage on the Southern plains. While no worse than that in upper Mexico, it is probable that the pony never attained his ancestor's proportions grazing on the vegetation that supported not only many horses but also buffalo, wild cattle, and others of the animal world.

The infiltration of Eastern horses into the mustang herds began at an early period, the Indian being the chief agent before the cattleman and farmer moved into the trans-Mississippi West. An army officer, stationed at Fort Gibson, wrote in 1835 of this distinction between the two types of wild horses in reply to a criticism of the wild horse made by another army man:

[When Major R. B. Mason made his observations, he was on the Texas or Spanish frontier] from where the Indians stole more than 7/8ths of the 4,000 horses he says he saw, the greater number having the Spanish brand upon their quarters..... I am in hopes when the Major again returns to the prairie he will have seen more of the true wild horse, and less of the cat-hammed, ewe-necked, spindle-shanked Spanish breed; a judge, but with half an eye, could most certainly tell the difference.

These horses [of the Osage Indians], I believe are the

Here in the mountain valleys had been developed a superior Indian pony

true American horses, equal to Arabia's best and fleetest sons, with all the marks and appearance of our best blooded stock, and not the descendants of European ancestors. They are generally found on the headwaters of the tributaries of the Arkansas river, two to three hundred miles west and southwest of this place, they are known and highly prized by the Indians, and when taken, it is rarely they will part with them.[10]

Major Mason had called attention to the preference of the Indians for horses stolen from the whites, "whilst those they have caught wild, they will sell for a blanket and a half a plug of tobacco."[11] Obviously the dragoon was wrong in his explanation of the origin of the horse, but presumably correct in noting that good horses existed in the wild state.

A Texan from the Red River area wrote in 1839 of the difference between the mustang and what he called the wild horse. In speaking of a trip he had recently taken, he said:

We saw large droves of Buffalo, and wild horses, by the latter I do not mean, mustangs, such as are found in western Texas.—The Ukraine cannot excel these prairies in the beauty and fleetness of its wild horses—They are said to be derived from various sources, but however derived, the mustang bears no proportion to them, and they sell when caught (persons follow it as business) for 3 to $500.[12]

A Santa Fe freighter of the early period, whose business activities took him into the upper Arkansas and Canadian River country, spoke of the mustang as being the "most noble" of the animals of the prairie. He stated that the buffalo was more important " 'though making no pretensions to the elegance and symmetry of the mustang..... ' "[13] He may have been making his observation on the horse herds commented on by other observers. So impressed was one Texan by the results of crossing mustang and American stock, which produced among the wild herds animals fifteen hands high as compared to the ordinary thirteen and one half hands, with vast improvements also in weight, power, and symmetry, that he started breeding Mexican mares to American blooded stallions.

It seems certain that by 1835 there had been built either through the infiltration of escaped "American" stock or the natural processes of breeding, some fair horse herds in the lower Great Plains. That many of these had come through the border area Indians seems a reasonable explanation. The mustangs of poor quality in west Texas may have shown the effect of Mexican and Texan horse runners who succeeded in capturing the best stallions.

It is known that the Indian tribes provided an excellent melting pot for the various strains of horseflesh which they gathered from here and there. Only a few were able to catch the best from the wild herds because they were never able to build trap corrals, which required a high type of guile and intelligent planning. Consequently the animals caught were in the main of inferior quality. A contemporary spoke of them as being a "small but very powerful animal, with an exceedingly prominent eye, sharp nose, high nostril, small foot and delicate leg....."[14] The ponies of the Arikara Indians impressed Washington Irving who saw them in the 1840's:

> The horses owned by the Arikaras are, for the most part, of the wild stock of the prairies; some however, have been obtained from the Poncas, Pawnees, and other tribes to the southwest, who had stolen them from the Spaniards..... These were to be known by being branded, a Spanish mode of marking horses not practiced by the Indians.[15]

Captain Randolph B. Marcy, exploring in the Red River of the South in 1849, spoke of the Waco Indians as having not only mustangs with the Mexican brand on them, but also others that were "large, well-formed animals .... undoubtedly stolen from the border white settlers."[16] Frederic Remington in discussing the Cherokee pony years later, said that this piebald animal was not of the broncho type, but was descended from American stock.[17] In the 1840's a traveler spoke of Pawnee horses as being "wild," some "Spanish," and some "American."[18] Francis Parkman, who went over the Oregon Trail in 1845, saw many Indian ponies at Fort Laramie:

> They were of every shape, size, and color. Some came from California, some from the States, some from among the mountains, and some from the wild bands of the prairie. They were of every hue, white, black, red, and

gray, or mottled and clouded with a strange variety of colors. They all had a wild and startled look, very different from the sober aspect of a well-bred city steed.....[19]

The Indians deserve the credit for introducing the Eastern and Western strains of horses, a factor that was of considerable importance in improving the quality of the mustang herds. The Indian himself, with few exceptions, was not a horse breeder.

Stock degenerated in his hands. He mistreated it by breaking the horse when it was very young, and by starving it. As long as he could steal from other tribes or from the whites, and could replenish his herds from the wild bands, he had horses. Yet at the same time he developed what became known as the Indian pony, which has many of the characteristics of the mustang. This suggests either selective breeding or stealing for color, and mistreatment and starvation, which caused the horse to become smaller. Some of the tribes had "special

medicine formulae" which supposedly increased
the number of colts, yet the Paduca and Comanche
said they could raise no colts.[20] It might be added
that perhaps these Indians did not have to increase
their herds in that way since they were so close
to the great reservoir of wild and Spanish stock.
Lewis and Clark commented that the natives seen
by them, excepting those of the Rocky Mountains,
appeared indifferent to the whole process, not even
taking pains in selecting stallions.[21] That the Indian's pony was largely dwarfish in size is probably explained by his inability to capture the good
horses from the prairie herds.

To the west of the Rockies Lewis and Clark found
horses that appeared like "fine English coursers
some of them are pied, with large spots of white
irregularly scattered, and intermixed with a dark
brown bay; the greater part, however, are of a
uniform colour, marked with stars and white feet,
and resembling in fleetness and bottom as well as
in form and colour, the best blooded horses of
Virginia. . . . . "[22]

Here in the mountain valleys had been produced
a superior Indian pony. It is probable that Lewis
and Clark were referring to horses of the Cayuse
Indians. In the 1840's when T. J. Farnham traveled among this tribe, he spoke highly of the horses:

These are a fine race of animals; as large and of better
form than most of the horses of the States. There is every
variety of color among them from shining coal-black to

milk-white. Some are pied very singularly; as a roan body with bay ears and white mane and tail. Some are spotted with white on a roan, or bay, or sorrel ground, with tail and ears tipped with black. They are better trained to the saddle than those of civilized countries..... [23]

By 1890, this horse, probably developed because of the restraining influence of the mountains over horse stealing, and because the animals could be well controlled, had gained a reputation all over the country as the cayuses. By the time the cattleman met this horse he was generally roan in color, strongly built and powerful, and about fourteen hands high. This was a good foundation upon which the cattleman could build.[24]

The cayuse seems to be the only distinctive Indian horse that may be said to have been produced by Indian breeding. Since the Indian preferred either colorful horses or colors that would take paint, the gray and the pinto were found among the Indian herds. Among the wild herds all colors were found. The ranchers of the West Indies, who supplied so many of the horses imported into Mexico, brought from Spain some good stock for breeding. Among them were certain sires—roans, pintos, and palominos—that had the ability to stamp succeeding generations.[25] The horses of South America never showed the variety of color seen in North America.[26] Seen among the herds of the Great Plains were all colors, with gray, roan, and bay predominant. Since the Indian pony came close to being a type—that is, he was small with fine legs, from thirteen to fourteen hands high, chunky and round with a large barrel, while his "head and neck join like the two parts of a hammer...."[27] it would seem that in spite of the lack of conscious breeding, the Indian did a certain amount anyway.

The paint, or pinto, so popular with the Indians, was found among the wild herds, but the color was more evident among crossbred and grade horses. The piebald is black and white, skewbald is bay, brown, or chestnut and white. Among the whites there has always been a belief that it was a poor horse with a mean disposition that came from inbreeding, or as an old Negro once said: " 'Dey is jus' good for soov'ners.' "[28] In a study of native breeds in north Europe, it was found that normally colored parents could foal a piebald, and the association between weakness and the splashed pattern was "pure imagination, which had no foundation in fact."[29]

The Nez Perce Indians are accredited with developing a specific color type known as the appaloosa. While the pinto had large splashes of color, the appaloosa had small spots, and those only on the rump and back, the rest being a solid color. A cowboy once explained this coloration by saying the horse " 'looks like he backed up to a squirt-gun loaded with pink paint.' "[30] How the Nez Perces may have come to breed this horse which they used especially as a war pony is told by one Westerner:

Anyway, some Nez Perce buck found an extraordinary spotted colt one day, and started himself in the business of breeding these unusual horses. They became so popular that the well-dressed warrior felt ashamed of himself if, when he rode to war or to any important festivity, he wasn't mounted on one of these spotted horses.[31]

The country in which the Nez Perces first lived —being western Idaho and eastern Washington— was known as the "Palouse country" and still is so known. Those Indians, being good horsemen, traded to other tribes of the Northwest, and thus they were distributed. Their horses later were taken by the whites.

The Indians of the lower plains were good horsemen but did not have to breed their horses. They contented themselves with the mustang or the Spanish and American horse which they stole. The Indians of the Northern plains could replenish their supply from the wild herds. Those of the upper Rocky Mountains were so located that they did not have a horse supply so readily at hand. Their ponies being somewhat protected from wild stallions, whereas the Plains Indians' horses were not, they could do some breeding. The Crows,[32] Nez Perces, and Cayuses are the recorded developers of the Indian pony type. All of them served as agents for the dilution of the mustang blood. The probability that the stallions (the Indians never practiced gelding) left their own herds for the wild state, and the fact that they could not catch the better horses, indicates that but few of the tribes would have had good ponies had not some "American" horse blood been infused into the Western bands.

More than the Indians, the cattle and horse rancher and the settler on the frontier were the avenues through which the mustang blood was chilled. The effect of the infiltration was that of breeding up the mustang stock. Considering the obvious fact that the horse runner captured the weakling, the laggard, and the scrub, and the rancher used his rifle on all and sundry, it is clear that the wild horse became a good animal. As early as the 1830's, as has been shown before, the horses of the Canadian River country showed either the influences of "American" blood or unusually selective breeding among the native ponies. On the staked plains in Texas, by 1872, were larger horses than the south Texas mustangs, being fourteen to fifteen hands high, with some of the stallions being larger. Parts of the plains "were alive with the biggest and best mustangs I ever saw, and the fastest....." wrote one mustanger.[33]

The wild herds in Kansas, reported in 1859, were only of the best, the product of the Indian pony, and the American estray, able to "defy alike the swiftest and longest pursuit; baffle the best skill and cunning of the hunter, and generally succeed in showing 'clean heels' in every attempt to capture..... The 'flowers of the flock' only remain....."[34] By 1900 the Utah mustangs were pretty well diluted. They still showed their Spanish and Indian pony ancestry in that many would not weigh over a thousand pounds, and more than a few were pintos. However, many fine horses, "escapes" from cattlemen, were found among them.[35] The horse herds of Colorado were described as having no pintos or cayuses, and "only tracings of the small Mexican mustang. They were larger and more stockily built. . . . . ."[36] A Nevada mustanger testified that years of shooting and trapping had improved the quality of the horses of that country at the time of his work there in 1911.[37]

In California where the wild herds were described as being "small and deficient in strength and beauty . . . . of a base and blotchy color, and neither honest nor gentle . . . . " it would seem that a minimum of larger ranch stock had escaped to the hills.[38] The feral herds of the northern United States showed a cross between the Indian pony and the imported stock of the rancher and settler that was obvious after the establishment of the cattleman's frontier. The breeder of the cayuse type of animal, as well as the rancher producing hot-blooded types of race horses, did much to improve the quality of the Indian pony breed of the Northwest wild herds.[39] It seems reasonable to conclude that in the South by 1890 and before, the domestic "American" horse had added his blood to that of the mustang in the wild state. Their identity had been largely lost except on the Indian

reservations and in some of the inaccessible mountain fastnesses of the West.[40] The mustanger reported that in nearly every band he found branded
stock. The ratio of branded to unbranded was reported by Will James, who hunted horses after the
turn of the century, to be twenty to one. That would
vary from place to place and, of course, would be
greater in 1940 than in 1860. In western Kansas,
so a story goes, a horse carrying a saddle escaped,
was not seen for two years, but when found in a
herd, it still carried the saddle in the proper position on the back.[41] This illustrates not only that
domestic stock escaped, but also that Kansas cattlemen used a tight girth!

The native horse of the Philippines, also introduced by the Spanish, never reverted to the true
wild state. He was a better horse than the American mustang, even though he had no blooded stock
of the "American" variety introduced to improve
him until the turn of the century.[42] The true horse
of South America, according to Graham, had disappeared by about 1900, and in the Argentine the
wild ones so plentiful there were mostly descendants of estrays.

When the concerted efforts of ranchers, the
Grazing Service of the Federal government, and
horse runners began the removal program of the
last two decades, they found very little mustang
blood left. In truth they found few horses that
had any market value other than at the packing

plants. Year after year the stockmen have crowded them back farther into the hills where the grazing is sparse. The winter range has been even
more restricted than that of the summer in the
highlands. Year after year the scrub stock of the
West has joined these bands. They have become
more isolated, and consequently inbreeding has
taken place. Suffering the cruel effects of these
many forces, they have become, in the main, small,
unattractive, and scrub remnants of what was
once a mighty horse herd. Seldom do they weigh
over 800 pounds, but these undernourished horses
still possess stamina and endurance.

From time to time have come reports of midget
animals existing in some isolated area where inbreeding and lack of forage have affected their
size. After having made an investigation of these
stories, Charles L. McNichols, a Western writer,
has confirmed them in the May-June, 1941, issue of
The Horse. He believes there are two or more
areas, one a canyon and the other an isolated mesa,
both south of the Grand Canyon, in which small
horses are to be found. Allegedly, these animals
weigh from 100 to 400 pounds, and are all colors
and conformation, some of which may be seen at
the Los Angeles County Museum.

Generally speaking, the horses of the northern
tier of mountain states are sturdier and heavier
than those of the Southwest where more mustang
blood remains. The infiltration of Percheron and

other draft stock, "escapes" from the wheat ranchers of the period of World War I, can be plainly seen. In the Montana roundups of a recent period they were described as "large and small, vicious and indifferent. . . . ."[43] The Secretary of the Montana Stockgrowers Association, E. A. Phillips, believes that among these horses largely of the cayuse type "you will find it impossible to obtain any authentic cases of mustangs at large in Montana today."[44] One horse found in the 1929 roundup bore a brand of a ranch that had gone out of business thirty years ago!

In Wyoming none of the horses showed any mustang breeding.[45] The Idaho horses had become "drafty."[46] In Oregon the horses found in the three areas where a few remain (Murder's Creek, Beaty Buttes, and Owyhee River breaks) are said to be "mostly the real blue, roan buckskin and pinto mustangs," apparently still showing the Indian pony influence. These "broomtails," so many of which were canned and smoked by a packing plant in Portland, Oregon, were small and mean in appearance, averaging 800 pounds in weight.[47] Many were ill-shaped, some actually deformed. Only a small porportion could be called saddle stock, many being of the child's pony type.[48]

Colorado had good horses a quarter of a century ago running on the range. In 1940 the stock showed less inbreeding and starvation than did the Nevada stock. Apparently these animals had spent only a few generations in the wild.[49] The Utah horses were described as weighing from 800 to 1200 pounds, and showing colors ranging from pinto to palomino. Most of them had originated from the ranchers' estrays, and apparently showed little of the ill effects of the forces of nature as seen in the Nevada herds. Horse hunters and ranchers had long before solved the problem of starvation and inbreeding by shooting or capturing them.[50]

The New Mexican roundup of 1932 gathered in hundreds of shaggy ponies, looking like Shetlands, with solid colors, duns, and pintos predominating.[51] Exclusive of the Indian reservations, the only area in Arizona where the wild bands still showed the mustang blood, and not that of "American" stock, was in the extreme southwestern part of the state on the International Boundary and probably those found on the lands of the Organ Pipe Cactus National Monument.[52] It is also possible that the mustang blood is fairly pure in the barren lands of the Arizona Strip. All other horses on the Arizona public domain show the influence of ranchers' estrays.

On the Indian reservations the horses removed were of the poorest type. On the San Carlos Reservation "at least half the horses .... were small wild animals practically worthless and almost impossible to gather ...." when the Bureau of Animal Industry started a removal program because of dourine.[53] The Fort Apache herds had as high a percentage of "wild mustang blood as any herds in the continental United States due to the relative isolation . . . ." of the reservation. The present-day Apache horse is described as follows:

. . . . sure-footed and often possesses a stamina and an ability to work on little feed that is quite remarkable, but they are small, averaging about 650 to 700 pounds which is too light for a good cow horse altho the Apaches do manage to do a lot of roping of heavy cattle on them. Many, while they may have been branded as colts or as yearlings, often have been handled only the one time. Some are condemned cow horses that, when they join a herd of wild horses, become almost as wild as though they had never been broken. Others are brood mares which are seldom broken to ride or to work altho they are branded whenever possible.[54]

On the Navajo lands where the horse problem has been so great, few of the ponies are of any value. The "typical sales horse," according to Superintendent E. R. Fryer, "is a decrepit, bony, half-starved creature, barely equal to the long trek from the sales corral to railroad shipping points. Literally hundreds of them have died en route, unable to make the slow drive across barren, draught-ridden ranges."[55]

The day of the magnificent animal has largely gone. The story book type of mustang never existed in any numbers. While he deteriorated little, if any, on the prairies, he was never anything in appearance but an inferior horse. When the mustang crossed with the rancher's estray the result was a fair horse. With a long mane reaching to the knees and a tail sweeping the ground, this animal often had some grace and good proportion. He lured many a mustanger down the beaten, glistening trails of the chaparral country and across the runways in the Western ranges. But nobody except the tourist wanted this horse on the range. Cattle and sheep ate the range grass, and starvation produced an unattractive, stunted horse no larger than a child's pony. Not only economic but humane considerations sent this animal to the cauldron and in so doing closed a chapter in the history of the West.

FOOTNOTES—CHAPTER FOURTEEN

1. This explanation is given by G. C. Robinson, "Mustangs and Mustangers in Southwest Texas," in J. Frank Dobie, Mody C. Boatright, and Harry H. Ransom, eds., *Mustangs and Cow Horses* (Austin, 1940), p. 3.

2. These terms are used by W. H. Carter, "Story of the Horse," *National Geographic Magazine*, XLIV (1923), 524; Stewart Edward White, "The Mountains," *Outlook*, LXXII (1904), 368; Owen P. White, "Montana Seals the Fate of 400,000 Wild Horses," *New York Times Magazine*, June 7, 1925; and *Prose and Poetry of the Live Stock Industry* (Denver and Kansas City, 1905), I, 138.

3. J. W. Moses, "A Mustanger of 1850," Dobie, Boatright, and Ransom, *op. cit.*, p. 39.

4. W. C. Barnes, *Western Grazing Grounds and Forest Ranges* (Chicago, 1913), p. 98.

5. *Prose and Poetry of the Live Stock Industry*, I, 137.

6. The writer in *Prose and Poetry* . . . ., pp 138-39, says they also became smaller and that the process was degeneration.

7. This point is strongly made by Robinson, *op. cit.*, p. 14.

8. Professor F. W. Wilson of the Department of Animal Husbandry, University of Nevada, calls attention to this practice among wild herds. Letter of September 8, 1939.

9. Frederic Remington, "Horses of the Plains," *Century Magazine*, XXXVII (1888-89), 334-35.

10. E. B. Nowland, letter in *American Turf Register and Sporting Magazine*, VII (1835-36), 60-62. *See also* the letter from Cantonment Jesup, Louisiana, *ibid.*, IV (1832-33), 501-2.

11. *Ibid.*, VI (1834-35), 166.

12. H. McLeod to M. B. Lamar, in *Lamar Papers* (Austin, 1922), II, 406. Edited by C. A. Gulick.

13. Quoted by E. Douglas Branch, *The Hunting of the Buffalo* (New York, 1929). pp. 108-9. Permission to quote given by D. Appleton-Century Company.

14. George Catlin, *Letters and Notes on the Manners, Customs, and Conditions of the North American Indians*, Vol. II, quoted in Dobie, Boatright, and Ransom, *op. cit.*, p. 148.

15. Washington Irving, *Astoria* (New York, n.d.), p. 155.

16. Grant Foreman, ed., *Adventure on Red River* . . . . (Norman, 1937), p. 126. Quoted by permission of the University of Oklahoma Press.

17. Remington, *op. cit.*, pp. 338-39.

18. C. A. Murray, *Travels in North America During the Years* 1834, 1835, & 1836 (London, 1841), II, 353.

19. Francis Parkman, *The Oregon Trail* (Boston, 1926), p. 275. Quoted by permission of Little, Brown and Company.

20. Clark Wissler, "The Influence of the Horse in the Development of Plains Culture," *American Anthropologist*, XVI (1914), 21, and James R. Mead, "The Pawnees as I Knew Them," *Transactions of the Kansas State Historical Society* (Topeka, 1910), X, 107, footnote.

21. Comments by the editor on "American Wild Horses," in *American Turf Register and Sporting Magazine*, IV (1832-33), 8.

22. *Loc. cit.*

23. T. J. Farnham, *Travels in the Great Western Prairies, the Anahuac and Rocky Mountains, and in the Oregon Territory* (New York, 1843), p. 82.

24. Remington, *op. cit.*

25. Robert M. Denhardt, "Spanish Horses and the New World," *The Historian*, Winter, 1938, p. 18.

26. R. B. Cunninghame Graham, *The Horses of the Conquest* (London, 1930), pp. 113-14, and C. H. Smith, *Horses* (Edinburgh, 1841), p. 179.

27. Remington, *op. cit.*, p. 339. *See also* Isaac P. Roberts, *The Horse* (New York, 1905), pp. 134-35; William R. Leigh, *The Western Pony* (New York, 1933), p. 39; and John A. Gorman, *The Western Horse* (Danville, Illinois, 1939), pp. 198-200.

28. John M. Hendrix, "'Paints' as Cow Horses," *The Cattleman*, November, 1934.

29. V. Kremola, "The 'Pied' and 'Splashed White' Patterns in Horses," *Journal of Heredity*, XXIV (1933), 67-69.

30. Quoted by Charles McNichols, "Cow Horses," *Western Story*, September 3, 1938. Permission to quote given by Street and Smith Publications.

31. *Ibid; See also* Gorman, *op. cit.*, pp. 196-98.

32. James S. Brisbin, *The Beef Bonanza*.... (Philadelphia, 1881), p. 148, says the Crows of the Yellowstone "raise the finest Indian horses I have ever seen."

33. Frank Collinson, "Fifty Thousand Mustangs," Dobie, Boatright, and Ransom, *op. cit.*, p. 71.

34. *Leavenworth Herald* (Kansas Territory), quoted in the *Kansas Messenger* (Baldwin), January 1, 1859, and the Grainfield, Kansas, *Republican*, quoted in the Atwood, Kansas, *Pioneer*, May 12, 1880.

35. Letter of August 26, 1939, from Zake Johnson, former cattleman, now Custodian of the Natural Bridges Monument, Blanding, Utah; also a letter of L. C. Montgomery, President of the Utah Cattle and Horse Growers Association, August 29, 1939.

36. Patrick Byrnes, *Wild Horses of Colorado*. (Pamphlet in the Colorado State Historical Society Library, n.d.)

37. Rufus Steele, "Mustangs, Busters and Outlaws of the Nevada Wild Horse Country," *American Magazine*, LXXII (1911), 759.

38. H. H. Bancroft, *History of California* (San Francisco, 1890), VII, 57.

39. Letter of Wayne Stewart, former mustanger, Dayville, Oregon, August 30, 1939.

40. This belief is expressed by Remington, *op. cit.*, 335, and by Louis Robinson in his article, "Wild Traits in Tame Animals," *North American Review*, CLVIII (1894), 483.

41. R. M. Wright, *Dodge City*.... (Wichita, 1913), p. 83.

42. J. C. Speed, "American Horses for the Philippines," *World's Work*, VIII (1904), 5300.

43. *New York Times*, June 6, 1929.

44. Letter, August 30, 1939.

45. Letter, September 28, 1939, from Russell Thorp, Secretary-Chief Inspector, Wyoming Stock Growers Association.

46. Professor E. F. Rinehart, College of Agriculture, University of Idaho, in a letter, September 11, 1939.

47. Letters from Rancher Tom Skinner, September, 1939, and Professor R. G. Johnson of the Oregon State Agricultural College, August 16, 1939.

48. Johnson, *op. cit.*; L. R. Brooks, Regional Grazier, Grazing Service, Reno, Nevada, letter of March 30, 1940; and Professor F. W. Wilson, letters of September 8 and 26, 1939.

49. Interview with Charles Moore, Regional Grazier, Grazing Service, Grand Junction, Colorado, in August, 1940.

50. G. R. Parry in a letter, October 5, 1939, and Rufus Steele, "Wild Horses as Scenery," *Outlook*, CXLI (1925), 85.

51. Forrester Blake, *Riding the Mustang Trail* (New York, 1935), pp. 17-18.

52. Statement in letter of September 5, 1939, of Andrew A. Nichol, National Park Service, Tucson, Arizona. *See also* Charles B. Roth, "Intelligence, Plus Speed, Plus Bottom, Equals Mustang," *The Horse*, November-December, 1937.

53. *Report of the Chief of the Bureau of Animal Industry*.... *1930* (Washington, D. C., 1930), p. 34.

54. L. E. Holloway, Agricultural Extension Agent, Fort Apache Indian Agency, in a letter, September 14, 1939.

55. "The Navajos Sell Their Range Robbers," *Indians at Work*, November, 1938, pp. 26-27.

Over the upland plateaus of Idaho, Oregon, Washington, Montana and Nevada there gallop fleet ponies and big-boned "pull horses" whose teeth have never champed a bit. In the remote reaches of the Pacific Northwest the wild horse —a symbol of pioneer America—is making its last stand.

Trapped by meat packers, harassed by predatory animals, the wild horse outspeeds these perils and continues to be the last remnant of the Old West.....

R. L. Neuberger, "Wild Horses of the West are Vanishing," *New York Times Magazine*, February 10, 1935. Quoted by permission of the author and the *New York Times Magazine*.

CHAPTER FIFTEEN

The Stallion in Fact and Fancy

Down the ribbons of concrete and macadam across the continent to the Pacific goes the American tourist every summer in search of some trace of the Old West. He is interested in the Indian, who parades in full regalia in the national parks and elsewhere where tourists are appreciative, in the museums where repose the personal effects of Kit Carson, Deadwood Dick, and others of the purple frontier, in the cowboy who conveniently can be found in flaming shirt and decorated leather-work, and lastly in the wild horse, that remnant of a day in our history when life was free and the West was a place of escape. In the creation of these desires, this nostalgia of modern man for a life that has fewer of the responsibilites than his has today, the feature writer and Hollywood deserve some credit. A recent romancer, writing for the readers of a Sunday magazine, gives this picture of the "broomtail":

On a high rock the traveler sees [today] an equine figure silhouetted against the sky. Near him other beautiful horses graze peacefully. Suddenly the lookout stallion takes alarm, leaps down from the rock and leads his herd down a boulder-strewn slope at amazing speed. Behind a bend in the mountain the wild band disappears. But in the beholder's memory this striking picture of these swift, keen-scented wild horses of the Great West remains forever.[1]

Other writers of fiction give their stories a setting in the post-Civil War period, and employ the professional mustanger or handsome cowboy to catch the beautiful leaders of the Western bands. Zane Grey perhaps stands as the best exponent of such writing among a great number of Americans. In his *Wildfire*, Lucy Bostil, daughter of a Southwestern rancher, was nearing her eighteenth birthday. What did she want for her present?

Oh, if I ever get the one I want to love! A wild horse— a desert stallion—pure Arabian—broken rightly by an Indian! .... [She wanted "Wildfire"] a giant of a horse, glistening red, with mane like dark-striped, wind-blown flame, all muscle, all grace, all power; a neck long and slender and arching to the small, savagely beautiful head; the jaws open, and the thin-skinned, pink-colored nostrils that proved the Arabian blood; the slanting shoulders and the deep, broad chest, the powerful legs and knees not too high nor too low, the symmetrical dark hoof that rang on the little stones—all the marks so significant of speed and endurance. A stallion with a wonderful physical perfection that matched the savage, ruthless spirit of the desert killer of horses.

Lucy Bostil was finally the owner of "Wildfire." Her lover pursued him for weeks until the horse

ran into a box canyon. Setting a fire at the other
end, the mustanger stood at the small opening and
lassoed him as he ran out. "Wildfire became an af-
fectionate and serviceable horse that won races and
otherwise showed his superior ancestry."[2]

In an old *Harper's Weekly* appeared a representative story of the eternal triangle which resolved
itself around a handsome stallion and a beautiful
girl who danced in a saloon in old Arizona. Carlotta
was loved by two vaqueros, Juan Alvarado and Len
Taylor. She loved both very much. To solve this
perplexing problem of the triangle, she told them
she would marry the one who captured "Red
King," an heroic stallion of the desert. As Len
rode home with her she told him, with apparent
foresight, to go to Coyote Wells that night. There
he went, found "Red King," ran him until his own
horse was exhausted. At this critical moment
appeared Carlotta on a fresh horse which she gave
to him. Still his lariat missed the wily horse. At
this moment Juan rode down the canyon wall. The
race was even. Finally Len roped the beauty, tied
him securely, and after some preliminary talk,
"took her in his arms, shaken almost to tears
by the completeness of her surrender."[3]

These illustrations set a good pace for romancers
of the wild horse. The setting is historical, the
description is accurate, the methods used by the
horse catchers are plausible. Even the yen of a
Western woman for a good horse is not far-fetched.

He lured many a mustanger down the beaten trails of the chaparral country

That there were such examples of horseflesh as "Wildfire" and "Red King" is not to be doubted. The only issue is that of representativeness: was this type of horse the usual leader of a band?

It is doubtful if more than a few stallions were magnificent animals. Unfortunately the records of the Spanish "escape" and his descendants who roamed the Southwest before the coming of white man do not reveal much information. The impression is general, however, that the heads of the Western herds were those animals showing the characteristics of the best horses of Arabia. That these stallions were the best animals on the plains in most instances is not to be doubted. The laws of survival operated strongly upon the leader of the herd. His position was often challenged by other stallions, either young or old, and the strongest one took all. It is likely that the early steeds seen by the army in its Western explorations of the 1830's were not pure mustang, but were the result of inter-breeding with "American" horses. The horse that "evinced such prodigious speed and wind, that, in the words of the ranger, he 'just stood still and looked at him . . . .' " was probably an "escape."[4] At a distance, standing silhouetted against the sky with arched neck and flowing mane and tail, the stallion looked good, but "near at hand he was likely to appear gimlet hammed and narrow chested, a scrub not worth catching."[5] In the Montana roundup of 1929, these animals were thus described:

> Contrary to popular belief and romantic fiction, the leader of a wild horse band is not a magnificent big-bodied stallion which races at the head of his followers. Close observation of the scores of leaders captured.... established the fact that the mustang leaders were small, ranging from 700 to 1,000 pounds. But they were as fleet as deer and they are vicious fighters.
>
> "Tough muscles, swift, sure feet and an uncanny ability to race at full speed through rough country that would block the domestic horse, are the chief marks of a wild leader," said Carl Skelton (who was in charge of that roundup). "A heavy horse would look well at the head of a band, the way the story writers put him. But he would be clumsy and couldn't get anywhere....."[6]

Legend insists that this was not true, that the Arabian led the herd. It must be admitted that there is some evidence to show that "throw-backs" may have been found. A careful student of the Spanish horse, Robert M. Denhardt, holds that certain sires of the mustang stock left their stamp on the horse herds, and that one can still find today the colors of roan, pinto, and palomino recurring in animals having symmetry and beauty.[7] It must be said that even this horse, if found, is seldom, if ever, a "throw-back" or an atavar. The beautiful stallion, regardless of color or features, was largely fictitious and when found at all proved to be a blooded estray that had escaped from some rancher's domestic stock.[8] The mustang stock has been so diluted since 1890 that a "throw-back" becomes less of a possibility. The cattleman's practice of holding the saddle stock as well as enclosing stallions in fenced areas has largely done away with the flaming stallion in the herds of the last few years.

The greatest horse legend in America is that of the beautiful stallion. It no doubt rose when the first white man saw native herds from a distance, it grew as estrays joined the herds and were chased by every cowboy in the country, and it will persist throughout all time. That good horses were in existence cannot be denied. A mustanger of 1850 for years knew of a large horse fourteen hands high "of a rich orange color, with a snow white mane reaching below his knees, and so heavy that it bent its neck over to one side while grazing . . . . and a tail that actually dragged the ground."[9] Later he had the opportunity of buying this animal. The same man once captured a sorrel stallion, "a fast pacer with a very long, beautiful mane, which reached to his knees. . . . . " A Colorado pioneer remembered a "big beautiful stallion, all black, with a tail dragging on the ground, and a flowing mane reaching down below his neck and to the end of his nose."[10] At the turn of the century, a thousand-pound black and white patriarch ruled for over ten years in the Nevada country, finally being shot at a water hole. The black splotches turned out to be places where he had been bitten in his struggle for power, and over which black hair had grown.[11] A large blue stallion, "Blue

Streak," which became a sensational race horse, was caught in Colorado at the same time. A living ex-mustanger tells of a friend living in Fredonia, Arizona ("whose word I would take on the subject") who caught a respectable horse that "was absolutely green."[12] Floyd Hanson, aerial cowboy of the Nevada roundups, drove into the corral in the 1930's a handsome white horse that had run the range for twelve years. After letting the men look at him, Hanson nonchalantly opened the gate and let this thunderbolt called "Silver King" escape to run up the mountain trail again.[13] For years in southern Utah "Red Volcano" outran the best horses and jumped out of corrals.[14]

These good horses became fewer as the years went by when the mustangers picked them over and the cattlemen enclosed their horse bands. But they did exist, even if they were "escapes" or their descendants.

The tradition of the famous white stallion, dating from the 1840's or thereabouts, has long had wide circulation. He was reported from the Rio Grande to the Canadian border. Stories tell of a Texan catching him and that refusing to eat or drink, he died. Another story tells of his being caught in southwest Texas, that he was the colt of a white mare lost by the army in 1846. Sometimes he was a single-footer, sometimes a trotter. It would seem that every locality had some such story and some must have had such a horse.[15]

The Blackfeet Indians once captured in a herd a steeldust stallion that later escaped. He became famous as a night killer of horses in Montana and Alberta. In the darkness his mane and tail gave off a phosphorescent glow, but his steel blue body could not be seen. Consequently, according to the story, he became the "Ghost Horse" of Alberta and Montana.[16]

In western Kansas, according to a frontier story, a Mormon wagon train lost some thoroughbred stock in a stampede. For thirteen years around Fort Wallace ranged a horse produced by this stock, known far and wide as "Black Kettle." In 1879, he had twenty-nine black and roan mares, and had been chased by every horse runner of the plains, including the U. S. Cavalry. Finally, he was captured by a mustanger of note, who kept him on the move for twenty-two days until his feet became so sore that he gave out.[17]

These horses were largely in legend and story. A few of the authentic horse runners, Rufus Steele, Will Barnes, and Will James, do not deny that there were some great horses that when seen excited lovers of horseflesh, and that when captured lived up to expectations. One such animal was "Stampede," a chestnut of Cortez Valley, Nevada. His mother was believed to be a mustang and his sire an escaped thoroughbred. This fast animal that was so sure-footed he would run down mountains and outdistance all the mustangers, was finally roped at a water hole by a Shoshoni Indian. The Indian choked him, put on a second rope, and gave a dance of joy. Broken, he became a good horse for the red mustanger who would run the wild bands down the side of the French Mountains, where trails diverted them from the brink of a canyon. One eventful day the Shoshoni came

helter-skelter down the hill only to realize too late that "Stampede" refused to change direction. The other horse runners could see that the great horse was running away for the last time. He did not tumble over the lip of the canyon, he leaped, and all the by-standers saw a man on a horse silhouetted against the blue sky. Three hundred feet below, upon the cactus and rocks, died a horse, and under him lay an Indian who stayed there to the end.[18]

In this Nevada country between 1900 and 1910

were thousands of horses, and among them were some fine stallions. "Sontag" was one of the outlaws. He was large, weighing twelve hundred pounds, brown in color, and he led a band of fourteen colored mares. Named after a California bandit, Sontag, he lived up to his reputation. Once surrounded, he dashed to freedom, leaving his band behind him. Within a week he had a new band, including three saddle horses of a mustanger. That season he was corralled along with the others, and the end looked near. Milling around the others, his sides heaved but his head was still high. Rufus Steele roped him from his horse but in the ensuing struggle found his saddle jerked up on the withers of the saddle horse. "Sontag" continued to rear and plunge as a helper rode in and grabbed the rope, only to lose hold. Together the two men watched this powerful horse tear away down the hill dragging behind him a twelve-dollar lariat. Two years later this piece of lightning was caught at a water hole corral made of wire. With food and water sufficient for the sixty in the corral the horse runners left for two weeks. When they returned the horses were gone. A gap in the wire, and the loose ends covered with blood and hair, showed them that "Sontag" had again left for the hills.[19]

Writing in 1923, Will James, an authentic product of the West, tells of his experiences catching a paint stallion, a young one, weighing eleven hundred pounds, and having but two fillies in his herd. James and his crew built a corral at a mountain gap, and the riders, scattered over a two-mile area, drove the horses toward it. In the net were many "broomtails" of every color, but no "Paint." These horses corralled, another drive was made. This time the stallion was there, but being wise, he led a break and escaped with seventy others, "their tails a-popping....." Three mustangers dashed away in pursuit, among them James, who succeeded in roping "Paint." The stallion kept going, and James' saddle slipped, throwing him on the ground in the midst of the escaping herd. He "saw more horses' legs at one setting, so to speak, than ever before....." The piebald bucked on down the mountain, dragging a good saddle, followed by James' horse. Later they roped this elusive animal and put him in the trap. The next morning he was found dead, his neck broken. "Unfortunately he had hit the corral a little too hard."[20]

The stallion, according to legend, was not only a magnificent animal, faster than all the others, but was also so sensitive that he seldom could live in captivity. There is some truth in this belief. Pete Barnum, college-bred mustanger of a quarter-century ago, once captured a large red stallion in Nevada. To quote him:

Until we saddled him we did not know his desperation. We fastened the riata to his front feet; when he tried to run away we jerked his feet from under him, throwing him heavily .... until exhaustion necessitated his capitulation. But his surrender was only temporary. For three years we tried to break him, using every artifice known to us—as quickly as one man gave up the task another would try to conquer him; but every time a human being approached or tried to bridle or saddle him he would bite viciously, while his eyes, protruding from the sockets, blazed fiery red with hate. As the cinch was drawn tight the outlaw, if upon his feet, invariably reared straight up, then hurled himself backward to the ground..... His end was as tragic as his career; in making an attempt to escape by jumping out of a stockade corral he misjudged the distance and became impaled on a jagged post, and a forty-four was turned loose upon him to end his suffering.[21]

Will James tells of a lone stallion that, after being captured, was released in a pasture with a herd. A month later he was dead. "It wasn't lockjaw or starvation that killed him. He was fat as a seal and had plenty of feed and water. He just died of a broken heart."[22]

There are other men of the West who have recorded or told stories of proud stallions whose aversion to captivity was so great that they died in corrals, leaped to freedom or death. There must be exceptions. Caught, gelded, and broken, these horses served many a good cowboy on the Western range. There were some horses that were good, those showing Eastern breeding, but most of them were not of the type that Hollywood or the fictionists can use.

FOOTNOTES—CHAPTER FIFTEEN

1. John Warrington, "Still Time to Save America's Wild Horses," *The American Weekly*, January 14, 1940.

2. The quotation given above taken from *Wildfire* by Zane Grey is quoted with the permission of Mrs. Zane Grey.

3. Jane Anderson, "The Red King," *Harper's Weekly*, LVI (1912), Part II, 16-18.

4. Letter from Fort Gibson, August 1, 1833, by "A Reader," given in *American Turf Register and Sporting Magazine*, V (1833-34), 73-74.

5. This is the opinion given by J. Frank Dobie in *A Vaquero of the Brush Country* (Dallas, 1929), p. 238, and Will C. Barnes, "The Passing of the Wild Horse," *American Forests and Forest Life*, November, 1924.

6. Russel A. Bankson in the *New York Times*, June 23, 1929. Quoted by permission of the *New York Times*.

7. "Spanish Horses and the New World," *The Historian*, Winter, 1938, p. 18. That these horses are found is held by John A. Gorman, *The Western Horse* (Danville, Illinois, 1939), p. 180, and by O. P. White in the *New York Times Magazine*, June 7, 1925.

8. This viewpoint is held by most of the mustangers who have left records.

9. J. W. Moses, "A Mustanger of 1850," in J. Frank Dobie, Mody C. Boatright, and Harry H. Ransom, eds., *Mustangs and Cow Horses* (Austin, 1940), p. 32. Quoted by permission of the Texas Folk-Lore Society.

10. A. J. Pearce, *Experiences of a Pioneer Family.* (Pamphlet, n.d.)

11. Rufus Steele, "Mustangs, Busters and Outlaws in the Nevada Wild Horse Country," *McClure's Magazine*, LXXII (1911), 764.

12. G. R. Parry, Superintendent of Motor Transportation, Utah Parks Company, Cedar City, Utah, in a letter, October 5, 1939.

13. Jeff Sparks, "Wild Horses Corralled from the Air," *Popular Mechanics*, LXX (1939), 120 A.

14. Kathleen Caesar, "With the Wild Horse Hunters," *ibid.*, XLVI (1926), 76.

15. J. Frank Dobie, "The Deathless Pacing Stallion," and G. C. Robinson, "Mustangs and Mustanging in Southwest Texas," in Dobie, Boatright, and Ransom, *op. cit.*, pp. 173-83 and 11-12.

16. Chief Buffalo Child Long Lance, quoted in the same.

17. Frank Lockard, quoted in the same, pp. 102-42, and the *Norton County People* (Norton, Kansas), August 19, 1880.

18. Steele, *op. cit.*

19. Rufus Steele, "Trapping Wild Horses in Nevada," *McClure's Magazine*, XXXIV (1909-10), 207-8.

20. Will James, "Piñon and the Wild Ones," *Saturday Evening Post*, May 19, 1923, pp. 24-25.

21. Told by Steele in *McClure's, op. cit.*, 764.

22. James, *op. cit.*, p. 156.

In time to come mayhap some man will take his small son up to a glass case and say "Son, that is what was once known as the Western pony."

Letter of Harry M. Ralston, Glacier Park, Montana, in *Life*, July 25, 1938.

CHAPTER SIXTEEN

Save the Wild Horse!

A frontier editor in 1832 called his readers' attention to the value of the wild horses as the tide of civilization rolled on toward the Pacific. Their abundance and cheapness, when purchased through the Indians, "will be extremely advantageous to those who may hereafter attempt the fur trade to the East Indies, by way of the Columbia river and the Pacific ocean."[1] The little horse never lived up to this prophecy except in a minor way, even though he did serve early fur traders trekking in from some Western rendezvous. Since that time he has been chased and captured, and used in many ways by man. Like the Indian, the good wild pony to many Westerners was the dead one, and never a voice was lifted in his behalf until recent years when suddenly it was realized that the horses were nearly gone. The University of Texas appropriately was said to be capturing the grace and beauty of the original mus-

They belong to that country of junipers and sage, of deep arroyos, mesas —and freedom

tang in 1940. The $80,000 group of statues, financed by one special lover of horseflesh and the American Legion, was to be placed on the Texas campus, showing the little horse in action.[2]

Now that the horse has largely disappeared, a few voices are raised in his behalf. In a recent issue of a Sunday magazine an appeal was made to preserve the mustang in the national parks. Yellowstone National Park could become a breeding ground for polo ponies, developed from the wild herds. Steeplechasing mounts could be bred in Rainier National Park where the lofty crags would give the horse the necessary environment for that sport. Zion or Bryce could be the "nursery for bronco-bucking outlaw horses" so needed by rodeos and Hollywood. From these reservations might come, also, the steeds necessary for the army, dude ranches, forest rangers, and others. To make certain that the wild ones serve these purposes, government-owned stallions could be released to provide the blood for good lines of horseflesh. Unless Congress acts soon, as it did to save the buffalo, it will be too late to save these "equine aristocrats, acknowledged by experts the finest wild horses in the world....."[3]

The reservation idea is not likely to take hold of the American mind, although the state of Idaho was reported to be considering "in co-operation with the Grazing Service, a proposition to provide a small area where a few specimens might possibly be preserved."[4] Idaho was probably moved as much by the desire to attract tourists as by sentiment. Westerners know that the wild horse of today is a tame horse gone wild. He is just like any horse found on a farm or ranch, except that he is smaller, scrawnier, and may even be disfigured. He is a starved animal that has no place to go if cattle and sheep continue to run the range. These people proposing reservations are not aware of the Taylor Act of 1934 which established the policy of this government, that being that the horse must go from the public domain if he is a nuisance and if he can be removed. Even the *New York Times* defended this policy when it said editorially:

These wild horses, of inferior stock, worth only $2 to $10 a head, eat as much grass as would feed valuable cattle. . . . .

It is a wise policy to permit land which supported almost worthless animals to be turned over to cattle worth $50 a head. Still it is hardly possible that these outlaw horses will be completely wiped out while there exist in this country, and even in Europe, vast audiences of movie fans who dote on Western thrillers. Motion picture companies will surely do something to save a few thundering herds from the reduction plants to range in security on grassy plains not too remote from Hollywood, disturbed only by actor-cowboys and camera men.[5]

If not critical of the removal of the horses, some objected to the way of doing it. Why use the airplane? In the popular *Life* magazine appeared a letter which probably reflected the thinking of many Americans:

Sirs:

With indignation and sorrow I viewed your pictures of the aerial cowboy who rounds up wild horses by airplane. I wonder if this man does not know that without man's best friend, the horse, this great West of ours could never have been pioneered as it was. In time to come mayhap some man will take his small son up to a glass case and say "Son, that is what was once known as the Western pony."

Our Government should take shame for allowing an insensible machine to so terribly frighten beautiful, innocent colts.[6]

Another letter in *Life* called upon "all lovers of horses and all real sportsmen" to petition Congress to stop this ruthless practice.[7] This pressure must have been felt in Washington, for the Department of Interior did send a man out to Nevada where the airplane was being used. The Grazing Service defended its use, saying that it saved the saddle horse from the long, hard, gruelling runs which oftentimes injured the animal; the wild ones did not have to run so hard as when pursued by riders;

and the young colts which always fell behind when saddle horses were used in the chase, were not left on the desert to die but were brought in by the mares.[8] That the accusation in the letter was true in one case was shown by a native rancher of that area who had in 1939 a *"two-year* old blue colt, caught two years ago last June. . . . ."[9]

The practice of shooting animals in the distant and inaccessible places because it was impracticable to do anything else brought some protests in recent years. Wanton waste, it was called. The use of these degenerate horses for chicken feed, dog food, and even human consumption must have irked many a cowboy who still loves the horse. One Westerner, in referring to this, wrote: "Which to my mind is very disgusting. For I sure like the horse."[10]   A cow hand suspect was once held, charged with attempting to dynamite a horse-meat canning plant. Pleading guilty, he said: "I couldn't help it. I am a cowboy and I love horses. I can't bear to think of people eating them."[11] Even literary Will James, lover of horses, says that he regrets it is all over.

I'm kind of sorry now so many were caught, 'cause I have a lot of respect and admiration for the mustang. The fact that he'd give us back the same medicine we'd hand him, with sometimes a little overdose, only made me feel that in him I had an opponent worthy of the game. Even though I'd get sore at them when they'd put it over on us and rub it in a little too hard, the satisfaction I'd get at catching some wise bunch didn't last very long when I'd remember they'd be shipped, put to work and maybe starved into being good by some *hombre* who was afraid of them and didn't savvy at all. For they really belong, not to man, but to that country of junipers and sage, of deep arroyos, mesas—and freedom.[12]

Had James caught horses in the last ten years when the removal of the starved critters was even sanctioned by several humane societies, he might have felt as did another bona fide Westerner: "As it was they fed a lot of happy bowwows and furnished a living to some riders who are having a tough time getting by."[13]

The little pony left his stamp not only on the hearts of the West and on the Western cow pony but also on geography. Several states have a "Wild Horse Plains," or "Wild Horse Mesa." In Texas there are twenty-seven "Mustang Creeks," and a town called "Mustang" in Culbertson County. If the mustang as he once was, a definite horse type with his long mane and tail, his protruding eyes, his bulky head, had been threatened with extermination in 1940, Congress would have rushed to his aid, appropriated money for his preservation. But that horse is gone. If the diluted horse found in the West as late as 1900 were today threatened with destruction, cowboys, Congressmen, and the rest of America would have raised voices against it. But that horse, too, is gone. Rather than preserve degenerate estrays, it is better to look backward to that which once was, and cease thinking of perpetuating that which does not exist. Texas has the idea. Build a statue to the horse that used to be, make it life size, include a stallion, some mares, and a few colts. Let this bronze symbol stand in a public place so that generations that are to come may see the type of horse that contributed the base stock to the Western range horse industry. And on this statue carve a caption taken from a letter to *Life* protesting the destruction of the wild horse herds in recent years:

"Son, that is what was once known as the Western pony."[14]

FOOTNOTES—CHAPTER SIXTEEN

1. *American Turf Register and Sporting Magazine*, IV (1832-33), 8.

2. *St. Paul Dispatch*, December 10, 1939.

3. John Warrington, "Still Time to Save America's Wild Horses," *The American Weekly*, January 14, 1940.

4. J. E. Stablein, Regional Grazier, Grazing Service, Pocatello, Idaho, in a letter, February 7, 1940.

5. Issue of June 28, 1928. Quoted by permission of the *New York Times*.

6. Issue of July 25, 1938, letter section.

7. *Loc. cit.*

8. Enclosure in a letter from Nic W. Monte, Acting Regional Grazier, Grazing Service, Burns, Oregon, January 23, 1940.

9. Letter of Tom Skinner, Jordan Valley, Oregon, September, 1939.

10. Murray Morton, Assessor, Malheur County, Oregon, letter of August 22, 1939.

11. Kathleen 'Caesar, "With Wild Horse Hunters," *Popular Mechanics*, XLVI (1926), 78. Quoted by permission of *Popular Mechanics*.

12. "Piñon and the Wild Ones," *Saturday Evening Post*, May 19, 1923.

13. Charles L. McNichols, "Cow Horses," *Western Story*, June, 1939, p. 76. Quoted by permission of Street and Smith Publications.

14. This Texas project consists of a stallion, several mares, and a colt, to be cast life-size in bronze at a cost of $60,000. Ralph Ogden of Austin offered to finance the cost of it if J. Frank Dobie of the University of Texas would care for all arrangements. The sculptor, A. P. Proctor, has been engaged, but the work will of necessity be held up for the duration because of priorities.

Bibliography

I. BOOKS

ADAIR, JAMES. *The History of the American Indians*. London: Edward and Charles Dilly, 1775.

ARNOLD, OREN and JOHN P. HALE. *Hot Irons*. New York: The Macmillan Co., 1940.

BAKELESS, JOHN. *Daniel Boone*. New York: William Morrow & Co., 1939.

BANCROFT, HUBERT H. *History of California*. Vol. VII. San Francisco: The History Company, 1890. Being Vol. XXIV of *The Works of Hubert Howe Bancroft*.

BARNES, W. C. *Western Grazing Grounds and Forest Ranges*. Chicago: The Breeder's Gazette, 1913.

BARTLETT, J. R. *Personal Narrative of Exploration and Incidents in Texas, New Mexico, California, Sonora, and Chihuahua*.... *1850, '51, '52, and '53*. Vol. II. New York: D. Appleton & Co. 1854.

BIRNEY, HOFFMAN. *Steeldust, The Story of a Horse*. Philadelphia: The Penn Publishing Co., 1928.

BISHOP, MORRIS. *The Odyssey of Cabeza de Vaca*. New York: The Century Co., 1933.

BLAKE, FORRESTER. *Riding the Mustang Trail*. New York: Charles Scribner's Sons, 1935.

BOLTON, HERBERT E. *The Spanish Borderlands*. New Haven: Yale University Press, 1921.

BOLTON, HERBERT E. and T. M. MARSHALL. *The Colonization of North America, 1492-1783*. New York: The Macmillan Co., 1927.

BRANCH, E. D. *The Hunting of the Buffalo*. New York: D. Appleton & Co., 1929.

BRAND, D. D. and FRED HARVEY, eds. *So Live the Works of Men*. Albuquerque: University of New Mexico Press, 1939.

BRISBIN, J. S. *The Beef Bonanza; or How to Get Rich on the Plains*. Philadelphia: J. B. Lippincott & Co., 1881.

BURPEE, L. J., ed. *Journals and Letters of Pierre Gaultier de Varennes de la Vérendrye and His Sons*.... Toronto: The Champlain Society, 1927.

CANNON, C. L., ed. *Scout and Ranger, Being the Personal Adventures of James Pike* .... Princeton: Princeton University Press, 1932.

CARVER, JONATHAN. *Travels Through the Interior Parts of North America, in the Years 1766, 1767, and 1768.* London: C. Dilly, 1781.

CATLIN, GEORGE. *North American Indians* .... Vol. I. Edinburgh: John Grant, 1926.

CHAPMAN, ARTHUR. *The Pony Express.* New York: G. P. Putnam's Sons, 1932.

CHAPPELL, P. E. "History of the Missouri River." *Transactions of the Kansas Historical Society,* Vol. IX. Topeka: State Printing Office, 1906., pp. 237-316.

COOK, J. R. *The Border and the Buffalo.* Topeka: Crane & Co., 1907.

CUNNINGHAME GRAHAM, R. B. *The Horses of the Conquest.* London: William Heinemann, Ltd., 1930.

DALE, E. E. *The Range Cattle Industry.* Norman: University of Oklahoma Press, 1930.

DOBIE, J. FRANK. *A Vaquero of the Brush Country.* Dallas: The Southwest Press, 1930.

DOBIE, J. FRANK, M. C. BOATRIGHT, and H. H. RANSOM, eds. *Mustangs and Cow Horses.* "Texas Folk-Lore Society Publications," Vol. XVI. Austin: Texas Folk-Lore Society, 1940.

FARNHAM, T. J. *Travels in the Great Western Prairies, the Anahuac and Rocky Mountains, and the Oregon Territory.* New York: Greeley and McElrath, 1843.

FERRIS, I. M. "The Sauks and Foxes in Franklin and Osage Counties, Kansas." *Transactions of the Kansas State Historical Society,* Vol. XI. Topeka: State Printing Office, 1910, pp. 333-95.

FOREMAN, GRANT. *Adventure on Red River, Report on the Exploration of the Headwaters of the Red River by Captain Randolph B. Marcy and Captain G. B. McClellan.* Norman: University of Oklahoma Press, 1937.

————. *Pioneer Days in the Early Southwest.* Cleveland: The Arthur H. Clark Co., 1926.

GORMAN, J. A. *The Western Horse.* Danville, Illinois: The Interstate Printers & Publishers, 1939.

GREY, ZANE. *Wildfire.* New York: Grosset & Dunlap, 1917.

————. *Wild Horse Mesa.* New York: Grosset & Dunlap, 1928.

GRINNELL, G. B. *The Fighting Cheyennes.* New York: Charles Scribner's Sons, 1915.

GULICK, C. A., ed. *Lamar Papers,* Vol. II. Austin: Texas State Library, 1922.

HALEY, J. E. *Charles Goodnight, Cowman & Plainsman.* New York: Houghton Mifflin Co., 1936.

HART, S. H. and A. B. HULBERT, eds. *Zebulon Pike's Arkansas Journal* .... Denver: Stewart Commission of Colorado College and Denver Public Library, 1932.

HENDERSON, J. C. "Reminiscences of a Range Rider," edited by J. B. Thoburn. *Chronicles of Oklahoma,* Vol. III. Oklahoma City: Oklahoma Historical Society. 1925, pp. 253-88.

HENRY, ALEXANDER. *Travels and Adventures in Canada and the Indian Territories between the Years 1760 and 1776.* New York: I. Riley, 1809.

HODDER, F. H., ed. *Audubon's Western Journal: 1849-1850.* With a biographical memoir by Maria R. Audubon. Cleveland: The Arthur H. Clark Co., 1906.

HOWEY, M. C. *The Horse in Magic and Myth.* London: William Rider & Son, Ltd., 1923.

HYDE, G. E. *The Pawnee Indians.* Denver: John Van Male, 1934.

IRVING, WASHINGTON. *Astoria. Bonneville.* Being one volume in *The Complete Works of Washington Irving.* New York: Thomas Y. Crowell & Co., n.d.

JONES, C. J. *Buffalo Jones' Forty Years of Adventure.* Compiled by Henry Inman. Topeka: Crane & Co., 1899.

KROEBER, A. L. *Anthropology.* New York: Harcourt, Brace & Co., 1923.

LEIGH, W. R. *The Western Pony.* New York: The Huntington Press, 1933.

LEWIS, ANNA. "Du Tisne's Expedition into Oklahoma, 1719." *Chronicles of Oklahoma,* Vol. III. Oklahoma City: Oklahoma Historical Society, 1925, pp. 318-22.

LA VÉRENDRYE, PIERRE GAULTIER DE VARENNES, SIEUR DE. *See* L. J. Burpee, ed.

LULL, R. S. *Organic Evolution.* New York: The Macmillan Co., 1932.

McCOY, J. G. *Historic Sketches of the Cattle Trade of the West and Southwest.* Kansas City: Ramsey, Millet, and Hudson, 1874.

MAJORS, ALEXANDER. *Seventy Years on the Frontier.* Chicago and New York: Rand, McNally & Co., 1893.

MARCY, R. B. *See* Grant Foreman, *Adventure, etc.*

MEAD, J. R. "The Pawnees as I Knew Them." *Transactions of the Kansas State Historical Society,* Vol. X. Topeka: State Printing Office, 1910, pp. 106-11.

MERWIN, R. E. "The Wyandott Indians." *Transactions of the Kansas State Historical Society,* Vol. IX. Topeka: State Printing Office, 1906, pp. 173-88.

MOREHOUSE, G. P. "History of the Kansa or Kaw Indians." *Transactions of the Kansas State Historical Society,* Vol. X. Topeka: State Printing Office, 1908, pp. 327-73.

MURRAY, C. A. *Travels in North America During the Years 1834, 1835, & 1836,* Vols. I and II. London: Richard Bentley, 1841.

NATIONAL LIVE STOCK ASSOCIATION. *Prose and Poetry of the Live Stock Industry,* Vol. I. Denver and Kansas City: National Live Stock Historical Association, 1905.

OSTERTAG, ROBERT. *Handbook of Meat Inspection.* Chicago: American Veterinary Publishing Company, 1919.

PAGE, ELIZABETH. *Wild Horses and Gold.* New York: Farrar & Rinehart, 1932.

PARKMAN, FRANCIS. *The Oregon Trail.* Boston: Little, Brown & Co., 1926.

PELZER, LOUIS. *Marches of the Dragoons in the Mississippi Valley* .... Iowa City: The State Historical Society of Iowa, 1917.

PERKINS, C. E. *The Pinto Horse.* Santa Barbara: Wallace Hebberd, 1927.

PIKE, ZEBULON M. *An Account of Expeditions to the Sources of the Mississippi and Through the Western Parts of Louisiana, to the Sources of the Arkansas, Kansas, La Platte, and Pierre Juan Rivers* .... Philadelphia: Carl and A. Conrad & Co., 1910.

PRESCOTT, W. H. *History of the Conquest of Mexico* .... Vols. I, II, and III. New York: Harper & Brothers, 1843.

RICHARDSON, R. N. and C. C. RISTER. *The Greater Southwest.* Glendale, California: The Arthur H. Clark Co., 1934.

RIDGEWAY, WILLIAM. *The Origin and Influence of the Thoroughbred Horse.* Cambridge, England: The University Press, 1905.

ROBERTS, I. P. *The Horse.* New York: The Macmillan Co., 1905.

ROLLINS, P. A. *The Cowboy.* New York: Charles Scribner's Sons, 1930.

ROOSEVELT, THEODORE. *Hunting Trips of a Ranchman.* From *The Works of Theodore Roosevelt*, prepared under the auspices of the Roosevelt Memorial Association. New York: Charles Scribner's Sons, 1927.

SMITH, C. H. *Horses. The Naturalist's Library*, Vol. XII. Edinburgh: W. H. Lizars, 1841.

SOLMS-BRAUNFELS, CARL, PRINCE OF. *Texas 1844-45.* Houston: The Anson Jones Press, 1936.

STONG, PHIL. *Horses and Americans.* New York: Frederick A. Stokes Co., 1939.

THOMPSON, DAVID. *See* J. B. Tyrrell, ed.

THWAITES, REUBEN G., ed. *Travels in the Interior of North America by Maximilian, Prince of Wied.* Vol. XXII, Part 2. *Early Western Travels, 1748-1864.* Cleveland: The Arthur H. Clark Co., 1904-7.

TOZER, BASIL. *The Horse in History.* London: Methuen & Co., 1908.

TYRRELL, J. B., ed., *David Thompson's Narrative of His Explorations in Western America, 1784-1812.* Toronto: The Champlain Society, 1916.

UNTERMEYER, LOUIS, ed. *Modern American Poetry.* New York: Harcourt, Brace & Co., 1930.

VERNON, ARTHUR. *The History and Romance of the Horse.* Boston: Waverly House, 1939.

VESTAL, STANLEY. *Sitting Bull, Champion of the Sioux.* New York: Houghton Mifflin Co., 1922.

WALTON, WILLIAM. *The Army and Navy of the United States* .... Vol. II. Boston: George Barrie & Son, Publishers, 1900.

WEBB, W. P. *The Texas Rangers.* New York: Houghton Mifflin Co., 1935.

———. *The Great Plains.* Boston: Ginn & Co., 1931.

WOESTERMEYER, I. F. and J. M. GAMBRILL, eds. *The Westward Movement.* New York: D. Appleton-Century Co., 1939.

WISSLER, CLARK. *The American Indian.* New York: Douglas C. McMurtrie, 1917.

——. *Man and Culture.* New York: Thomas Y. Crowell Co., 1923.

——. *Indians of the United States.* New York: Doubleday, Doran & Co., 1940.

WRIGHT, R. M. *Dodge City, The Cowboy Capital and the Great Southwest....* Wichita, Kansas: *Wichita Eagle* Press, 1913.

——. "Reminiscences of Dodge." *Transactions of the Kansas State Historical Society,* Vol. IX. Topeka: State Printing Office, 1906, pp. 66-72.

II. MAGAZINES

"A Wild Horse," *American Turf Register and Sporting Magazine,* IX (1838), 360-63. Quoting *Audubon's American Ornithological Biography.*

ALPHONSO, DON. "Horsemanship of the North American Indians," *American Turf Register and Sporting Magazine,* I (1829), 73-74.

"American Wild Horses," *American Turf Register and Sporting Magazine,* IV (1832-33), 8.

ANDERSON, JANE. "The Red King," *Harper's Weekly,* LVI, Part 2 (1912), 16-18.

AULD, R. C. "As to the 'Extinction of the American Horse,'" *Science,* XX (1892), 135.

BARNES, W. C. "The Passing of the Wild Horse," *American Forests and Forest Life,* XXX (1924), 643-48.

——. "Wild Burros," *American Forests and Forest Life,* XXXVI (1930), 640-42.

——. "Wild Horses," *Atlantic Monthly,* CXXXIV (1924), 616-23.

——. "Wild Horses," *McClure's Magazine,* XXXII (1908-9), 285-94.

BEASLEY, W. L. "Evolution of the Horse," *Scientific American Supplement,* LXXXVIII (1903), 451-52.

BECKER, L. I. "Verily, This Product Goes to the Dogs," *Printers' Ink Monthly,* January, 1935.

BIGELOW, POULTNEY. "Emperor William's Stud-Farm and Hunting Forest," *Harper's New Monthly Magazine,* LXXXVIII (1893-94), 742-55.

BLAKE, FORRESTER. "Wild Horses Run," *Scribner's Magazine,* XCVII (1935), 248-51.

BOONE, A. R. "The Wild Herd Passes," *Travel,* LX (1933), 20-23, 56.

BRISH, COL. H. C. "On the Wild Horses of the Far South-West," *American Turf Register and Sporting Magazine,* V (1833-34), 463-64.

BURSEY, J. A. "Horses of the Southwest," *New Mexico Magazine,* September, 1933.

"Business in the Bow-wows," *Business Week,* August 17, 1936.

CAESAR, KATHLEEN. "With the Wild-Horse Hunters," *Popular Mechanics,* XLVI (1926), 76-80.

CARTER, MAJOR GENERAL W. H. "Story of the Horse," *National Geographic Magazine,* XLIV (1923), 455-566.

CASEMENT, D. D. "The Western Cowhorse," *The Producer*, XV (1934), 3-7.

"Colorado's Sensational Wild Horse," *Current Literature*, XXXII (1902), 330-33. Quoted from *Chicago Inter-Ocean*.

COOPER, J. M. and DEWEY DISMUKE. "The Sheep Industry of Indians in the Southwest," *Indians at Work*, August, 1939, pp. 13-19.

DENHARDT, R. M. "The Role of the Horse in the Social History of Early California," *Agricultural History*, XIV (1940), 13-22.

———. "The Equine Strategy of Cortés," *Hispanic American Historical Review*, XVIII (1938), 550-55.

———. "The Southwestern Cow-Horse," *The Cattleman*, December, 1938, January and February, 1939.

———. "Spanish Horses and the New World," *The Historian*, Winter, 1938.

———. "The Truth About Cortés's Horses," *Hispanic American Historical Review*, XVII (1937), 525-32.

DENMAN, RT. HON. LORD. "The War Office and Remounts," *Nineteenth Century*, LII (1902), 746-53.

DETZER, KARL. "Portrait of a Pioneer," *Reader's Digest*, June, 1939.

DOBIE, J. FRANK. "The Spanish Cow Pony," *Saturday Evening Post*, November 24, 1934.

DODGE, T. A. "The Horse in America," *North American Review*, CLV (1892), 667-83.

EWART, J. C. "The Possible Ancestors of the Horses Living Under Domestication," *Science*, New Series, XXX (1909), 219-23.

ENGEL, C. P. "The War-Horse Business," *Colliers*, LV (1915), 13-14, 34-36.

FRYER, E. R. "The Navajos Sell Their Range Robbers," *Indians at Work*, November, 1938.

GIDLEY, J. W. "American Wild Horses," *The Scientific Monthly*, XXV (1927), 265-71.

HAINES, FRANCIS. "Where Did the Plains Indians Get Their Horses," *American Anthropologist*, New Series, XL (1938), 112-17.

———. "The Northward Spread of Horses Among the Plains Indians," *American Anthropologist*, New Series, XL (1938), 429-37.

HENDRIX, J. M. "'Paints' as Cow Horses," *The Cattleman*, November, 1934.

HOLT-LOMAX, R. "The 'Amgrey' Horse," *Harper's Weekly*, LI (1907), 1505.

"The Horse Trade of the United States With Foreign Countries," *Scientific American Supplement*, LIII (1902), 22054.

"Horses Nobody Wants," *Literary Digest*, LXXXIV (1925), 20-21.

HOYT, HOMER. "Catching Wild Horses," *Colorado Magazine*, XI (1934), 41-45.

"The Inheritance of the Centaur," *Atlantic Monthly*, LXXII (1893), 575-76.

JAMES, WILL. "Piñon and the Wild Ones," *Saturday Evening Post*, May 19, 1923.

KNOWLES, LEES. "Horseflesh," *Nineteenth Century*, LII (1890), 592-607.

KREMOLA, V. "The 'Pied' and 'Splashed White' Patterns in Horses and Ponies," *The Journal of Heredity*, XXIV (1933), 65-69.

LIVINGSTONE, A. "Wild Steeds of the Pampas," *Outing*, XXVIII (1896), 127-30.

LUNDBERGH, HOLGAR. "Last of Sweden's Wild Horses," *Nature Magazine*, XXIII (1934), 169.

LUCAS, F. A. "The Ancestry of the Horse," *McClure's Magazine*, XV (1900), 512-17.

MASON, R. B. "All Aback! Wild Horses!" *American Turf Register and Sporting Magazine*, VI (1834-35), 166.

MATTHEW, W. D. "The Horse and the Llama," *Outlook*, CXXIII (1919), 318-19.

MAUR, H. S. "His Majesty—Horse," *Outing*, LIII (1908), 52-54.

McNICHOLS, C. L. "Cow Horses," *Western Story*, September 3 and December 17, 1938; February 4, October 15, and a clipping from the June issue, 1939.

MILES, D. S. "Osage Stallions Procured," *American Turf Register and Sporting Magazine*, VI (1834-35), 30-31.

MOHLER, J. R., ADOLPH EICHHORN, and J. M. BUCK. "The Diagnosis of Dourine by Complement Fixation," *Journal of Agricultural Research*, I (1913), 99-108.

"Natural History," *American Turf Register and Sporting Magazine*, I (1829), 19-26.

NICHOLS, M. W. "The Spanish Horse of the Pampas," *American Anthropologist*, New Series, XLI (1939), 119-29.

NOTSON, R. C. "Horses! Horses!" *Sunset Magazine*, LIX (1927), 29, 78-81.

NOWLAND, E. B. "Wild Horses of the West," *American Turf Register and Sporting Magazine*, VII (1835-36), 60-62.

"On the Origin and Qualities of the Wild Horses of the Prairies of the Southwest," *American Turf Register and Sporting Magazine*, VI (1834-35), 118-24.

"On This Ranch Wild Horses are Made Wilder," *Popular Science Monthly*, CXIX (1931), 40-41.

Overland Monthly, XIX (1891), 478-93.

PHASMA. "Indians Hunting the Buffalo," *American Turf Register and Sporting Magazine*, XI (1840), 648-49.

PHILLIPS, RUFUS. "Early Cowboy Life in the Arkansas Valley," *Colorado Magazine*, VII (1930), 165-79.

POND, W. P. "The Horse in America," *Country Life in America*, XIX (1910), 27-30, 70, 72, 74, 76.

RAMSDELL, C. W. "General Robert E. Lee's Horse Supply, 1862-1865," *American Historical Review*, XXXV (1930), 758-77.

REMINGTON, FREDERIC. "Horses of the Plains," *Century Magazine*, XXXVII (1888-89), 332-43.

RHODES, C. D. "Uncle Sam's Four-Footed Friends," *Lippincott's Magazine*, LX (1897), 837-43.

ROBINSON, LOUIS. "Wild Traits in Tame Animals," *North American Review*, CLVIII (1894), 477-83.

RODNICK, DAVID. "An Assiniboin Horse-Raiding Expedition," *American Anthropologist,* XLI (1939), 611-16.

ROTH, C. B. "Trapping Wild Horses," *Popular Science Monthly,* CXXXI (1937), 38-39, 140-41.

———. "Intelligence, Plus Speed, Plus Bottom, Equals Mustang," *The Horse,* November-December, 1937.

"Santa Fe Trail Traveler." A letter from Little Rock, Arkansas. *American Turf Register and Sporting Magazine,* VII (1835-36), 204-5.

SASS, H. R. "Hoofs on the Prairie," *Country Gentleman,* CVI (1936), 5-6, 68-69.

Scientific American Supplement, LXXI (1911), 18.

SCHWARTZ, ERNST. "The Story of the Horse," *Nature Magazine,* XXXI (1938), 162-64.

SHALER, N. S. "The Horse," *Scribner's Magazine,* XVI (1894), 567-86.

SHEAF, E. T. "The Ponies of the New Forest," *Outing Magazine,* XLI (1903), 415-18.

SIGMA. "Catching Wild Horses," *American Turf Register and Sporting Magazine,* V (1833-34), 129-31. A letter.

SPARKS, JEFF. "Wild Horses Corralled from Air," *Popular Mechanics,* LXX (1938), 541-43, 120 A, 121 B.

SPEED, J. G. "The Horse in America," *Century Magazine,* LXVI (1903), 667-83.

———. "American Horses for the Philippines," *World's Work,* VIII (1904), 5299-5304.

STEELE, RUFUS. "Killing an Army of Horses to Rebuild San Francisco," *Harper's Weekly,* LI (1907), 580-81.

———. "Mustangs, Busters and Outlaws of the Nevada Wild Horse Country," *American Magazine,* LXXII (1911), 756-65.

———. "Trapping Wild Horses in Nevada," *McClure's Magazine,* XXXIV (1909-10), 198-209.

———. "Wild Horses as Scenery," *Outlook,* CXLI (1925), 84-86.

STROPE, A. M. "Catching Wild Horses in the '60's," *Outdoor Life,* August, 1914. A clipping in the Colorado State Historical Society Library.

Subscriber. "On Crossing our Bred Horse with the Wild or Prairie Horse," *American Turf Register and Sporting Magazine,* IV (1832-33), 501-3. A letter from Cantonment Jesup, La.

TAYLOR, F. J. "The Golden Horse," *Colliers,* July 27, 1940.

TROUESSART, E. L. "Did the Horse Exist in America Before this Continent was Discovered by Europeans," *Scientific American Supplement,* LXXVI (1913), 387.

———. "The Fiction of the American Horse and the Truth on this Disputed Point," *Science,* XX (1892), 188-89.

———. "Wild Horses," *Popular Science Monthly,* XXXVII (1890), 626-31.

TSCHIFFELY, A. F. "Buenos Aires to Washington by Horse," *The National Geographic Magazine,* LV (1929), 135-96.

TURRELL, G. B. "Livestock," *Country Life,* LXXVI (1939), 90.

UNDERHILL, B. M. "The Evolution of the Horse," *Scientific American Supplement*, LXIV (1907), 412-14.

"The Vanishing Mustang," *Current Literature*, XXX (1901), 616-17.

VISCHER, PETER. "Albinos," *Country Life*, LXXVI (1939), 80.

WARRINGTON, JOHN. "Still Time to Save America's Wild Horses," *The American Weekly*, January 14, 1940.

———. "Wild Horses of the Old Frontier," *Travel*, November, 1939.

WENTWORTH, E. N. "The Horse—From Then to Now," *The Producer*, XV (1933), 3-6.

WHITE, S. E. "The Mountains," *Outlook*, LXXVII (1904), 368-74.

"Wild Horses—The Game and the Sports of the West," *American Turf Register and Sporting Magazine*, V (1833-34), 70-75.

"Wild Horse Round-Up," *Time*, February 20, 1939.

WISSLER, CLARK. "The Influence of the Horse in the Development of Plains Culture," *American Anthropologist, New Series*, XVI (1914), 1-25.

III. GOVERNMENT PUBLICATIONS

BARKER, E. C., ed. *The Austin Papers. Annual Report of the American Historical Association for the Year 1922*. Vol. II. Washington, D. C.: Government Printing Office, 1928.

BARNES, W. C. *The Story of the Range*. U. S. Department of Agriculture, Forest Service. Washington, D. C.: Government Printing Office, 1926.

BRYMNER, DOUGLAS. "Report on Canadian Archives (1889)," pp. 1-29. An appendix to the *Report of the Minister of Agriculture*. Printed by the Government, Ottawa, 1890.

DORSEY, J. O. "A Study of Siouan Cults," *Eleventh Annual Report of the Bureau of Ethnology (1889-90)*. Washington, D. C.: Government Printing Office, 1894.

EWART, J. C. "The Multiple Origin of Horses and Ponies," *Annual Report of the Smithsonian Institution, June 30, 1904*. Washington, D. C.: Government Printing Office, 1905, pp. 437-55.

MALLERY, GARRICK. "Picture-Writing of the American Indians," *Tenth Annual Report of the Bureau of Ethnology (1888-89)*. Washington, D. C.: Government Printing Office, 1893.

McGINNIES, W. G., and OTHERS. *The Agricultural and Range Resources of the Navajo Reservation in Relation to the Subsistence Needs of the Navajo Indians*. Issued by the Indian Office, U. S. Department of Interior. Washington, D. C.: Government Printing Office, 1936.

MOONEY, JAMES. "Calendar History of the Kiowa Indians," *Seventeenth Annual Report of the Bureau of Ethnology (1895-96)*. Washington, D. C.: Government Printing Office, 1898.

MUCK, LEE, and OTHERS. *Grazing on Indian Lands*. Part 22. Hearings Before a Subcommittee of the Committee on Indian Affairs. Senate, 71st Congress, 2nd Session.

NIMMO, J. G. "The Range and Ranch Cattle Traffic," *House Executive Document No. 267*, 48th Congress, 2nd Session, Serial No. 2304.

REESE, H. H. *Breeding Horses for the United States Army*. From the Yearbook of the U. S. Department of Agriculture for 1917. Washington, D. C.: Government Printing Office, 1918.

ROMMEL, G. M. "The Army Remount Problem," *Twenty-seventh Annual Report of the Bureau of Animal Industry for the Year 1910*. Washington, D. C.: Government Printing Office, 1912.

TEIT, J. A. "The Salishan Tribes of the Western Plains," *Forty-fifth Annual Report of the Bureau of American Ethnology (1927-28)*. Washington, D. C.: Government Printing Office, 1930, pp. 23-396.

U. S. DEPARTMENT OF AGRICULTURE. *Annual Reports . . . . for the Years Ended June 30, 1918, 1919, 1920 1921, 1922, 1923*. Washington, D. C.: Government Printing Office, 1919-24.

————. *Reports of the Bureau of Animal Industry, 1926-38*. Washington, D. C.: Government Printing Office, 1926-38.

————. *Twenty-eighth Annual Report of the Bureau of Animal Industry for the Year 1911*. Washington, D. C.: Government Printing Office, 1913.

U. S. CONGRESS. HOUSE. COMMITTEE ON INDIAN AFFAIRS. "Authorizing the Secretary of the Interior to Determine Claims of Certain Members of the Sioux Nation in South Dakota." *House Reports No. 443*, 68th Congress, 1st Session, Serial No. 8228.

————. *Indians of the United States*. Hearings before the Committee on Indian Affairs, Vol. I. House of Representatives, 66th Congress, 1st Session.

————. Senate. Committee on Indian Affairs. *Survey of Conditions of the Indians of the United States*. Hearings before a Subcommittee of the Committee on Indian Affairs. 70th Congress, 2nd Session, Part 4, February 4-6, 27; March 1, 1929.

U. S. DEPARTMENT OF THE INTERIOR. *Annual Reports . . . . for the Years Ended June 30, 1905, 1906, 1914, 1915, 1916, 1917, 1918, 1919, 1934, 1936, 1937, 1938*. Washington, D. C.: Government Printing Office, 1906-39.

————. *Annual Reports of the Commissioner of Indian Affairs . . . . for the Fiscal Year Ended June 30, 1920, 1921, 1922, 1923, 1924, 1925, 1926*. Washington, D. C.: Government Printing Office, 1920-26.

————. *Extracts from the Annual Reports . . . . for the Fiscal Years 1927 and 1928 Relating to the Bureau of Indian Affairs*. Washington, D. C.: Government Printing Office, 1927-28.

————. *Memorandum to the Press*. Released June 9, 1939, by the Office of Indian Affairs.

————. Division of Grazing. *The Grazing Bulletin*, April, 1939, and June 28, 1939.

WINSHIP, G. P. "The Coronado Expedition, 1540-1542," *Fourteenth Annual Report of the Bureau of Ethnology*. Washington, D. C.: Government Printing Office, 1896, pp. 339-615.

IV. PAMPHLETS

BYRNES, PATRICK. *Wild Horses of Colorado.* Publisher and date not given. In Colorado State Historical Society Library.

JACKSON, W. H. *Broncho Drive from the Pacific to the Missouri River in 1867.* Letters of Jackson to Thomas F. Dawson. In Colorado State Historical Society Library.

MATTHEW, W. D., and S. H. CHUBB. *Evolution of the Horse.* American Museum of Natural History, No. 36. 7th Edition.

PEARCE, A. J. *Experiences of a Pioneer Family.* Publisher and date not given. In Colorado State Historical Library.

PROBST, T. K. *Roping Wild Horses.* Publisher and date not given. In Colorado State Historical Society Library.

V. NEWSPAPERS

Chicago Sunday Mirror, January 27, 1940.
Daily Sentinel (Grand Junction, Colorado), August 2, 1940.
Dodge City (Kansas) *Times,* August 4, 1877.
Kansas Messenger (Baldwin, Kansas), January 1, 1859.
News (Sherman Center, Kansas), March 24, April 2, and August 4, 1887.
New York Times, June 30, 1914, "Montana Horses in Demand for Army Service."
New York Times, January 27, 1918, "See Harm to Army Horses."
New York Times, March 17, 1918, "Dix Cowboys Shun Mule."
New York Times, July 15, 1920, "New Game for Hunters."
New York Times, February 6, 1927.
New York Times, June 28, 1928, "Horse Nobody Wants." Editorial.
New York Times, September 23, 1928, "Wild Horses Take Their Last Trail."
New York Times, February 18, 1929, "The Menace of Wild Horses." Editorial.
New York Times, May 27, 1929, "Wild Horse Round-up Starts in Montana."
New York Times, June 6, 1929, "Wild Horse Roundup Herds all Varieties."
New York Times, June 9, 1929, "Wild Horses are Passing." Editorial.
New York Times, June 23, 1929, "Expect to Capture 5,000 Wild Horses."
New York Times, July 7, 1929, "Wild Horses are Outlawed on the Ranges of the West."
New York Times, July 14, 1929, "Pony Coat Demand Spurs Slaughter of Wild Horses."
New York Times, November 21, 1930, "Rounding Up Wild Horses." Editorial.
New York Times, May 8, 1931, "Ask War on Wild Horse in Alberta."
New York Times, May 17, 1931, "Wild Horses in Arkansas."

New York Times, September 6, 1931, "To Kill 10,000 Wild Horses."

New York Times, July 23, 1933, "Wild Horses Being Trained."

New York Times Magazine, June 7, 1925, "Montana Seals Fate on 400,000 Wild Horses."

New York Times Magazine, August 9, 1931, "A Wild-Horse Hunt in Arkansas."

New York Times Magazine, February 10, 1935, "Wild Horses of the West are Vanishing."

Norton County People (Norton, Kansas), August 19 and October 14, 1880.

Republican (Granfield, Kansas), quoted in the *Pioneer* (Atwood, Kansas), May 12, 1880.

St. Paul Dispatch, December 10, 1939, "Texas Campus to Get Statues of Mustang."

St. Paul Dispatch, February 4, 1940, "Canadian Wild Horses to be Rounded Up, Shot."

St. Paul Pioneer Press, August 9, 1939.

St. Paul Pioneer Press, July 13, 1941, "Navajos Declare War Against U. S."

St. Paul Pioneer Press, September 17, 1939, "Navajos Sadly Head Horses into Last Round-Up."

St. Paul Pioneer Press, September 24, 1939, "Europe Looks Again to U. S. for More Horses."

St. Paul Pioneer Press, February 23, 1941.

Sherman County Republican (Itasca, Kansas), December 10, 1886.

VI.   PERSONAL LETTERS AND COMMUNICATIONS

BLOOM, L. B., Department of History, University of New Mexico, Albuquerque, New Mexico, May 22, 1940.

BRANDT, D. C., Acme Poultry Products Company, Hayward, California, November 2, 1939.

BROOKS, L. R., Regional Grazier, Grazing Service, U. S. Department of Interior, Reno, Nevada, September 29, 1939, and March 30, 1940.

BURBACK, H. J., Regional Grazier, Grazing Service, Rawlins, Wyoming, February 9 and 10, 1940.

BUTLER, W. J., State Veterinary Surgeon, Livestock Sanitary Board, Helena, Montana, January 17, 1940.

CHAPPEL BROS. Inc., Rockford, Illinois, August 29, 1939.

DAVIS, B. F., Secretary of Colorado Stock Growers and Feeders Association, Denver, Colorado, August 15, 1939.

DICKENS, W. F., Superintendent, Cheyenne River Indian Agency, Cheyenne Agency, South Dakota, February 29, 1940.

DOUGLASS, E. K., Assistant Range Examiner, Navajo Service, Soil Conservation Service, Window Rock, Arizona, July 2, 1940.

DUCKWORTH, C. U., Chief, Division of Animal Industry, California Department of Agriculture, Sacramento, California, August 22, 1939.

EXLINE, J. C., Bureau of Animal Industry, U. S. Department of Agriculture, Olympia, Washington, January 15, 1940.

FRYER, E. R., Superintendent, Navajo Indian Reservation. A four-page mimeographed statement, entitled "The Navajos Sell their Range Robbers," sent by W. V. Woehlke, Assistant to the Commissioner of Indian Affairs.

GRAVES, C. L., Superintendent, Blackfoot Indian Agency, Browning, Montana, February 20, 1940.

HACKEDORN, H., Department of Animal Husbandry, State College of Washington, Pullman, Washington, September 1, 1939.

HOLBROOK, M. L., Marketing Director, Utah State Board of Agriculture, Salt Lake City, Utah, January 17, 1940.

HOLLOWAY, T. D., Agriculture Extension Agent, Fort Apache Indian Agency, Whitewater, Arizona, September 14, 1939.

JOHNSON, R. G., Department of Animal Husbandry, Oregon State Agricultural College, Corvallis, Oregon, August 16, 1939.

JOHNSON, ZEKE, Custodian, Natural Bridges National Monument, Blanding, Utah, August 26, 1939.

JOSS, E. C., Chief, Meat Inspection Service, U. S. Department of Agriculture, August 11, 1939.

KAY, J. L., Carnegie Museum, Pittsburgh, Pennsylvania, January 15, 1940.

KIETH, MRS. J. M., Secretary, Arizona Cattle Growers' Association, Phoenix, Arizona, August 17, 1939.

LYTLE, W. H. Chief, Division of Animal Industry, Oregon Department of Agriculture, Salem, Oregon, August 10, 1939.

McCRAY, E. R., Superintendent, San Carlos Indian Agency, San Carlos, Arizona, November 27, 1939. Also an enclosure by James B. Kitch.

McNICHOLS, C. L., Los Angeles, California, August 25, 1939.

MARNEY, DR. F. L., Veterinary, Yuma, Arizona, January 23, 1940.

MELVIN, F. H., Bureau of Animal Industry, U. S. Department of Agriculture, Cheyenne, Wyoming, January 17, 1940.

MONTE, NIC W., Acting Regional Grazier, Grazing Service, Burns, Oregon, January 23, 1940. Also enclosure by district grazier.

MONTGOMERY, L. C., President, Utah Cattle and Horse Growers Association, Heber City, Utah, August 29, 1939.

MOORE, C. F., Regional Grazier, Grazing Service, Grand Junction, Colorado, April 3, 1940. Also an interview, August, 1940.

MORGAN, R. E., Regional Grazier, Grazing Service, Billings, Montana, January 31, 1940.

MORTON, MURRAY, Assessor, Malheur County, Oregon, August 22, 1939.

MURRAY, HENRY, Department of Animal Husbandry, Montana State College, Bozeman, Montana, August 30, 1939.

NEWMAN, H. L., Superintendent, Mescalero Indian Agency, Mescalero, New Mexico, August 22, 1939.

NICHOL, A. A., Associate Wildlife Technician, National Park Service, Tucson, Arizona, September 5, 1939.

PAINTER, J. R., Acting Regional Grazier, Grazing Service, Phoenix, Arizona, January 29, 1940.

PARRY, G. R., Superintendent, Motor Transportation, Utah Parks Company, Cedar City, Utah, October 5, 1939.

PIERSON, ED, Acting Regional Grazier, Grazing Service, Alburquerque, New Mexico, January 23, 1940.

PHILLIPS, E. A., Secretary, Montana Stockgrowers Association, Helena, Montana, August 9, 1939.

RINEHART, E. F., Extension Animal Husbandman, College of Agriculture, University of Idaho, Boise, Idaho September 11, 1939.

ROSS, DR. W. J., Dr. W. J. Ross Company, Los Alamitos, California, October 5, 1939.

RUTLEDGE, R. H., Director, Grazing Service, U. S. Department of Interior, August 23, 1939.

RYAN, A. D., Acting Director, Grazing Service, U. S. Department of Interior, July 7, 1939.

SEELEY, C. P., Regional Grazier, Grazing Service Salt Lake City, November 10, 1939.

SCHLESSER BROTHERS, Packers, Portland, Oregon, August 7, 1939.

SKINNER, T. L., Rancher, Jordan Valley, Oregon, September, 1939.

STABLEIN, J. E., Regional Grazier, Grazing Service, Pocatello, Idaho, February 7, 1940.

STANLEY, E. B., Animal Husbandman, College of Agriculture and Agricultural Experiment Station, University of Arizona, Tucson, Arizona, September 18, 1939.

STEWART, WAYNE, former mustanger, Dayville, Oregon, August 30, 1939.

THORP, RUSSELL, Secretary-Chief Inspector, Wyoming Stock Growers Association, Cheyenne, Wyoming, September 28, 1939.

TRAGER, E. A., Acting Supervisor of Research and Information, National Park Service, July 1, 1940.

WESTERN CALIFORNIA PRODUCTS COMPANY, San Francisco, California, October 2, 1939.

WILSON, F. W., Chairman, Department of Animal Husbandry, University of Nevada, Reno, Nevada, September 8 and 26, 1939.

WILSON, J. W., County Extension Agent, Elko County, Nevada, August 22, 1939.

YELLOWTAIL, ROBERT, Superintendent, Crow Indian Agency, Crow Agency, Montana, February 26, 1940.

ZUMWALT, A. R., Bureau of Animal Husbandry, U. S. Department of Agriculture, Phoenix, Arizona, January 27, 1940.

Index

A NOTE ABOUT THE AUTHOR

WALKER D. WYMAN is Professor of History at Wisconsin State College, River Falls, Wisconsin, where he is also Chairman, Division of the Social Sciences, and Director of Graduate Studies. He holds degrees from Illinois State Normal University (B.S., 1929) and State University of Iowa (M.A., 1931; Ph.D., 1935). Professor Wyman is the author of *California Emigrant Letters* (1952) and *Nothing But Prairie and Sky* (1954). With Clifton B. Kroeber, he edited *The Frontier in Perspective* (1957).